SEXUAL MISCONDUCT IN EDUCATION

PREVENTION, REPORTING AND DISCIPLINE

Grant Bowers, B.A. (Hon.), LL.B.
Rena Knox, Ph.D., LL.B.
Consulting Editor: Justice Marvin A. Zuker

Sexual Misconduct in Education: Prevention, Reporting and Discipline
© LexisNexis Canada Inc. 2003
October 2003

Members of the LexisNexis Group worldwide

Canada	LexisNexis Canada Inc, 75 Clegg Road, MARKHAM, Ontario
Argentina	Abeledo Perrot, Jurisprudencia Argentina and Depalma, BUENOS AIRES
Australia	Butterworths, a Division of Reed International Books Australia Pty Ltd, CHATSWOOD, New South Wales
Austria	ARD Betriebsdienst and Verlag Orac, VIENNA
Chile	Publitecsa and Conosur Ltda, SANTIAGO DE CHILE
Czech Republic	Orac sro, PRAGUE
France	Éditions du Juris-Classeur SA, PARIS
Hong Kong	Butterworths Asia (Hong Kong), HONG KONG
Hungary	Hvg Orac, BUDAPEST
India	Butterworths India, NEW DELHI
Ireland	Butterworths (Ireland) Ltd, DUBLIN
Italy	Giuffré, MILAN
Malaysia	Malayan Law Journal Sdn Bhd, KUALA LUMPUR
New Zealand	Butterworths of New Zealand, WELLINGTON
Poland	Wydawnictwa Prawnicze PWN, WARSAW
Singapore	Butterworths Asia, SINGAPORE
South Africa	Butterworth Publishers (Pty) Ltd, DURBAN
Switzerland	Stämpfli Verlag AG, BERNE
United Kingdom	Butterworths Tolley, a Division of Reed Elsevier (UK), LONDON, WC2A
USA	LexisNexis, DAYTON, Ohio

National Library of Canada Cataloguing in Publication

Bowers, Grant
    Sexual misconduct in education : prevention, reporting and discipline / Grant Bowers, Rena Knox ; consulting editor, Marvin A. Zuker.

Includes bibliographical references and index.
ISBN 0-433-44170-4

    1. Child sexual abuse by teachers—Ontario—Prevention. 2. Sexual harassment in education—Law and legislation—Ontario. Student Protection Act, 2002. I. Knox, Rena II. Zuker, Marvin A. III. Title.

KE8928.B685 2003	371.5'8	C2003-905774-7
KF3467.B69 2003		

Printed and bound in Canada.

FOREWORD

From a moral perspective, the issue is straightforward and non-contestable: sexual abuse of students and sexual misconduct on the part of teachers and others within the school environment are abhorrent and must be stopped. From a legal perspective, the issue is more complex: definitions of abuse and misconduct are more variable, and the specific peculiarities of individual situations are often less clear, especially for those not trained in the study of law. Of course, the most sensational breaches of fiduciary duty and gross violations of children at the hands of those in positions of authority and trust are well publicized by the media. But what of the less obvious cases that we rarely hear about and of the far-reaching implications that the criminal and/or unprofessional behaviour of the few have on everyone within the education context?

As a teacher educator in the discipline of professional ethics, I encounter students longing for direction and clarification as to what is both moral and legal in this sensitive and critical area of schooling. Obviously, as essentially good people, they are well aware that harming children is wrong. However, their questions revolve around such concerns as what constitutes harm; whether student age and consent are relevant factors; what to do about colleagues they suspect of harmful behaviour; what the burden of proof is; who is ultimately responsible for the formal reporting of abuse; what happens to them personally if their suspicions prove to be unfounded or incorrect; how to protect themselves from false allegations; whether there is a distinction between on and off duty responsibilities; and whether teachers should always avoid touching a child, even a youngster in need of a comforting hug.

In this important and timely book on sexual misconduct in education, authors Grant Bowers and Rena Knox, in consultation with editor Justice Marvin Zuker, provide the answers to these and other questions in an accessible and informative way that captures the essence of such concerns and the urgency of their significance. Theirs is not a book for would-be predators and criminals intent on perverting the spirit of *in loco parentis*, but rather for the vast majority of educators and others of good faith within the sphere of the educational authority who, like my student teachers, have to be both aware of their own professional behaviour and alert to the potential dangers of that of others.

Sexual Misconduct in Education documents real cases, presents hypo-thetical scenarios for consideration, and clarifies the changing reality in

Ontario schools that has been ushered in by Sydney Robins' influential report entitled *Protecting Our Students* that subsequently led to significant changes in provincial legislation in the form of the *Student Protection Act, 2002*, S.O. 2002, c. 7. Changes in the law regarding definitions of terms, liability, reporting, procedures and investigations, among other issues, are addressed here in exhaustive detail, and implications for teachers and others are raised for information and discussion.

While this book does refer to the legal requirement more generally to report suspected child abuse at the hands of parents or others outside the school community, its primary focus is on the perhaps even more complicated issue of abuse and misconduct within the community. It bravely takes on issues of disclosure, reporting and investigation within both the legal and professional contexts. It distinguishes between criminal and civil liability and extends its attention beyond the school itself to school boards and the ramifications of vicarious liability as well as to professional policies and regulations governing misconduct as interpreted by the Ontario College of Teachers and teachers' federations.

Among the book's many points of interest are its accounts of the "low threshold" for reporting abuse, which is designed to encourage early identification and intervention; the distinction between reasonable suspicion and reasonable belief; the dangers and potential obstructiveness of premature internal investigations in advance of formal reporting; the fact that the legal duty to report falls squarely on the individual teacher, principal or other who harbours the initial suspicion; and the important observation that teachers are governed not only by the *Criminal Code*, R.S.C. 1985, c. C-46, the *Child and Family Services Act*, R.S.O. 1990, c. C.11, the *Education Act*, R.S.O. 1990, c. E.2 (as amended), and the *Student Protection Act, 2002*, but also by professional responsibilities as defined by the College. In this latter respect, both the convergence and divergence of law and professional ethics are noteworthy as misconduct may or may not involve actual criminal activity. By extension, it further notes that teachers are never truly "off duty" or exempt from adhering to standards of acceptable moral behaviour in their role as models and exemplars, regardless of time and place.

If one were to extract from Bowers and Knox's text pithy and concise phrases to serve as a primer for educators, one could identify such lines as, "There will be no liability for reporting," "The reporting duty overrides the duty to confidentiality," "The duty to report is paramount," "Any disclosure of sexual misconduct by a student (should) be believed for the purpose of forming a reasonable suspicion," "The Ontario

College of Teachers forbids sexual relationships by teachers with a student of any age," and "It is essential that school boards make it clear in protocols and procedures that it is an expectation that teachers never follow 18(1)(*b*) [Adverse Report Regulation] when reporting suspicions of sexual misconduct."

This latter invocation of "Adverse Report" flags, from my perspective, one of the most significant, controversial, yet forward thinking changes in the law, and the book explains it powerfully. Defining the Adverse Report Regulation as being not a normal law passed by provincial legislation but rather a policy enacted by the Board of Governors of the Ontario Teachers' Federation, the book refers to the undisputed "chilling effect" it has had on teachers who have been traditionally reluctant to report on other teachers for any reason because of the duty embedded in the Regulation to notify the suspected colleague of the report within three days of making it. The Robins Report made clear the potentially devastating consequences on children that have resulted from the kind of collegial solidarity and covering-up of misconduct that the Adverse Report Regulation has enabled and fostered. While in theory the Regulation should not inevitably lead to this, in reality it has eroded the teacher's capacity as an individual professional to take responsible action in harmful situations because of both real and imagined fear of negative personal repercussions. Research evidence supports the claim that both the pressures of the informal teacher culture and the influence of federations or unions, which actively discourage teachers from reporting on colleagues, militate against exposure of abuse, neglect, incompetence and other forms of misconduct. Furthermore, as the authors note from the Robins Report (p. 92), Children's Aid workers issued a common complaint against the unions for "thwart(ing) investigations by delaying the investigative process and disciplinary process, by causing teachers to close ranks and not cooperate in the investigation". Consequently, on the recommendation of the Robins Report, the law took a step that it is hoped will address this problem by making the concept of Adverse Report non-applicable to situations involving sexual misconduct.

The laws around sexual misconduct in Ontario schools have been clarified; however, will the practice of educators be able to keep up with the changes? In order to establish new norms that govern the daily life of teachers and others within the educational community, the professional culture needs to respond to the spirit and intent of the legislation not only as a matter of law but also as a matter of professional ethics. Educational practitioners need to embrace the policies and procedures aimed at ensuring the best interests of students, confident in their own sense of professionalism and moral authority that comes from being in a position of societal trust. Bowers, Knox and Zuker's *Sexual Misconduct in Education* offers concrete, informative and thought-provoking guidance to augment the professional confidence that comes in part from a thorough awareness and understanding of some of the most critical legal dimensions of schooling.

Elizabeth Campbell
Associate Professor
The Ontario Institute for Studies in Education of the
University of Toronto (OISE/UT)

PREFACE

The purpose of this book is to provide school administrators, teachers, parents and students who shape the playing field we call education with a source of information that will allow them to help make schools safe and respectful places for learning and teaching.

This book in many ways could not have been written but for the Robins Report (*Protecting Our Students*), released on April 7, 2001, and its many recommendations that have led to identifying and dealing with sexual misconduct in education through legislative and regulatory changes as well as changes in school board policies, procedures and protocol.

An old cliché says an ounce of prevention is worth a pound of cure. It is all about building a respectful, caring and learning environment by enhancing a student's sense of belonging. The vulnerability of our students as potential victims through the opportunity of individuals within an educational context to abuse their power is what we must protect against. Exploitation of relationships is unacceptable.

This book examines the moral and legal interaction of the participants in the educational system from the time sexual misconduct is first identified.

Important as well, of course, is the realization that the players in the education system are not only subject to the legislation covering education in their particular province, but may also be subject to federal criminal laws that identify crimes involving children, to their own College of Teachers, where applicable, as well as to child protection proceedings, which vary from province to province.

Even if certain misconduct cases have commonalities, the combination of circumstances is usually different in each situation. When you read this book and, in particular, the extensive appendices included, you should at the same time thoroughly review your own school board or district policies, your own contractual or collective agreements, and the statutes relating to misconduct in your own particular jurisdiction.

The book is both comprehensive and brief. It is comprehensive because it covers virtually every legal challenge faced by schools today dealing with sexual misconduct. It is brief because the issues are summarized, emphasizing only the most important concepts.

The book combines the experiences of a practising lawyer with the largest school board in Canada, the Toronto District School Board, and the experiences of a practising lawyer with the Catholic Children's Aid Society, virtually the largest agency of its kind in Canada. In every chapter, an attempt has been made to merge legal concerns with educational concerns.

Chapter 1 deals with the history of sexual abuse in Canada. Highlighted is the Badgley Report of 1984, its recommendations and the subsequent amendments to the *Criminal Code*, R.S.C. 1985, c. C-46. Case law is also provided to demonstrate how our courts have interpreted the *Canadian Charter of Rights and Freedoms* and other relevant legislation.

Chapter 2 has its focus on tort law and civil actions in an educational context, an area where the Supreme Court of Canada has been particularly creative and proactive in utilizing tort law to assist victims of sexual wrongdoing. The Court's emphasis on social and public policy considerations has led to its rejection of the traditional test for vicarious liability.

Chapter 3 outlines the role of the Children's Aid Society and the criteria for state intervention. When is a child in need of protection? What reporting obligations exist? Are there protocols in place? Investigation, documentation, police intervention and the taking of evidence are set out in practical language, as a guide and directive.

Chapter 4 deals with the types of sexual misconduct and the proactive responses to them, having regard to the extensive concurrent and overlapping legislation provincially and federally. The handling of an investigation from beginning to end is discussed. The operative word is prevention. One does not have the luxury of applying the law or making the rules after the fact.

Chapter 5 deals with the consequences after an investigation. Criminal charges may be laid, charges may be withdrawn, or there may be no criminal charges. Where do you place an "accused" employee in the educational system? How do you address the concerns of the school community and the public? These issues are discussed in detail.

Chapter 6 has as its focus the issue of internal investigations that the Board itself should undertake. Discussed are the process of interviews and the gathering of evidence that may be the subject of disciplinary action. As they say, justice must not only be done, but must be seen to be done. Emphasis is placed on procedural due process, given issues such as terms and conditions of employment.

Chapter 7 provides various hypothetical scenarios and suggests how best to deal with them. The scenarios are not designed as statements of final authority. They provide suggested guidelines for the avoidance of litigation. They allow the reader to quickly find and identify important legal points to consider during decision-making processes when such decisions will have legal consequences.

Special gratitude and appreciation are extended to Bev Freedman of York University and to The Catholic Principals' Council of Ontario, specifically Lou Rocha, Executive Director, and Paul Game, for their review and criticism of the book.

We would also like to thank Vicki Kelman, Investigations Advisor to the Toronto District School Board, who taught Grant Bowers everything he knows about sexual abuse.

A special and personal thank you is extended to Caroline Knox, as well as to Stefanie Upshaw and Geisa Roveri of the Catholic Children's Aid Society for their assistance. We most heartily thank the social workers, legal department, and other staff at Catholic Children's Aid who over the years have made Rena aware of the challenges that children face when growing up. We would also like to thank Dr. Sherwin Desser and the gang at Hart House for their insight into the culture of sports.

Finally, we all extend a personal thanks to Myrsini Rovos of LexisNexis Butterworths, who not only had the vision and motivation to see the importance of this book but also had the vigilance to see it to its completion.

Let us all work together to end sexual misconduct. Reading this book, we hope, will be the first step toward change.

Note: As this book goes to press, a decision of the Supreme Court of Canada has more clearly defined the limits on vicarious liability of a school board for employees' sexual assault of students. In *E.D.G. v. Hammer*, 2003 SCC 52, a school board was found not liable for a sexual assault committed by a janitor on a student.

Grant Bowers
Rena Knox
Marvin A. Zuker

Toronto, Ontario
July 2003

ABOUT THE AUTHORS

Grant Bowers is Counsel with the Toronto District School Board. He is currently responsible for developing a Child Abuse and Neglect policy. From 1998 to 2001 he was Chair of the Board's Child Abuse and Neglect Taskforce. Mr. Bowers has been a superintendent or senior manager at five Ontario school boards.

Rena Knox is Counsel with the Catholic Children's Aid Society – Toronto. She has 13 years of experience in child protection litigation, specializing in the areas of sexual abuse, physical abuse and neglect. She represents the CCAS in carrying out its mandate under the *Child and Family Services Act*. Dr. Knox has a Ph.D. in History from the University of Toronto.

Justice Marvin A. Zuker is with the Ontario Court of Justice. He currently sits in Family Court in North York, Ontario. He is an Associate Professor in the Department of Theory and Policy Studies at the Ontario Institute for Studies in Education. Justice Zuker has published extensively in the area of education law.

TABLE OF CONTENTS

CHAPTER 1

THE HISTORY OF INSTITUTIONAL SEXUAL ABUSE IN CANADA

It is often said that children are our most precious resource. It is certainly true that they are our future. How we treat our children and how we allow them to be treated reveals much about ourselves and our values as a society. ... Those questions become even more urgent when the abuse continues undetected or ignored for long periods.[1]

INTRODUCTION

Sexual abuse of children is a complicated and widely misunderstood phenomenon. Most sexual abuse occurs at the hands of people known to the victim such as family, friends, and babysitters. Often the abuser has power over the child. The victim is told not to reveal the "secret" or he or she will get in trouble. Often abusers have more than one victim. Some have been estimated to have had over 500.[2]

The popular stereotype of the stranger with candy at the playground represents a very small percentage of sexual abuse cases. Men perpetrate most abuse, with either male or female children. As described below, much of the early focus on abuse has been on young children, but increasingly society is becoming aware of individuals who prey on adolescents, often in educational settings or on the Internet. In addition, the concept of sexual abuse has been broadened over the last few years to encompass exploitative behaviours involving adolescents and other forms of harassment not amounting to "abuse" as described in child protection legislation. Sexual abuse is now commonly referred to as sexual misconduct.

The abuse of children in institutions follows the pattern of abuse of victims by persons who are known to the child or who have authority over the child. Such abuse in Canada remained undetected or ignored for far too long. In Ontario sexual abuse went undetected at a girls' residential training school called Grandview for 50 years. At Mount

Cashel orphanage in Newfoundland, reports of sexual abuse only emerged in the 1970s after decades of abuse and it took a further 16 years to prosecute some of the abusers. Compensation for victims is still unresolved, a further 17 years later.

Child sexual abuse has been "… a largely hidden and pervasive tragedy that had damaged the lives of ten of thousands of children and youth."[3]

The concept of sexual abuse is a modern notion. The language of child sexual abuse developed in the 1970s.[4] It grew out of the discovery made by physicians that children were being abused, not by strangers, but by those closest to them — family members.

PHYSICAL ABUSE

The physical abuse of children was first identified by physicians as a medical problem in accordance with the vernacular of the medical profession.[5] In 1965, the term "child abuse" was first listed as a new medical category. Before 1965 there were no books on child abuse published and in Canada medical reports on physical child abuse only began appearing in the 1970s. They attempted to identify and categorize child abuse, and in a few instances to describe the experiences of children who had been treated for what was termed "child abuse".[6] Physicians had great difficulty in believing that parents, relatives or caregivers could have assaulted their own children. In fact it was easier for a physician to deny "the possibility of such an attack [on a child] than to have to deal with the excessive anger that surges up in … [the physician] when he realizes the truth of the situation".[7] It was claimed at the time that since a physician's training and personality were not similar to those of a police officer or prosecutor, physicians found it difficult to ask questions as if they were investigating a crime and also found it difficult to report what they had observed to the proper authorities, such as child welfare agencies or the police.[8]

In Canada, the path toward public awareness of sexual abuse was paved in the 1970s. Sexual abuse was mentioned rarely and when it was, it was listed in passing as a component of physical abuse. "There was a tendency to apply the results of research in other countries to the Canadian situation, in the absence of research and reliable information."[9]

There was divided opinion on the establishment of procedures for a more effective reporting system in order to assist in the identification of child abuse and in the establishment of more effective treatment programs. Articles were written by physicians for and against mandatory reporting. Some advocated the continuing practice of a physician's right to exercise discretion as to reporting abuse to the proper authorities such as child welfare agencies or the police. Several advocated for mandatory reporting procedures once an accusation of battering had been made."[10] Other articles claimed that "mandatory reporting along general lines would achieve little as it would be too difficult and costly to effect."[11]

It was not until 1984 that the government introduced legislation referring specifically to child *sexual abuse*. This was the result of a massive federal study on the issue called the Badgley Report.

THE BADGLEY REPORT AND SEXUAL ABUSE

In August 1984 The Badgley Committee produced the *Report of the Committee on Sexual Offences Against Children and Youth*.[12] This report, consisting of two volumes and 1,314 pages based upon 14 research studies, made recommendations on child sexual abuse. It recommended extensive revision of the criminal law.

The Badgley Report took the position that any sexual activities with children were harmful to children in and of themselves. The prevailing view at that time was that children were not harmed by non-assaultive sexual activities with adults, but rather by societal and parental reaction to their having engaged in those activities. The Committee recommended that restrictions be placed on the capacity of children to consent to any sexual conduct with adults. The age of consent fluctuated depending upon the nature of the forbidden sexual activity. In some cases 16-year-olds were defined as capable of giving consent and were no longer deemed to be young persons. In other cases 14-year-olds were deemed capable of giving their consent. The Committee's views were publicly criticized as infringements on a child's autonomy. In the Committee's view, the special vulnerabilities of children and young persons made it imperative that the state provide them with protection. The support for the sexual autonomy of children and young persons is described by the Badgley Report as "transparent, dangerous, and intellectually dishonest".[13]

The Report set out a series of detailed amendments that were based upon a thorough review of the various sexual offences in the *Criminal Code*.[14] It also identified the fact that there was little protection in the *Code* for children and young persons. The Committee asked two basic questions: what kinds of conduct involving children and young persons should be made criminal, and what are the appropriate penalties? Implicit in this was the question of at what age one is deemed a young person for the purposes of child protection before the law. With respect to criminal conduct and with respect to sentencing, the Committee recommended that crimes involving children be treated differently:

> The offences proposed by the Committee proscribe behaviours with children and youths which are unacceptable for reasons independent of the issues of "consent" and assault, the age of the young person, the nature of the sexual act engaged in, the abuse of legal or social trust by the offender, and the harms which may be incurred by the young person as a consequence of the sexual act. Consequently the Committee urged that there continue to be an absolute prohibition against a male having sexual intercourse with a woman who was not his wife and who is under the age of 14.[15]

The were several other important recommendations regarding the criminal law and children that resulted in reforms to the *Criminal Code*. The new laws specifically dealing with children and adolescents are discussed in detail in Chapter 3.

THE EVOLUTION OF ATTITUDES TOWARD SEXUAL ABUSE IN EDUCATIONAL INSTITUTIONS

United States

If attitudes toward children and law with respect to children were slow in changing, what could be said of the level of awareness of the problem of sexual abuse in education? In 1982, research on sexual relationships and sexual conduct between teachers and students did not appear in education journals. There were a few student-conducted surveys in the 1970s that assessed the degree of sexual misconduct on university campuses but there were questions as to the validity of the surveys. What the surveys found, however, was that about one-fourth of the professors who responded admitted to having sexual contact with their students and about one-fourth of the female students who responded reported sexual contact with their professors.[16]

"Speak Out" programs were also organized throughout the 1970s on campuses in order to attempt to get public recognition of the problem that women's groups thought to be pervasive. In the 1970s few women came forth to name their harassers or those with whom they engaged in some form of sexual conduct. A review of case law in the United States in the 1970s and in the early 1980s seemed to indicate that the male teachers or professors enjoyed respect that translated into greater credibility in the courts. Cases that did go to court most often favoured the defendants, not the complainants. Fear of being removed from school for laying charges may have prevented young girls from laying charges.[17]

Fear of cross-examination about the student's sexual character also played a role in determining whether to proceed against a teacher.

In the 1980s there was a growing awareness of the exploitative nature of the professor-student relationship. Not only could students be rewarded for submitting to sexual misconduct, they could be punished for blowing the whistle. Some cases in the United States illustrated that complainants did fear retaliation if they brought the situation to the attention of higher authorities or before the court.[18] In one instance, a student was thrown out of West Point, and in another poor grades were given when the student refused to grant sexual favours.[19]

Increasing awareness of the potential abuse of power in the university setting was on the agenda of the women's rights movement. However, the analogy to secondary and elementary school settings was not as apparent. Popular misconceptions about pedophilia still lingered and the issue of abuse of authority by teachers in those settings was not widely perceived.

Despite a generally held community expectation that teachers exhibit high standards of moral conduct, very few cases involving child sexual abuse by teachers were litigated in the 1970s in the United States. It has been argued that the test was a difficult one for the individual litigant to demonstrate. Commentators maintained that sexual misconduct against a student by a teacher did not necessarily result in unfitness to teach. It has also been argued that there was a conspiracy of silence throughout the educational systems in the United States. Parents and victims waited for school districts to act, but little was done.

Canada

A similar situation existed in Canada. Some have alluded to a conspiracy of silence, others have suggested that priests, teachers and educators remained in a state of denial. The disclosures made in recent years by native residents in institutions, adults who were children in residential schools and orphanages, as well as "... the law reports, the disciplinary cases, the arbitration cases and media accounts indicate a significant number of cases ... in which teachers have engaged in sexual misconduct against students".[20]

In a 1983 Nova Scotia labour arbitration dismissal case, the grievor was a janitor, approximately 50 years of age, who had worked in the District School Board for nearly 14 years with a perfect performance record. There was one incident where he was witnessed hugging and kissing a 12-year-old child while on duty. The result was suspension and later termination. Several days prior to the incident, the grievor had bought a birthday card with five dollars inserted. The child was one of the many students who assisted the janitor in his duties. The grievor did not have benefit of counsel when he put his case before the school board. The arbitration board acknowledged that it had dealt with a serious incident but found few reported arbitration cases as precedents involving board of education employees. It indicated that "[s]exual conduct is certainly misconduct for which an employer may discipline an employee."[21] The test it relied on was whether or not the misconduct interfered with and prejudiced the safe and proper conduct of the business of the company. The arbitration board concluded that the incident of hugging and kissing was not serious, and it was not a culminating event, but only a single event. The hugging and kissing "involved a serious error in judgment because the grievor was placed in a position of trust which he breached", but his long and good service resulted in his being reinstated following a suspension without pay.[22] It was suggested by the arbitration board that for one year it would be inappropriate for the grievor to work as a caretaker in any school and that he should be offered a utility position, one not involving children.[23]

The same year, the Alberta Public Service Grievance Appeal Board found in favour of the employer that had dismissed a child care counsellor who had been carrying on a sexual relationship with a 15½-year-old female who was in its treatment centre.[24]

In a 1988 Ontario decision an arbitrator reinstated a caretaker who had been terminated for sexual harassment of another employee.[25] He had a history of having been disciplined for sexual conduct and had demonstrated an inappropriate interest in female students that led to transfers on several occasions. In 1988 the grievor began paying unwanted attention to a female employee. He began frequently visiting her office, making advances that she rejected, albeit subtly. She did not tell him she was rejecting his advances. The grievor continued to pursue her. The Board rejected the "reasonable person test" in the context of employee discipline and looked for evidence of a clear and unequivocal rejection by the victim of his advances. The grievor was not to be faulted for not having interpreted her reply as discouraging, and his failure to detect subtle indications that his advances were unwelcome and offensive was not sufficient to support discipline. The board found that the employee had no actual knowledge that his advances were being rejected and thus the charge of sexual harassment was not upheld. The Board placed little weight on the history of harassing behaviours of the grievor as previously documented.[26]

CRIMINAL COURTS

Of concern to criminal courts was how to sentence convicted educational workers. Did the punishment fit the crime? The principal of a high school was convicted on two counts of indecent assault on male students. He had put his hand between the legs of a student and had offered him Playboy magazine. On another occasion, he talked about homosexuality with a male student and felt his private parts. The principal was married with three young children and a prominent member of the community. He had no prior criminal record. He lost his job as a result, his standard of living declined and he was only able to find part-time employment with his church. The issue here was the appeal of the 16-month sentence imposed on the accused. The court characterized the offences as "technical" assault, serious but not sufficiently aggravated to justify imprisonment for the benefit of punishment alone.[27] The court took into consideration that the offences were never repeated and assessed the extent of shame and economic punishment suffered by the principal set against the necessity of his remaining in jail. The appeal court came to the conclusion that he had already suffered enough.[28]

In another case a 32-year-old school teacher and school principal pleaded guilty to sexual assault involving sexual touching in the genital area. No force or violence was used.[29] Quoting a case called *R. v. Hoskins*,[30] the court imposed a sentence of three months, to be followed by probation.[31] The rationale for the term of imprisonment in *R. v. Hoskins* was as follows:

> What the applicant did was on the lower end of the scale of seriousness. … This is a case where deterrence … ranks ahead of rehabilitation … it is also important that a message should go out to those people in positions of trust dealing with young people … that they … must not allow [their sexual preferences] to be satisfied at the expense of young children… .[32]

In another case involving a principal, the Ontario Court of Justice recognized that the very nature of the relationship between principal and student "… gave rise to a coercive atmosphere, in which the accused was in control".[33] The accused "was in a position of power and authority over the complainant, who knew that [the accused] was widely respected".[34]

The off-duty conduct of a teacher is also increasingly being held to a higher standard since the Malcolm Ross case was decided by the Supreme Court of Canada (see below).[35] In a British Columbia arbitration, the suspension without pay of two married teachers for placing a picture of the wife in a "girlie magazine" was upheld on the basis that teachers must model appropriate behaviour at all times.[36] Sexual misbehaviour of any kind was cause for increased scrutiny of teachers because it compromised the ability of a teacher to perform his or her duties and to set an example for students. Oddly enough, the physical and emotional harm to actual victims had not attracted the same response from the courts or labour tribunals.

Many cases of sexual abuse or impropriety were still not being reported into the 1990s. "The reported cases are only the tip of the iceberg", as Sydney Robins reported in 2000 in his study of educational abuse in Ontario, described later in this chapter.[37] Robins concluded that teachers who had sexually abused students would not admit what they had done and had often taken measures to ensure that the victims remained silent. This silence was finally broken in 1989.

THE IMPACT OF MOUNT CASHEL

In 1989, a cover-up by church and government officials of widespread sexual and physical abuse at a church-run orphanage in Newfoundland outraged a nation. It was revealed that priests had perpetrated in unspeakable acts of abuse on the residents of Mount Cashel Orphanage. This orphanage was operated by the Order of Christian Brothers of Ireland and was an associate order of the Catholic Church. The Order operated 29 schools across Canada.

At first the Catholic Church responded by convening a special Archdiocesan Commission of Enquiry headed by Gordon White. The Commission was not empowered to summons witnesses or to order the production of documents. Despite this the Commission felt it necessary to follow a process modelled upon that of a public inquiry to address the anger and pain of the public.[38] The Commission held public meetings in parishes that had been directly affected. The Commission found "that at the center of the abuse were men with fiduciary responsibilities who abused their priestly status and power by acting out their regressed sexuality with children".[39] What was also discovered was that the Archdiocesan leadership had had knowledge of the deviant sexuality and inappropriate behaviour since the 1970s. The Church either denied the problems, admonished the clergy and established self-help programs, or transferred the priests to other communities.[40]

A public outcry resulted in the government of Newfoundland and Labrador establishing a Royal Inquiry headed up by Commissioner the Honourable S.H. Hughes. Unlike the Church inquiry, this was a full public inquiry with the power to subpoena evidence. It was revealed that the Archbishop had known about allegations of sexual abuse and had prevented a full investigation by police who were also complicit in the failure to protect the students. As more witnesses came forward, it became clear that many priests had physically, emotionally or sexually abused children for decades and that many others knew and failed to act. The most important aspect of the Inquiry was that it did clearly demonstrate a conspiracy of silence that could only be broken by empowering victims to speak out.

The subsequent uproar created a crisis of confidence within the Catholic community across Canada. It empowered children of other residential schools to come forward with their own experiences of abuse, including resident students at a Christian Brothers School in California and another in Ireland.[41] In addition, two other institutions run by the Order, one in British Columbia and another in Newfoundland, were investigated for similar abuse.[42]

Subsequent criminal proceedings resulted in many priests being convicted. More importantly, subsequent civil proceedings found that the Christian Brothers Order itself was liable to the victims because it stood *in loco parentis* in regards to children in its care. The Order was found liable for breach of fiduciary duty for failing to protect the children or to act in their best interests. Even more importantly, the Order was found to be negligent and vicariously liable for the acts of abuse by the individual brothers. The Brothers failed to take precautionary measures to decrease the likelihood of abuse, had knowledge of the abuse, failed to prevent further contact between abusive priests and their victims, and failed to report such information to the proper authorities.[43] The value of these claims is $36 million and growing. Victims were frustrated in recovering on these judgments for several years because the Brothers were an incorporated entity and the property they owned, which had to be sold to pay these debts, was protected by a claim that it was held in trust for a charitable purpose and could not be sold.[44]

GRAHAME WISHART

A student who had heard first-hand the stories of abuse at Mount Cashel from a victim realized that he too was the victim of a sexual predator. That predator was not a priest or an employee of a residential facility. He was Grahame Wishart, a well-respected 46-year-old music department head at Toronto's Oakwood Collegiate. The disclosure and subsequent criminal charges split the school community. Many were angry that allegations had been made and felt that the teacher was the victim of a witch-hunt. Others, primarily those who knew the victims, felt betrayed by the teacher. Many of Wishart's colleagues did not believe the charges. The school community endured almost a year of anger and recrimination. Then, Wishart pleaded guilty to 11 counts of sexual assault and one count of sexual exploitation. He was sent to jail for two years and placed on probation for a further three years.

The agreed statement of facts prepared for the guilty plea revealed that on weekends, Wishart took several male students up to one of his two Ontario cottages. He drove them in his car or he flew them up in his bush plane. Once there, he bought their favourite liquor or beer and encouraged them to drink in the evenings. When they were drunk, he gave them a pill that he said would reduce the effects of a hangover, but that was really a sleeping pill. Later in the night, while they were "stupefied" by the pill and alcohol, he molested and fondled them, the Crown attorney said. Wishart's strong personality drew the students to him and he became like a surrogate father for several boys from broken homes.[45]

This case had a profound impact on the Toronto Board of Education. It determined to develop clear rules regarding disclosures of abuse, dealing with implicated employees as well as informing and supporting the school community. As a result, by 1993, the Toronto board had prepared a detailed policy, which was updated by the new amalgamated Toronto District School Board in 1999. Extracts from that policy may be found in Appendix 8. Once this policy was in place the entire staff were trained in the procedures. Again, after amalgamation, all of the staff of the Toronto District School Board were trained in the procedures.

Further disclosures of abuse by educational employees at the Toronto board occurred with increased frequency. Some were historical as in Mount Cashel, while others were contemporary. In several cases the accused was a prominent, well-respected teacher. In one case the abuser was a principal. In several, there was a pattern of previous complaints with transfers to other schools or even other boards. Clearly the comprehensive new policy was empowering students to come forward and put an end to the cycle of abuse.

ST. GEORGE'S CATHEDRAL BOYS CHOIR

The fact that a person in a position of authority could misuse that authority to exploit young persons and to cover up the abuse, hiding behind a reputation as a well-respected community member, was a pattern that was becoming all too familiar. In Kingston, Ontario, a choirmaster at St. George's Cathedral used this same *modus operandi* to sexually molest hundreds of young boys. One victim came forward but the Diocese failed to act on the advice of its lawyer. However, the suicide of an adult ex-choirboy who was emotionally affected by the abuse brought the matter to public attention. In 1990, John Galliene pleaded guilty to 20 counts of sexually abusing 13 boys. The charges ranged from molestation to fellatio and sodomy. Two of Galliene's victims are dead, by suicide. Later 11 former choirboys won a landmark $2.1 million out-of-court settlement against St. George's Cathedral and the Synod of the Anglican Diocese of Ontario.[46] It is significant that the Church assumed liability for the actions of an individual as well as for the Church's failure to act to prevent abuse. This is a situation that is increasingly facing school boards and is the subject of Chapter 2.

JERICHO HILL

In 1993, a special counsel was appointed to look into allegations of sexual abuse of students at the Jericho Hill School for the Deaf in British Columbia.[47] Reporting to the Deputy Attorney General of British Columbia, the special counsel was to conduct an informal investigation "to avoid requiring the victims to relive the trauma of their abuse and to avoid the risk of compromising innocent persons".[48] The objective was to avoid disrupting the deaf community. The abuse occurred at the hands of staff and other residents. The inquiry revealed that the abuse allegations were first disclosed to the school authorities in 1982. Generally it was found that the school did not report the disclosures to the parents. The abused received no therapy. The employees involved were dismissed or transferred; one had resigned. No charges were laid.

In 1986 there was a suicide in the group home. In 1987 one student attempted suicide after having abused his siblings sexually. He alleged that a childcare counsellor had sexually abused him.

It was not until 1987 that a real investigation took place. Once the investigation was completed, it was ascertained that there had been no proper training for the staff. There were no official policies and procedures for the appropriate management and operation of the school. Sleeping arrangements were inappropriate; for example, students slept in a gender-mixed dormitory. There was very poor supervision by the staff and too few staff for the number of students. Students were isolated from their parents, who most often were unable to communicate with their children, as they could not use sign language. The special counsel found that disclosures had been made to the psychologist at Jericho Hill School. The psychologist informed the Ministry of Education but it had taken no steps to investigate the reports.[49] The overall atmosphere of the school was described as a "culture of sexual abuse".[50]

INSTITUTIONAL AND TRAINING SCHOOL ABUSE

In 1990 two Ontario institutions were the subject of major police investigations of physical and sexual abuse of resident students. St. John's Training School in Uxbridge and St. Joseph's Training School in Alfred were both operated by the lay order of the Brothers of the Christian Schools under the supervision of the Ontario government. The residents of the schools were varied. There were orphans, "delinquents", Children's Aid Society referrals, physically and perceptually challenged students, children from Indian reserves and children from homes whose parents could not support them. The abuse occurred mainly between 1930 and 1974, although there were some isolated cases in the 1980s.

The Ontario Provincial Police began their investigation in the early 1990s. They laid charges against 28 Christian Brothers from both schools. The charges covered 200 counts of abuse. Indecent assault and sodomy were among the charges laid. Some of the accused were convicted and the Government of Ontario and the Roman Catholic Archdioceses negotiated a redress program. The abused victims received financial compensation, and access to various benefits such as counselling and therapy, to "help restore lost trust in the spiritual and secular institutions of … society".[51]

In 1991, the Waterloo Regional Police and the Ontario Provincial Police began a joint investigation into the claims of physical and sexual abuse at Grandview, a training facility for adolescent girls operated by the Ontario provincial government from 1932 to 1976 in Galt, later part of Cambridge, Ontario. The girls became wards of the province and their parents relinquished all rights over them. There were approximately 100 girls housed in the institution annually and of those one-quarter were in a secure facility. The population of Grandview was varied. Some girls had committed petty crimes and others were sent because they were described as unmanageable under the *Juvenile Delinquents Act.*[52]

The girls were extremely vulnerable, as family members had physically and sexually abused many. Others were orphans. Several came from homes where parents were unable to care for them due to extreme poverty. Students were physically, emotionally and sexually abused during their residency there. The most serious instances of abuse occurred between the mid-1960s and the 1970s. The school was closed in 1976 as a consequence of the allegations of abuse against staff and guards. Some women were interested in filing legal suits, while others sought collective compensation. The Province of Ontario, through mediation, attempted to settle the Grandview claims through an out-of-court settlement, and in 1994 a draft agreement with the government was reached. The government's compensation package did not restrict individuals' rights to bring civil actions against individual perpetrators of abuse. Not only did the package include monetary compensation, but it also provided access to therapy and counselling and to vocational training. Most importantly, it allowed the women a forum for the disclosure of their abuse and its acknowledgement.[53]

In 1992 the issue of institutional abuse arose at the New Brunswick Training School in Kingsclear operated by the Ministry of the Solicitor General. It housed "delinquents" and those who were wards of the state awaiting foster placement. A Commission of Inquiry was held and a compensation package was established to provide redress to the victims. In 1985 the first allegation of sexual abuse by an employee against a male student was reported. The employee was transferred. A few years later other allegations against the employee were filed. The regional police and RCMP investigated the complaints but no charges were laid. In 1991 an employee named Karl Toft was arrested and charged with 27 counts of sexual abuse. Twelve additional charges were laid in 1992. Toft pleaded guilty to 34 counts of sexual abuse and was sentenced to 13 years in prison. Others have since been convicted.[54] It is now believed that Toft may have been one of the worst serial abusers in Canadian history.

In or about 1992, the New Brunswick government set up a Commission of Inquiry to investigate allegations of physical and sexual abuse in three provincial institutions. One of the institutions was a hospital school operated by the New Brunswick Department of Health for mentally challenged minors and other wards of the state. The Department of Justice announced a compensation program in 1996 in an effort to redress the wrongs, compensate the victims, and provide counselling and vocational training. The process called for the thorough investigation of the claimant's allegations, in order to safeguard against fraudulent claims.[55]

In 1993, the same issue again arose, this time in Nova Scotia. Damages were sought by residents of the Shelburne Youth Centre for sexual abuse perpetrated by a youth counsellor named Patrick MacDougall who had been convicted of 11 charges of sexual abuse involving 10 complainants. At trial information surfaced that when allegations were brought against MacDougall, government officials transferred him from Shelburne to the Sydney Children's Training Centre.

In 1994 the Nova Scotia government took the initiative to investigate the extent of the sexual and physical abuse that occurred in Shelburne from 1956 to 1975. The government was interested in knowing the practices and procedures that were in place that "permitted or hindered detection of abuse of children".[56] The government was also interested in developing a compensation package for the victims if the investigation revealed liability. The report was completed in 1995, and concluded that there was ongoing sexual, physical and emotional abuse of the residents who were held in custody at the Shelburne Youth Training Centre and at the Nova Scotia Youth Training Centre.[57]

The findings indicated that there were no mechanisms in place for reporting abuse and consequently young offenders and staff did not report the abuse. The report also stated that there were no appropriate mechanisms in place to ensure proper communication and follow-up between responsible departmental authorities and police agencies in the event of allegations of sexual and other abuse of young persons held in custody. In 1996 the government provided a compensation program. Subsequent complaints about the government's compensation package for victims of institutional abuse resulted in an independent review.[58]

MAPLE LEAF GARDENS

The duty of other members of the educational community came under close scrutiny with revelations of abuse of young boys by part-time employees at Maple Leaf Gardens between the 1960s and 1980. The convicted abuser was a volunteer and part-time employee at two school boards who had misused his position. It was revealed that nearly 90 children, most of them boys, had been sexually abused over 20 years, after being lured to the hockey arena with promises of souvenirs or free admission to NHL hockey games or musical events. The first complainant was Martin Kruze. He took his case to Gardens officials, who failed to act for many years. Even though he was later vindicated, Kruze could never escape the emotional demons of the abuse and committed suicide in 1997. The same year, former Gardens assistant equipment manager Gordon Stuckless was sentenced to two years less a day for sexually abusing 24 boys.[59] In 1998, the Court of Appeal increased the sentence to five years.

There were other Gardens staff involved as well: George Hanna, another employee of the Gardens implicated in the abuse, died in or around 1983. An usher, John Paul Roby, was charged with 60 counts of varying sexual offences involving 42 boys.

What is important to note about Stuckless is that he was not only an assistant equipment manager employed by Maple Leaf Gardens, but was also a teacher's assistant at two public schools: Park Public School and Lake Wilcox Public School. At Park School, in the Regent Park area of Toronto, Stuckless assisted with athletic programs in the school at lunch hour and coached city lacrosse and hockey teams at a facility adjacent to the school. He became involved in the personal lives of some of the boys, even visiting their homes and becoming friends with their parents. Some of the assaults took place in classrooms and at the Gardens in public view during hockey games and other events.[60]

When the Crown appealed the original sentence, the Ontario Court of Appeal looked at the manner in which Stuckless and Hanna enticed the boys with favours and gifts. This was set out in the agreed statement of facts signed by Stuckless when he pleaded guilty to 24 counts of indecent and sexual assault. The Court of Appeal noted that the sentencing judge did observe that Stuckless established a relationship of trust with the boys and "… consistently and without apparent hesitation, violated the trust reposed in him".[61] Watt J., the sentencing judge, considered Stuckless' conduct purposeful. "The boys were means to an end, the sexual gratification of Gordon Stuckless."[62]

The sentencing judge also recognized that the offences left "a profound and enduring impression" on the victims.[63] Watt J. relied on the principle that the sentence fit the gravity of the offence and the degree of responsibility of the offender. He viewed the crimes as on the less serious side of the spectrum in that no weapons were used and there was no force, no threats, no anal intercourse and no col-lateral crime. Another factor taken into consideration by him was Gordon Stuckless' apparent remorse. The guilty plea was viewed as an acknow-ledgement of responsibility for the crimes he committed. Watt J. also con-cluded that "the disorder from which [Stuckless] and others suffer is not cured or deterred by imprisonment", but is "controlled or can be by med-ication willingly taken and some insight into the disorder". Given those mitigating factors, he imposed a less onerous sentence and gave credit for Stuckless' time spent in jail.[64]

The Court of Appeal took a different view. It regarded the original sentence imposed as insufficient. It focused on the need to protect the public and to provide a denunciatory sentence reflecting Stuckless' moral culpability and society's outrage. The sentence had to reflect society's condemnation of the particular offender's conduct. It viewed the sexual offences continuing over 20 years and the premeditated manner in which Stuckless gained and abused the trust of the boys to gratify his sexual needs as "reprehensible" and serious in nature. "These offences were, individually and collectively, unconscionable".[65] The Court of Appeal described the sexual abuse of children as acts of violence and the magnitude of the crime could not be diminished because apparently no force or weapons were used and no threats were uttered.[66] Rehabilitation was considered important. "The public has an undeniable interest in protecting itself through the rehabilitation of Stuckless", but the Court of Appeal considered general deterrence to be a relevant factor in sentencing pedophiles.[67] It was now clear, in the post-Mount Cashel world, that the courts were taking the issue of abuse by persons in authority more seriously.

ABORIGINAL RESIDENTIAL SCHOOLS

The growing awareness of the vulnerability of students in institutional settings was accelerated by the explosion of claims by aboriginals who had been students in the "residential school system".

The federal government began to play a role in the development and administration of school systems for aboriginal children as early as 1874, mainly to meet its obligation under the *Indian Act*[68] to provide an education to aboriginal people, as well as to assist with their integration into the broader Canadian society. Although the schools varied in their structure and programming — some were industrial schools and some were boarding schools, while others were schools where students lived for up to 10 months away from the reserve — all have come to be known as "residential schools". Approximately 100 such facilities were located in every province and territory, except New Brunswick and Prince Edward Island. It is estimated that approximately 100,000 children attended these schools over the years in which they were in operation.

Until April 1, 1969, the schools were run jointly by the government and various religious organizations, including the Catholic and Anglican Churches and what is now known as the United Church of Canada. The schools were slowly phased out and the last federally run residential school in Canada closed in Saskatchewan in 1996.

In recent years, individuals have come forward with personal and painful stories of physical and sexual abuse at residential schools. Today, while it is not uncommon to hear some former students speak about their positive experiences in these institutions, their stories are overshadowed by disclosures of abuse and criminal convictions of perpetrators that tell of the tragic legacy the residential school system has left with many former students. They, and their communities, continue to deal with issues such as physical and sexual abuse, family violence, and drug and alcohol abuse.

The problem was studied first by the Royal Commission on Aboriginal Peoples and later by the Law Reform Commission of Canada. While there was great concern over the assimilation policies, the loss of culture and language and the separation of children from their families, what has received the most attention was abuse at the hands of religious and lay staff at the schools.

The relative isolation of the schools and the atmosphere of total authority resulted in terrible cases of abuse. While many complaints involved mistreatment by priests and lay brothers, what is notable about many of the cases that have been litigated is that institutional authority of the churches and the government created an atmosphere where children could be preyed on by any employee of the school. Recent decisions have described seven-year-old boys strapped down and sexually assaulted by a school administrator in a government-run school in Saskatchewan in 1975.[69] Even though he was not a teacher, his apparent authority in school administration gave him *de facto* power over children. In another case a lay dormitory supervisor sexually assaulted students. This supervisor was in a parental position with prolonged and intimate contact with the children in his care; the children were away from their home and parents, making them particularly vulnerable; the social architecture of the school ensured that the dormitory supervisor was not viewed just as a parent, but as the most powerful influence in the children's lives; the supervisor was white, as were all the staff, making the supervisor even more unassailable; and the supervisor's room was immediately adjacent to the dormitory.[70]

The liability for support staff in residential schools was extended in a recent British Columbia Supreme Court decision.[71] The court found that the plaintiff, while attending a residential school near Tofino, British Columbia, was sexually assaulted by a baker at the school when he was seven years old, and that the assaults continued on a regular and frequent basis until he was 11 or 12 years old. The school was operated by the Order of the Oblates of Mary Immaculate in the Province of British Columbia. All of the assaults took place in the baker's living quarters, which were situated in a building on the school grounds. The court found that the Order was liable even though it had no knowledge of the abuse at the time and had given the cook no authority over, or responsibility for, the children at the school. The court found that the Oblate disciplinarians made it clear to the children that they were supposed to listen to and obey the lay staff and this was sufficient to establish liability in the Oblate Order for the actions of the baker.

It was determined by the Law Reform Commission that three factors contributed to the abuse of aboriginal students:

- The children came from marginalized groups in society.
- A significant power imbalance existed between the children and the adults who were imbued with the institutional authority to discipline and the moral authority of a religion.
- There was little independent monitoring of internal activities of such schools and the desire to preserve reputation often overcame concern for the welfare of children.[72]

Today, aboriginal people want recognition of what was done to their communities as a result of the residential schools. Aboriginal people have demanded, and received, official apologies from the Anglican, United and Roman Catholic churches, which operated residential schools. As more and more former students of residential schools come forth with stories about the sexual and physical abuse they experienced, several religious authorities that administered the schools are being charged criminally. In addition, the liability of churches has resulted in financial problems for the Anglican, United and Catholic Churches, which have to sell assets and develop church properties to pay for settlements.

The federal government offered a Statement of Reconciliation that included an apology to aboriginal survivors of the schools. In addition, the Government committed $350 million in support of a community-based healing strategy to address the healing needs of individuals, families and communities arising from the legacy of physical and sexual abuse at residential schools. On May 4, 1998, the Aboriginal Healing Foundation was formally launched. The Foundation was created to design, implement and manage the healing strategy, including providing financial support to eligible community-based healing initiatives that complement existing aboriginal and government programs.

Thousands of victims filed legal actions, some of which were successfully litigated against many religious institutions, but the vast majority await full settlement by the federal government. The government has set up a special program that encourages survivors of residential schools to report allegations of abuse to the police, and to participate in a mediation process to determine appropriate treatment and financial terms of settlement.

All of these actions, of course, will not undo the damage of the past. Recognizing and acknowledging the history is a start, but what was needed was a proactive approach to protect young persons.

ABUSE OF YOUTH IN SPORTS AND EDUCATION: TWO STUDIES, ONE RESULT

The Kirke Report

In 1996, the hockey community was shocked by revelations by Sheldon Kennedy, a National Hockey League player with the Boston Bruins, that he had been sexually assaulted by Graham James, his junior hockey coach in Saskatchewan, over 300 times between 1984 and 1990. In January 1997, Graham James pleaded to guilty sexual assault and was sentenced to three-and-a-half years in prison. As a result, the Canadian Hockey League comprising the Ontario Hockey League, the Quebec Major Junior Hockey League, and the Western Hockey League, commissioned the Players First Report, known as the Kirke Report because it was prepared by Gordon I. Kirke Q.C. The report seemed to be a response to the disclosures made by Kennedy. It confronted the issues of sexual harassment and abuse within the Canadian Hockey league:

> The mission was not to investigate instances of harassment or abuse which may have occurred in the past, rather it was a clear directive to bring forward policies and procedures designed to (a) decrease the likelihood of it happening in the Canadian Hockey League in the future and (b) to provide an appropriate environment and support mechanism in the event that it does happen.[73]

The mandate of the Report was to provide strategies to ensure that abuse and harassment could be prevented. Such strategies included the screening of personnel and the educating of players regarding the causes of abuse and the consequences of abuse and harassment. The report was also commissioned to provide recommendations for the reporting of abuse and harassment, and the creation of a support framework and counselling services for players and employees who experienced harassment and/or abuse. The Report also contained a policy manual and a procedure manual for initiating complaints, as well as a mission statement and clear definitions of what constitutes sexual harassment.

In researching the Report, Kirke found that one in three males reported unwanted sexual touching in his lifetime.[74] Though numbers of reported male sexual abuse victims are high, disbelief and scepticism follow the reports. There is a hostile social climate that wishes to avoid facing the fact that there is abuse and harassment in arenas where myths of masculinity and strength continue to be treasured.[75] Research indicates that the harassment of males is infrequently reported and largely overlooked.

Kirke recommended that there be screening procedures for the Canadian Hockey League. This recommendation is necessary because the Canadian Hockey League "is the springboard for careers in the National Hockey League, minor professional leagues, Canadian University hockey clubs and Olympic teams".[76] The coaches, the management and the staff of these organizations have come to be viewed as the trusted guardians of the players at any level. According to Kirke, the coaches were endowed with tremendous power. The relationship between coach and player was unbalanced and consequently had the potential for abuse. Coaches had the power to influence players in many ways.

Generally speaking, the majority of the coaches were described as having integrity, but research has demonstrated that predators seek out positions of trust and authority with young persons to sexually exploit and harm them.[77] Screening was viewed by Kirke as a possible deterrent to those who fear background inquiries. Screening procedures would include completing local police record checks as well as making full use of the federally operated Canadian Police Information Centre and the Automated Canadian-United States Police Information System. All applicants should consent to the full record checks. There should also be reference checks for applicants. Applicants should provide a list of three references and consent to their references being assessed. There should also be ongoing evaluation by parents and players of the employees and volunteers with whom they interact. Players and parents could submit their evaluations anonymously. If a pattern of complaints emerged, steps could be taken to do whatever was necessary and reasonable with respect to the subject of the pattern of complaints.

Other recommendations in the report focused on education strategies as protective mechanisms. The Report dispels the myth that removing players from their homes and sending them away as part of the draft procedures places them at greater risk of sexual abuse or harassment. The Report asserts that children are best served by making them aware of the issues of harassment and abuse. The Report identifies early childhood education as the key to protecting players from harassment. Younger children are being targeted by predators and, according to Kirke, they must be taught and reassured that they have rights as autonomous beings. They also should be taught that victimization is not their fault. Children should be made aware that predators are often people that they trust. The Report also recommends that parents educate their children, not only in recognizing abusive situations but also in developing coping mechanisms and learning how and to whom to report abuse. The Report recommends that the Canadian Hockey League take reasonable steps to lend its support to educational programs. Advisors should be appointed and made responsible for educating employers and players with respect to what constitutes harassment and abuse, and how to be aware of it, prevent it and report it.

The development of a policy was another recommendation made by the Report. Integral to the policy was the development of a complaint process that was intended to work in conjunction with any external procedures. It was also recommended that the Canadian Hockey League appoint a committee to oversee the implementation and administration of the policy.

Given the sensitivity of young people, and the shame attached to the disclosure of sexual abuse or harassment, the Kirke Report recommended that the Canadian Hockey league establish a system of nationwide toll-free telephone support services for players who have disclosed or wish to disclose or report sexual harassment and abuse. The Kirke Report indicated that there could be no effective response to harassment or abuse when the experience is shrouded in secrecy. Once the disclosure is made, the player should be connected to the appropriate individualized counselling. It recommended that the Committee establish an appropriate counselling and support service system for the victims of abuse or harassment. It also recommended that there be an appropriate insurance scheme designed to assist with the cost or subsidize the counselling. The Report recommended that mechanisms be put in place to ensure that the complainant's right to privacy would be protected.

The Robins Report

In 1999, the issue of abuse of day students at an Ontario school board was the subject of a provincial inquiry in Ontario. The Honourable Mr. Justice Robins was by Order in Council appointed to conduct a review and prepare a report as a result of the conviction of Kenneth DeLuca, a schoolteacher employed by the Roman Catholic Separate School Board in Sault Ste. Marie. DeLuca pleaded guilty to having sexually assaulted female students over 20 years. Justice Robins was not only to inquire into the particulars of the DeLuca case but was to make recommendations regarding protocols, policies and procedures that would assist in the identification and prevention of "sexual assault, harassment or violence" in the publicly funded schools of Ontario.[78]

The DeLuca story was yet another example of a sexual abuser in a position of trust and authority who had abused his position of trust repeatedly, but who nevertheless was able to continue abusing within an institutional setting, a school board. He has been described as a sexual predator. He was arrested and charged with 41 offences involving 21 complainants in 1994. All but one of the complainants was a former student. Their ages ranged from 10 to 18. The non-student complainant was a female teacher with the school board. On April 9, 1996, prior to the commencement of his trial, DeLuca pleaded guilty and was convicted of 14 offences: six counts of indecent assault, seven counts of sexual assault, and one count of counselling a person to touch for a sexual purpose. The convictions related to 13 of the complainants. DeLuca was sentenced to 40 months' imprisonment. Eight of the victims were between 10 and 13 years old. Four were high school students.

DeLuca began his teaching career at St. Joseph's School in 1970. A complaint about DeLuca was made with respect to his use of excessive force in 1972. He was transferred to Canadian Martyrs School in 1972. The official reason given for the transfer was declining enrolment at St. Joseph's. The information regarding DeLuca's use of excessive force was never communicated to Canadian Martyrs at the time of the transfer. Complaints were made about DeLuca at Canadian Martyrs as early as 1973. The complainant at the time was between 11 and 12 years old. She lodged a complaint with respect to improper advances. The principal acknowledged her complaint, but no written report was prepared. The complainant remained at home, left the school and was enrolled in the public school system for the following year. More allegations surfaced with respect to other young girls aged 11 and 12 between 1972 and 1974. Some of these allegations of unwanted sexual advances made by DeLuca became the focus of a meeting held in 1974 at Canadian Martyrs, attended by a large group of parents. The principal of Canadian Martyrs and the Assistant Superintendent of Schools were among the officials present. As a consequence of the meeting DeLuca was verbally reprimanded and a vague report regarding the allegations of improper behaviour toward his students was placed in the file. DeLuca was transferred to St. Theresa's School in 1974. The official reason was declining enrolment at Canadian Martyrs.

DeLuca remained at St. Theresa's School from 1974 to 1981. No details of DeLuca's previous record or of any of the allegations were transferred with DeLuca. The reprimand letter was not forwarded to St. Theresa's School. There were many incidents of sexualized conduct and abuse during the course of DeLuca's tenure at St. Theresa's School, involving 11 young girls between the ages of 9 and 14. The parents of the children recollected that they had complained to the principal, but that their complaints were either ignored or minimized. They were unaware of any resulting investigation. The principal had only vague recollections of the incidents of sexual assault reported by the parents. In 1981, DeLuca was transferred to St. Veronica's School. The nature of the complaints was never conveyed to the principal of St. Veronica's. In 1984-85 five young girls alleged sexual abuse of them by DeLuca. An investigation was conducted at the school and board levels. There was no indication that DeLuca was interviewed with respect to the allegations. DeLuca was exonerated. However, he was reprimanded for "behaving in a less than professional manner".[79] The students' parents were not informed of the allegations against DeLuca. No report was placed in DeLuca's file at the school.

DeLuca left to teach at Mount St. Joseph's College. He remained there from 1985 to 1988. During the period of time that DeLuca was there, one young girl was charged criminally for harassing him. DeLuca transferred to St. Mary's College in 1988. The official reason for the transfer was the advancement of DeLuca's career. No information regarding the past allegations of sexual abuse came to the attention of the principal of St. Mary's College. At St. Mary's College, sexual assault allegations were made against DeLuca by a few of his students. Complaints on the part of students surfaced with respect to DeLuca in 1989, 1992, and 1993.

The police were finally brought into the case in a serious way due to the actions of the coordinator of Community Schools and Continuing Education (called Ms. Doe in the subsequent legal proceedings). In 1989, DeLuca made unwanted advances to Ms. Doe when she attempted to discuss with him a complaint brought to her by a student regarding his inappropriate conduct. A meeting was held to discuss certain issues regarding DeLuca's lack of professionalism. Suggestions were made to DeLuca that he seek help. The issues at the meeting remained general and vague. In 1992 the Sault Ste. Marie Police were contacted by the principal of St. Mary's College, but the investigation was aborted. It was not until 1993 that Ms. Doe and the principal of St. Mary's College, Mr. Barsanti, approached the Sault Ste. Marie Police independently with complaints regarding certain inappropriate sexual behaviour on the part of DeLuca. The investigation resulted in DeLuca's arrest in 1994.

The subsequent inquiry noted that there appeared to be a reluctance to proceed with any form of investigation on the part of the school board authorities. Instead of investigating, it appeared that school authorities simply transferred the problem to a new school. Each new school was provided with no information regarding DeLuca. Furthermore, information regarding DeLuca took a great deal of effort to secure. The system seemed to be complicit in the abuse. There was reluctance to believe the accounts of the students or their parents. There was a reluctance to talk specifically about sexual misconduct with either DeLuca or the school authorities. There did not appear to be any mechanisms for reporting, investigating or addressing the complaints.

Students who did complain were either threatened or made to feel as if they would be the cause of DeLuca becoming impoverished and humiliated. The complainants were filled with dread of their teacher and felt humiliated. School authorities either minimized their complaints, blamed the students, or drove them away. Even Ms. Doe, an adult who was the recipient of unwanted sexual advances, was hesitant and reluctant to confront DeLuca specifically and directly. She was informed early of the complaints regarding DeLuca but only stepped forward and followed through four years after her first encounter with DeLuca's sexual misconduct against her.

There were long-lasting effects of the trauma suffered by the complainants and victims of abuse. The experiences affected their interpersonal relationships and their self-esteem.

Research indicates that there are many incidents of sexual abuse and misconduct between teachers, principals and students that remain unreported. The sexual abuse of students has been very difficult to acknowledge. Empirical data on sexual abuse or sexual misconduct in the school system usually has been limited to those cases that have become public. Robins has described "public domain cases as those that have been reported by the press and other forms of news media, the cases that are the subject of civil litigation, discipline hearings, grievance hearings, or criminal court proceedings.[80]

According to Robins, between 1989 and 1996 the Ontario Teachers' Federation, in its role as the regulatory body for Ontario teachers, dealt with over 100 cases of sexual misconduct by teachers.[81] From 1997, when the Ontario College of Teachers took over the jurisdiction of discipline, until the publication of the Robins Report, there have been approximately 20 cases of discipline involving students and teachers.[82] When a school board discovers sexual misconduct there is often a dismissal which is then grieved by the teacher's union. This can result in a labour arbitration. There have been numerous cases of sexual misconduct dealt with in the context of grievance proceedings before labour arbitration boards. They have involved school staff as well as teachers. Those recorded seem to appear with more frequency in the 1980s. The behaviours range from sexual harassment, hugging and kissing, to actions involving more egregious conduct. Writing in 1999-2000, Robins has also indicated that since 1986 there have been approximately 100 reported cases of criminal proceedings against teachers, principals, volunteers and other school employees.[83]

ROBINS' RECOMMENDATIONS: THE TERM "SEXUAL MISCONDUCT" IS COINED

As a result of the DeLuca scandal and after hearing submissions from school boards, teachers' federations and other interested parties, Robins drafted a list of over 100 recommendations for changes to the *Education Act*[84] and other statutes to provide further and better protection for students.

Many of the lessons learned by the Canadian Hockey League are applicable to the education system. Both authors recommend that the best approach to predatory sexual behaviour by persons in authority is to create a safe environment that educates and encourages youth to report abuse. Such an environment is very unfriendly to potential abusers and discourages them from taking advantage of vulnerable youth.

A detailed breakdown of Robins' recommendations can be found in subsequent chapters of this book, particularly in Chapter 3. In brief, Robins recommended in *Protecting Our Students* that all boards establish a comprehensive policy on sexual misconduct, covering all school board employees and volunteers, that outlines sexual abuse and exploitation, sexual harassment and sexual relationships generally. This broad stroke approach would make such conduct subject to internal discipline, up to and including dismissal, and would require internal reporting and internal formal investigations into all complaints, disclosures or observations in the case of non-criminal behaviours. No longer could problem teachers be transferred to new settings where the behaviour would recur. In addition, boards should screen new teachers before hiring and should check criminal records and references. Justice Robins recommended that boards go beyond the traditional definition of sexual discrimination and include behaviour that is incompatible with the role of a teacher, regardless of whether students regard the behaviour as "unwelcome". Examples may be teasing, telling off-colour jokes, asking students on dates or on trips. These may be types of "flirting" or similar social behaviours that adolescent students might welcome or enjoy but that are not appropriate in a learning environment.

Justice Robins suggested the following behaviour be deemed to be sexual misconduct: objectionable comments or conduct of a sexual nature that may affect a student's personal integrity or security or the school environment. These may not be overtly sexual but nonetheless demean or cause personal embarrassment to a student based on a student's gender.

Sexual relationships with older or adult students have presented a problem for educators, particularly when the age gap is relatively small, or the adult student is actually older than the teacher. There are many examples of students in such relationships actually marrying their teachers. Because both parties to the relationship are adults, it is often assumed that if a student consents, there is no reason for concern. However, the relationship between a teacher and a student is a professional relationship very similar to that of a doctor with a patient or a lawyer with a client. The teacher is in a powerful position *vis-à-vis* a student, since the teacher has the power to grant or withhold a credit. When a sexual relationship develops, the integrity of the credit-granting process is in question. In addition, the relative bargaining power of the parties is not equal and there is always a danger that the student is being exploited. It is possible that students will not feel secure and protected in an environment where a teacher is openly courting a student. It may also raise a suspicion of unequal treatment or favouritism. Some students may be reluctant to resist advances, fearing retribution. There is also a concern that a student who leaves school may return later. That is why Robins recommended a province-wide prohibition upon sexual activity between a teacher and a former student under the age of 18. "Responsibility for ensuring that a teacher-student relationship is appropriate rests with the teacher, and not the student. This remains the case even if it is the student who attempts to initiate the relationship."[85]

Justice Robins recommended that the definition of sexual misconduct include the following:

> any sexual relationship with a student, or with a former student under the age of 18, and any conduct directed to establishing such a relationship.[86]

Ultimately, the Robins Report led to the passage of the *Student Protection Act, 2002*,[87] an omnibus Bill that amended several pieces of legislation and implemented approximately 20 of Robins' recommendations.

THE ROLE OF A TEACHER

At the same time as attitudes towards and awareness of sexual misconduct were changing radically, so too was the societal view of the role of the teacher. A landmark decision in the area of teacher misconduct was made by the Supreme Court of Canada in *Ross v. New Brunswick School District*.[88] Even though the conduct was not sexual abuse or criminal in nature, the Court emphasized the duty of a teacher to always model good behaviour for students and not to compromise a healthy learning environment. This decision is very consistent with the post-Cashel concern that the special relationship between a teacher and a student not be abused.

The question before the Court was whether or not a school board should terminate the employment of Malcolm Ross if his off-duty activities create a poisoned educational atmosphere. The Court also considered whether the off-duty conduct of the teacher affected on his ability to teach. The teacher uttered and published anti-Semitic statements in the community but not in the course of his duties in the classroom. The matter was brought to the attention of the Human Rights Commission of New Brunswick by a Jewish parent of a student who had suffered from discrimination by other students, not Ross directly. The Commission ordered the board of education to place Ross in a non-teaching position, and if none was available to terminate his employment. Ross asserted that the curtailing of his off-duty activities was in violation of his right of freedom of expression under the *Canadian Charter of Rights and Freedoms*.[89] It is important to note that the Supreme Court of Canada found that the Board of Inquiry indicated correctly that a school board has a duty to maintain a positive school environment for all persons served by it:

> The conduct of a teacher bears directly upon the community's perception of the ability of the teacher to fulfil such a position of trust and influence, and upon the community's confidence in the ... school system as a whole.[90]

The Supreme Court of Canada went on to note that:

> The reason why off-the-job conduct may amount to misconduct is that a teacher holds a position of trust confidence and responsibility. If he or she acts in an improper way, on or off the job, there may be a loss of public confidence in the teacher and in the ... school system, a loss of respect by students for the teacher involved, and other teachers generally, and there may be controversy within the school and within the community which disrupts the proper carrying on of the educational system.[91]

The Supreme Court of Canada also found that the off-duty comments of Ross impaired his ability to fulfil his teaching position. Therefore it concluded that the continued employment of Ross contributed to "an invidiously discriminatory or 'poisoned' educational environment …".[92]

The special duty of a teacher was underscored in an Ontario court dealing with the offence of inviting, counselling and inciting a young person to touch the teacher's body for a sexual purpose.[93] While the teacher was acquitted, the court stated that the defendant, who was a music teacher, was in a position of trust and authority with respect to the complainant and that by being intimate with the student and showing him pornographic videos the teacher had engaged in unprofessional conduct. The court stated that a teacher "assumes a heavy mantle of responsibility".[94] His conduct should have been "irreproachable".[95] One significant factor for the court was that the teacher had a relationship that was conducted outside school hours and off school property, in a private residence.[96]

CONCLUSION

This chapter has attempted to briefly trace the history of child sexual abuse in Canada. It has tried to demonstrate that the values and norms of society have impeded society's ability to recognize that child abuse existed and that it was morally wrong and socially harmful. It has demonstrated that the public awareness of the issue of child sexual abuse arose out of the public's awareness of childhood as a separate and distinct stage of human development. It also arose out of an awareness that it was morally and socially wrong to physically abuse children. Once the concept of physical abuse came to the public's attention, the concept of child sexual abuse followed. It took a long time before society and the public were able to face the reality that children were being sexually abused not by strangers, but by alleged loved ones and those in positions of trust and authority over them. It was only when repeated, vindicated complaints of widespread institutional abuse came to public attention that attitudes changed.

This chapter has also tried to demonstrate how the provincial and federal governments responded to the awareness of child sexual abuse as an issue warranting their attention, and how they attempted to address the enormity of the problem as it manifested itself in their institutions and throughout their educational systems. In addition, increased scrutiny has expanded the scope of the issue from sexual assault of children to a wide range of exploitative behaviours. First "child abuse" was differentiated from other criminal conduct, then it was expanded to a wide array of behaviours, labelled "sexual misconduct".

Ultimately, young persons must be protected from abuse or exploitation by those entrusted with their care. This is only possible when the schools are vigilant and the judicial system repudiates such conduct in the strongest terms.

ENDNOTES

[1] Law Reform Commission of Canada, "Institutional Child Abuse Discussion Paper", cited at http//:www.lcc.gc.ca/en/themes/mr/ica/1998/discussion.asp (1998), p. 6.

[2] J. Steed, *Our Little Secret: Confronting Child Sexual Abuse in Canada* (Toronto: Random House, 1994), p. 5.

[3] Canada, *Sexual Offences Against Children: Report of the Committee on Sexual Offences Against Children and Youth* (Ottawa: Ministry of Supply & Services, 1984) ("the Badgley Report"), p. 29.

[4] T. Sullivan, *Sexual Abuse and the Rights of Children: Reforming Canadian Law* (Toronto: University of Toronto Press, 1992), p. 34.

[5] *Ibid.*, p. 33.

[6] Badgley Report, p. 646.

[7] *Ibid.*

[8] *Ibid.*

[9] *Ibid.*, p. 647.

[10] *Ibid.*, citing G. Bell, "Parents Who Abuse Their Children", in *Canadian Psychiatric Association Journal* 18: 223, 1973.

[11] Badgley Report, p. 647, citing J. Jacobs, "Child Abuse, Neglect, and Deprivation and the Family", in S. Smith, ed., *The Maltreatment of Children*, 1978, p. 265.

[12] *Supra*, note 3.

[13] J. Robertson, "Sexual Offences Against Children: The Badgley Report", Current Issue Review (Library of Parliament: Research Branch). Reviewed: 6 January 1988, p. 3.

[14] R.S.C. 1985, c. C-46.

[15] Badgley Report, pp. 43-44.

[16] P. Winks, "Legal Implications of Sexual Conduct", in 11 *Journal of Law and Education* (1982), p. 439.

[17] *Ibid.*, p. 441.

[18] *Ibid.*, citing *Alexander v. Yale*, 631 F.2d 178 (2nd Cir. 1980).

[19] Project on the Status and Education of Women, Sexual Harassment: A Hidden Issue, 3 (1978).

[20] Sydney Robins, *Protecting Our Students: A Review to Identify and Prevent Sexual Misconduct in Ontario Schools* (Toronto: Ministry of the Attorney General (Miller Graphics), 2002), p. 3.

[21] *Re Dartmouth District School Board and Nova Scotia Union of Public Employees, Unit No. 2* (1983), 12 L.A.C. (3d) 425 (N.S.), p. 431.

[22] *Ibid.*, p. 433.

[23] *Ibid.*, citing LeBel J. in *Stilwell v. Audio Pictures Ltd.*, [1955] O.W.N. 793 (C.A.), p. 794.

[24] *Re Government of the Province of Alberta* (1983), 8 L.A.C. (3d) 1 (Alta.) (Joliffe).

[25] *Re Ottawa Board of Education and Ottawa Board of Education Employees' Union* (1988), 5 L.A.C. (4th) 171 (Ont.).

[26] *Ibid.*, p. 180.

[27] *R. v. Pilgrim* (1981), 64 C.C.C. (2d) 523 (Nfld. C.A.), p. 532.

[28] *Ibid.*, p. 523.

[29] *R. v. Quigley* (1987), 66 Nfld. & P.E.I.R. 24 (Nfld. S.C.).

[30] *R. v. Hoskins* (1987), 63 Nfld. & P.E.I.R. 111 (Nfld. C.A.).

[31] *R. v. Quigley, supra*, note 29, p. 28.

[32] *Ibid.*, p. 28, citing *R. v. Hoskins, supra*, note 30, p. 115.

[33] *R. v. Kennedy*, [1993] O.J. No. 1434 (Gen. Div.) (QL), para. 17, citing *R. v. Palmer* (1985), 7 O.A.C. 348, which cites *R. v. M. (G.)* (1993), 77 C.C.C. (3d) 310 (Ont. C.A.).

[34] *Ibid.*, para. 17.

[35] *Ross v. New Brunswick School District No. 15*, [1996] 1 S.C.R. 825.

[36] *Shewan v. Abbotsford School District No. 34* (1987), 47 D.L.R. (4th) 106 (B.C.C.A.), affirming (1986), 26 D.L.R. (4th) 54 (B.C.S.C.).

[37] Robins, *Protecting Our Students*, p. 3.

[38] *Report of the Archdiocesan Commission of Enquiry into the Sexual Abuse of Children by Members of the Clergy*, 1989, p. viii.

[39] *Ibid.*, p. 2.

[40] *Ibid.*

[41] David C. Day, Q.C., "From Mount Cashel to the Latest Report of the Law Commission of Canada. Where Do We Go from Here?", paper presented to Vicarious Liability for Sexual Assault/Abuse Conference, Canadian Institute, 1999.

[42] Douglas Garbig, "Liquidation of Assets Re: Christian Brothers of Ireland in Canada", paper presented to Institutional Liability for Sexual Assault and Abuse Conference, Canadian Institute, 2002.

[43] *Re Christian Brothers of Ireland in Canada* (1998), 37 O.R. (3d) 367 (Gen. Div.), varied (2000), 47 O.R. (3d) 674 (C.A.).

[44] Garbig, *supra*, note 42.

[45] *Toronto Star*, July 6, 1991.

[46] *Toronto Star*, November 5, 1995.

[47] *Report of the Special Counsel Regarding Claims Arising Out of Sexual Abuse at Jericho School for the Deaf*, 1993.

[48] *Ibid.*, p. 1.

[49] *Ibid.*

[50] Law Reform Commission, Institutional Child Abuse Discussion Paper, *supra*, note 1, p. 14.

[51] *Ibid.*, pp. 12-13.

[52] Now the *Youth Criminal Justice Act*, S.C. 2002, c. 1.

[53] Nova Scotia Department of Justice, *Searching for Justice: An Independent Review of Nova Scotia's Response to Reports of Institutional Abuse* ("Kaufman Report") (January 2002), Chapter XVI, "Events Outside Nova Scotia", cited at http://www.gov.ns.ca/JUST/kaufmanreport/chapter16.htm, pp.1-44, at p. 2.

[54] *Ibid.*, p. 23.

[55] *Ibid.*, p. 24.

[56] The Honourable Fred Kaufman, C.M., Q.C., D.C.L., *Searching for Justice: An Independent Review of Nova Scotia's Response to Reports of Institutional Abuse* (Executive Summary and Recommendations), p. 9.

[57] *Ibid.*

[58] *Ibid.*

59   Hollie Shaw, "Goodbye, Gardens!", cited at http://www.canoe.com/GoodbyeGardens/ feb11_scandal.html, February 11, 1999, p. 1.
60   *R. v. Stuckless* (1998), 41 O.R. (3d) 103 (C.A.).
61   *Ibid.*, p. 107.
62   *Ibid.*
63   *Ibid.*
64   *Ibid.*, pp. 113-14.
65   *Ibid.*, p. 117.
66   *Ibid.*
67   *Ibid.*, p. 121.
68   *Indian Act*, R.S.C. 1985, c. I-5.
69   *P. (V.) v. Canada (Attorney General)*, [2000] 1 W.W.R. 541 (Sask. Q.B.).
70   *M. (F. S.) v. Clarke*, [1999] 11 W.W.R. 301 (B.C.S.C.).
71   *B. (E.) v. Order of the Oblates of Mary Immaculate in the Province of British Columbia*, 2001 BCSC 1783.
72   Law Reform Commission of Canada, *Restoring Dignity: Responding to Child Abuse in Institutional Settings* (Ottawa: Ministry of Public Works and Government Services, 2000).
73   Canadian Hockey League, *Players First Report*, Prepared by Gordon I. Kirke, Q.C., 1997, cited at http://www.canoe.com/PlayersFirst/home.html, p. 1.
74   *Ibid.*, p. 1, citing the statistics found in "Prevalence of Child Physical and Sexual Abuse in the Community", a study conducted by the Ontario Health Supplement.
75   *Ibid.*, p. 2.
76   *Ibid.*, p. 1 of Screening Procedures.
77   *Ibid.*, p. 1.
78   Robins, *Protecting Our Students*, p. 4.
79   *Ibid.*, p. 64.
80   *Ibid.*, p. 111.
81   *Ibid.*
82   *Ibid.*
83   *Ibid.* See *Re Brant County Board of Education and Ontario Secondary School Teachers' Federation*, Brant District Five (January 6, 1997) (Devlin); *Re Ottawa Board of Education and Ontario Secondary School Teachers' Federation* (March 22, 1995) (Kaplan); *Re Ontario Public School Teachers' Federation and Northumberland-Clarington Board of Education* (October 20, 1994) (Mitchnick); *Re Ontario Public School Teachers' Federation and Perth County Board of Education* (April 19, 1995) (McKechnie); *Re York Region Board of Education and Ontario Secondary School Teachers' Federation* (February 18, 1999) (Shime); *Re Simcoe County Board of Education and Ontario Secondary School Teachers' Federation, Dictrict 27* (June 24, 1996) (Kaplan); *Re Ontario Public School Teachers' Federation and Perth County Board of Education* (April 22, 1988) (Hunter). For cases involving custodians, see *Re York (City) Board of Education and Canadian Union of Public Employees, Local 994* (1993), 37 L.A.C. (4th) 257 (Ont.); *Re Ottawa Board of Education and Ottawa Board of Education Employees' Union* (1989), 5 L.A.C. (4th) 171 (Ont.).
84   R.S.C. 1990, c. E.2.
85   Robins, *Protecting Our Students*, p. 312.
86   *Ibid.*, pp. 311-14.
87   S.O. 2002, c. 7 (Bill 101).
88   *Ross*, *supra*, note 35.

[89]   Part I of the *Constitution Act, 1982*, being Schedule B to the *Canada Act 1982* (U.K.), 1982, c. 11.

[90]   *Ross, supra*, note 88, p. 857.

[91]   *Ibid.*, p. 858, citing *Shewan v. Abbotsford School District No. 34* (1987), 47 D.L.R. (4th) 106 (B.C.C.A.), p. 110.

[92]   *Ibid.*, p. 886.

[93]   *R. v. Seymour*, [1995] O.J. No. 2700 (Prov. Div.).

[94]   *Ibid.*, para. 47.

[95]   *Ibid.*

[96]   *Ibid.*

CHAPTER 2

SEXUAL MISCONDUCT IN SCHOOLS: WHO IS LIABLE AND WHY

A member of a religious order sexually assaults a child in an orphanage. A priest abuses an aboriginal student in a residential school. A hockey coach sexually exploits a young Junior A hockey player. A choirmaster is estimated to have serially abused over 200 children in his church choir. A Boy Scout leader fondles young boys on overnight camping expeditions. A female teacher writes sexually explicit letters to a 13-year-old male student. A high school music teacher flies his students to his remote island cottage, drugs them and sexually molests them. A schoolteacher sexually abuses female students aged 10 to 18 and a female colleague over a 21-year period. A worker at a residential care facility for emotionally troubled youth sexually abuses young children in his care. These are all recent Canadian incidents that have been widely reported in the media. They are all examples of the gross misuse of authority and breach of trust by an individual, yet in every case, victims and their families have sought to have the institution that employed these predators held liable for damages in the millions of dollars. In many cases they have been successful.

With increased public awareness of sexual abuse, exploitation and harassment, the incidence of civil suits against institutions is also growing. While the vast majority of abuse cases involve family members or adults in close affinity with children, such as babysitters, the phenomenon of institutional abuse has received intense public scrutiny because of high-profile cases in schools, churches and childcare agencies. In addition to recent abuse cases in the news, older historical cases are continuing to surface because there are no effective statutes of limitations on sexual abuse claims. The cost of such cases to institutions is staggering. In March 2003, the federal government agreed to limit the liability of co-defendant Anglican Church of Canada in aboriginal residential schools cases to *only* $25 million.[1]

How can an institution be held liable for the individual actions of an employee? This chapter will examine the law of civil liability and how it specifically applies to school boards and actions for damages caused by sexual misconduct of school board employees.

CIVIL ACTIONS AND "TORTS"

In law, an intentional or negligent act that harms another person is a "tort". A tort can include assault and battery, a negligent operation of a motor vehicle or failure to clean a sidewalk of ice. "Battery" is defined as offensive or hostile contact with the plaintiff. Intentional unwanted sexual contact is battery.[2]

To be liable to another for damages it has to be proved that the person owed a duty of care to the plaintiff, that the defendant breached that duty and the damage was caused by that breach. A person could include a corporation or institution such as a school. This law has developed in Anglo-Saxon jurisprudence over hundreds of years. Until recently most such legal actions were tried in front of juries. Juries tended to favour the underdog. Large corporations or wealthy businessmen who were well insured often found themselves on the losing side of such suits. Insurance companies in particular made very unsympathetic defendants. Defendants who were seen as "having deep pockets" were at a major tactical disadvantage.

Today, very few civil liability cases go to trial and even fewer are heard by juries. Nevertheless, defendants that appear to have big pockets still attract litigation. School boards are often one of the larger institutions in a community and even though they are non-profit public institutions, they are well insured, appear to have deep pockets and are therefore very attractive to prospective litigants.

In the past one strong disincentive to filing a lawsuit was the cost associated with prosecuting such an action. In the United States lawyers have been permitted to act for clients on the basis of speculation, taking a percentage of the resultant damages as the fee. This has resulted in an overwhelming number of negligence lawsuits. In Ontario, until recently this "contingency fee" approach was illegal and lawyers had to get at least a partial retainer from a client. A recent Ontario Court of Appeal decision[3] has cast doubt on this prohibition and it may be that in Ontario lawyers may institute civil liability suits on speculation. It is anticipated that the number of civil liability cases will increase. Additionally, in

Ontario a private member's bill (Bill 178) was tabled to amend the *Solicitor's Act*[4] to permit contingency billing. This has since been incorporated in a *Justice Statute Law Amendment Act*[5] which will come into effect in Ontario in January 2004.

Sexual misconduct suits are usually settled before trial. A protracted civil case can be complex, time-consuming and very expensive. Judges may, depending on the procedure, require the parties to go to a form of alternative dispute resolution, such as mediation. Such processes usually permit the plaintiff to present their case informally to the defendant and then the lawyers negotiate a monetary settlement.

If a case is perceived as "frivolous or vexatious" a defendant may seek to have the case stopped in its tracks by having the "pleadings struck" or having their client withdrawn as a defendant. If a determined plaintiff can get a matter actually set down for trial, a defendant or the defendant's insurer must then weigh carefully the possibility that the cost of the litigation may be more that the cost of settling the case, even where there appears to be little merit to the plaintiff's case. When the parties settle before trial because of the fear of the expense the matter is said to have been settled on a "nuisance basis".

Principals and other school officials are often named in lawsuits against school boards. This is because lawyers for plaintiffs are compelled to name every possible defendant in the initial proceedings of a lawsuit. Failure to name the correct party may cause the action to be lost. School officials who are named in such actions and who are said to have been acting "with the scope of their authority" are usually represented either by board counsel or the lawyers for the insurer. In case of doubt a principal can always consult his or her professional organization such as the Ontario Principals' Council, the Catholic Principals' Council of Ontario or the Association des directions et des directions adjointes des écoles franco-ontarienne.

Boards are covered for civil liability either by insurance companies or as part of a self-insured pool or cooperative. Public school boards in Ontario, for example, are usually members of the Ontario School Boards Insurance Exchange or "OSBIE". Such insurance providers, as part of the contract of insurance are "subrogated" to any legal action for damages covered by the policy. This means that the insurer takes over the legal defence of the case in order to limit its exposure to paying the claim. Nevertheless, a school board still has an interest in such cases because liability policies may have large deductibles, often in the six figures. Principals should be aware that lawyers acting for the insurer in an abuse claim are also acting on behalf of the board. Therefore principals should cooperate with these lawyers subject to any advice the board's counsel may provide.

Only in situations where there has been an alleged gross dereliction of duty, or where the official is alleged to be the abuser, would it be necessary for the official to obtain his or her own counsel. Nevertheless, in complex legal proceedings it may be advisable for a school official to obtain independent legal advice to ensure his or her interests are protected.

The board employee who is alleged to have engaged in the misconduct is usually required to obtain his or her own lawyer. Lawyers retained by the union or federation represent accused teachers and other unionized school employees. Non-union employees must pay for their own legal representation and often if cleared seek to be reimbursed by the employer. Policies on such matters vary widely from board to board.

THE EVOLUTION OF VICARIOUS LIABILITY

Until recently institutions were not held civilly liable for the individual sexual misconduct of employees without evidence of some culpability on the part of the institution or an agent of the employer, such as a supervisor or a school principal. It had to be demonstrated that the employer had been careless and had not acted on suspicions, had actually known of the propensity of the individual to abuse children, or had been warned and had not done anything to prevent the continuation of the abuse. This conforms to the long-established law of "negligence" as described earlier in the chapter. However, in Canada, since the Supreme Court of Canada decisions in *Bazely v. Curry* and *Jacobi v. Griffiths*,[6] it is clear that a school board may be held vicariously liable for sexual assaults committed by an employee in a position of trust equivalent to that of a parent (*in loco parentis*). This so-called "no-fault" liability has the legal name "vicarious liability".

THE LAW AS IT USED TO BE

In addition to proving facts a plaintiff in a civil action for negligence had to establish that the school board owed a "duty of care" to the plaintiff. The court also had to be satisfied that the school board failed to meet this standard of care and that this breach of duty caused damage to the plaintiff. In Canada courts held that a duty of care did not exist unless there was sufficient "proximity" between the school board as an employer and the victim. This proximity has been found to exist between a landlord and a tenant, a church and its congregation, a child welfare agency and a child in need of protection, and a school board and a student.

In any negligence action it was also necessary to demonstrate that it was reasonably foreseeable that an action ("commission") of the defendant, or lack of action ("omission") was likely to cause harm to the plaintiff. This standard of care was often described as that of the "reasonably careful person". What was reasonable depended upon the social context, including community standards and public awareness of the issues at the time. The effect of changing awareness is demonstrated in a case where a female student who was molested in the late 1970s by a teacher who was also her running coach did not succeed in her negligence action against the school board launched 20 years later. The plaintiff student never complained at the time. Thus, a duty to act was not established. The evidence did disclose, however, that the teacher often openly engaged in flirtatious acts with young female students. The court held that by contemporary standards such behaviours should have caused a suspicion that would have triggered a duty to act. However, sexual misconduct was not a live issue in the 1970s and the board could not have reasonably foreseen the consequences of its failure to act.[7] In such circumstances in the 1990s, however, it would have been reasonable for suspicion of misconduct to have arisen and for an investigation to have been undertaken, and the board may have been liable for its failure to discover the misconduct. In fact, misconduct is now commonly identified and litigated. In December 2002 alone, the Supreme Court of Canada considered three abuse cases, one involving a school janitor and two others involving foster care.

A school board and its teachers are expected to act without self-interest in the best interests of its students. This relationship is similar to that of a parent or guardian. The duty imposed on someone that is in such a position of trust is called a "fiduciary duty". Where a person (such as a teacher) has the power to act unilaterally and the victim (a student) is vulnerable or at the mercy of the other, a fiduciary relationship exists. This raises the duty of care and the degree of liability established in negligence law. Nevertheless in one case it was found that there had to be some element of intentional dishonesty, disloyalty or bad faith in order to establish a breach of fiduciary duty.[8] Where, for example, an employer tries to cover up incidents of abuse to preserve its reputation, a breach of fiduciary duty may well be found.

The actions of a principal can bind a school board on the basis of a breach of fiduciary duty. In one case[9] the plaintiff was a residential student of a school run by the Anglican Church of Canada and reported sexual abuse by a dormitory supervisor to the principal. Although the principal promised to report the disclosure, he met with the employee and, in an effort to preserve the reputation of the school and the church, simply asked him to resign. This action established a fiduciary liability. In the same case the plaintiff alleged negligence. Negligence was established when it was shown that there was widespread suspicion among staff about the supervisor and that the abuse had continued for eight years. The court imputed knowledge to the Anglican Church and found that institutions ought to know the prevalence of sexual abuse and the risks faced by children in the setting.

It has been conventional wisdom for many years that while school boards may be likely to be sued due to employee sexual misconduct, a strong preventative program, clear and well-communicated policies, protocols for reporting and intervening in abuse and eliminating situations of potential risk for students would make it difficult for plaintiffs to successfully sue in negligence. However, one case has changed all that.

THE LAW AS IT IS NOW

In the case known as *Bazley v. Curry*[10] the Children's Foundation of British Columbia was held liable for the actions of its employee Curry. The Foundation was a non-profit organization that operated two residential care facilities for emotionally troubled children between the ages of six and twelve. These were facilities of last resort for children who could not otherwise be served by the child welfare system. The philosophy of the organization was to act as a substitute parent and the employees were to care for the children physically, emotionally and mentally as if they were the parents. The tasks of the employees included bathing children and putting them to bed. Unknown to the Foundation, Curry, who was a pedophile, was sexually abusing children in his care. As soon as a complaint was received the Foundation dismissed Curry and called the police. Curry was subsequently convicted of 19 counts of abuse. Two of the convictions involved the plaintiff Bazley.

The plaintiff successfully claimed that the Children's Foundation as the employer was vicariously liable for the actions of Curry without alleging negligence. It was not disputed that the Foundation had a reasonable belief that it had hired a reputable employee. Curry had been a Hong Kong police officer for 18 years. It was not alleged that the employer had been warned of Curry's sexual predisposition. There were not even suspicions that were disregarded. There was, in fact, nothing the Foundation could have done to have prevented this specific abuse.

Vicarious liability is usually created when an employee's acts fall within the employee's "scope of employment". This usually includes acts that are specifically authorized by the employer, although in some cases the acts are so closely connected to authorized acts that they may be regarded as modes of doing the authorized acts. Curry's acts were clearly not authorized but in the original hearing a judge ruled that they were unauthorized modes of doing an authorized act. An example of this would be a dishonest bank employee who has the authority to manage a depositor's money but embezzles these funds instead of investing them wisely.

On appeal, the Supreme Court of Canada agreed with the trial judge but attempted to develop a clear framework for vicarious liability for sexual misconduct. The majority decision written by McLachlin J. found that where the employee's conduct is closely tied to a risk that the employer's enterprise has placed in the community, the employer may be justly held liable for the employee's wrong. The Court then described factors to take into account when assessing whether vicarious liability exists in any particular fact situation:

- the opportunity given to the employee to commit the abuse (being alone with permission);
- the nature of the opportunities (assistance with bathing);
- the nature of the relationship between the employee and the child (surrogate parent);
- whether the employee is required to touch the child's intimate body zones; and
- time and place considerations (during or outside work hours).

While it may be that the types of sexual misconduct that occur in schools may not meet all of these criteria, it is generally considered that school boards are much more likely to be found vicariously liable for the misconduct of board employees because of the following rationale, quoted from McLachlin J. speaking for the majority:

> In summary, the test for vicarious liability for an employee's sexual abuse of a client should focus on whether the employer's enterprise and empowerment of the employee materially increased the risk of the sexual assault and hence the harm. *The test must not be applied mechanically,* but with a sensitive view to the policy considerations that justify the imposition of vicarious liability — fair and efficient compensation for wrong and deterrence. This requires trial judges to investigate the employee's specific duties and determine whether they give rise to special opportunities for wrongdoing. Because of the peculiar exercises of power and trust that pervade cases of child abuse, *special attention should be paid to the existence*

of a power or dependency relationship, which on its own often creates a considerable risk of wrongdoing.[11] (Emphasis added)

The Supreme Court of Canada issued another decision on vicarious liability, *Jacobi v. Griffiths*,[12] the same day as the *Curry* case. Griffiths was the Program Director for a Boys' and Girls' Club that provided recreational activities for children, including camping and sporting trips. He supervised volunteers, coordinated some activities and participated in others. Many of the children who participated were from troubled homes or were disadvantaged or vulnerable in some way. There were no residential or overnight programs and while the staff were encouraged to cultivate trust and respect, they had no actual authority or power over the children. The plaintiffs were two siblings, a boy and a girl who were sexually abused by Griffiths when they were 11 and 13, respectively. To the plaintiffs the Club was a sanctuary from a troubled home. All but one of the assaults took place off the premises of the Club and outside regular work hours. While the original trial judge found the Club liable, the British Columbia Court of Appeal that had found the Children's Foundation liable in *Curry* reversed the judge's decision. By a narrow majority of four judges to three, the Supreme Court of Canada found the employer was not vicariously liable for the sexual misconduct of their employee, Griffiths.

The distinction from the *Curry* case lay in that fact that the Court did not find Griffiths to be in a position of special trust with respect to care, protection or nurturing, but found he was encouraged to befriend the children and not become a surrogate parent. Therefore, while the facts established a job-created opportunity to abuse children, the employer did not create a position of inherent power/dependence such as Curry had enjoyed and insufficient job-created power and intimacy existed to establish vicarious liability.

Not surprisingly, McLachlin J., who wrote the majority decision in *Curry*, disagreed with the majority and found that the children were entrusted to the Program Director who mentored them. McLachlin J. also cites testimony that Griffiths had God-like authority over children who, because they were troubled disadvantaged adolescents, were particularly vulnerable. She found the required job-created power and intimacy to establish vicarious liability.

Clearly, a school teacher that abuses students will meet the *Curry* test. The question is, will misconduct by other types of support staff, who are not authorized by the *Education Act*[13] or specifically by the employer to develop intimate relationships, be covered by the *Jacobi* decision? It should be noted that this distinction was made by a very narrow majority of the Court. It is likely that plaintiffs will continue to cite Justice McLachlin's broader test as to whether the employer created an opportunity for intimacy and abuse, the degree of vulnerability of the victim and the social objective served by compensating sexual abuse victims. A case currently before the Supreme Court of Canada involving a school janitor may resolve this ambiguity.[14]

Even where a plaintiff succeeds in establishing liability, the plaintiff is still required to prove a causal connection between the damages suffered and the breach of duty. Research shows that the sexual abuse of children can have wide-ranging and long-lasting effects. Sexual assault of adults can induce Post-traumatic Stress Disorder, which is characterized by hyper-alertness, sleep problems, survival guilt, memory and concentration problems. For children in the immediate aftermath of sexual abuse there is often fear, aggressiveness and inappropriate sexual behaviours, including sexual aggression towards other children.[15]

For adult survivors of child abuse studies have shown that 20 to 50 per cent of abused women have identifiable mental health impairments, including anxiety, depression, dissociation, sexual problems and substance abuse. Victims are often at great risk of re-victimization. Other effects include poor self-esteem, hostility toward parents, men or others, feelings of isolation, sleep disturbances and eating disorders.[16]

Children who are abused have been described as having their cognitive or emotional orientation to the world altered. This in turn can cause them to be sexually traumatized, to feel betrayed, stigmatized or powerless. These feelings in turn cause a long list of behavioural manifestations. For example, sexually traumatized children can become pre-occupied by sex or become sexually compulsive. Others become sexually aggressive, promiscuous or turn to prostitution. Still others develop sexual dysfunction such as phobic reactions to intimacy or the inability to be aroused. A sense of betrayal may result in: vulnerability to subsequent abuse, allowing one's own children to be abused, social isolation, marital problems or delinquency. Stigmatization may result in social isolation, substance abuse, criminal involvement, self-mutilation or suicide. Feelings of powerlessness may cause nightmares, eating and sleeping disorders, depression, disassociation, running away, truancy, employment problems or bullying. Sometimes the powerless victim asserts power by becoming a sexual abuser.[17]

In any event, there is a strong likelihood that an abused child will be a damaged adult who must undergo extensive long-term therapy. The social cost is enormous in lost productivity and the impact on the health care and criminal justice systems. So too is the financial liability for the abuser or the institution that employed the abuser. The defendant in a civil action will be asked to compensate the victim for pain and suffering as well as "making the victim whole again" by paying for expensive therapies. In addition, many plaintiffs claim for lost earnings attributable to the individual's inability to reach his or her full educational potential and therefore not having the employment opportunities he or she might otherwise have had. In cases where the effects of the abuse are discovered decades after the abuse occurred, the resultant financial claims will be in the hundreds of thousands, if not millions of dollars. In addition, many plaintiffs seek punitive damages where it is alleged that the conduct of the institution was especially egregious, selfish or uncaring.

HISTORICAL CASES

Since the 17th century, most English-speaking courts have recognized a limitation to civil actions based on the passage of time. In Ontario, for example, the limitation period for personal injury tort actions for assault and battery was four years.[18] This will soon be reduced to two years.[19] In the case of victims under the age of majority, the limitation period begins to run from the time that victim reaches age 18.[20] Each province has its own legislation. Limitation periods or limitation defences ensured that defendants were not placed at the disadvantage of defending a case when the evidence had disappeared or witnesses were no longer available. As well society had an interest in achieving closure and not leaving liability issues in limbo for decades. Nevertheless, there is no limitation period in Ontario for a breach of fiduciary duty as described above.

It has become clear in the last 20 years that a significant number of sexual abuse victims have come forward to complain about their abuse many years after limitation periods had apparently expired. In many cases victims felt that their allegations would not have been believed at the time the events occurred. After the Mount Cashel Inquiry in 1989, and subsequent disclosures such as those discussed in Chapter 1, more victims have felt empowered to come forward. In other cases victims simply refused to think about the events because they were too painful to deal with. Others, through therapy for example, discovered that they had been emotionally or psychologically damaged by the abuse. In some cases the damage, depression for example, only emerged years after the causative events. It has been claimed that some victims were so traumatized by their experiences that they actually repressed their memories of the events. This theory has yet to be proven.

The limitation period and its application to sexual abuse came under the scrutiny of the Supreme Court of Canada in 1992. In *M. (K.) v. M. (H.)*[21] a victim of incest had her action for damages dismissed under the Ontario *Limitations Act*, which will soon be amended. The Supreme Court on appeal held that the claim was indeed subject to a limitation period, but the limitation period could only start running once the plaintiff was actually aware of the damages she had suffered. This is called the "discoverability principle". A subsequent Ontario decision[22] held that the limitation period only starts to run once the victim has substantial awareness of the harm done and the likely cause of the harm. The realization may only come once the victim has received counselling that enables him or her to see a connection between the abuse suffered in childhood and difficulties experienced as an adult.

The discoverability principle will soon be enshrined in Ontario in the new *Limitations Act, 2002*, which states that:

> 5(1) A claim is discovered on the earlier of,
>
> > (*a*)   the day on which the person with the claim first knew,
> >
> > > (i)   that the injury, loss or damage had occurred ...
> >
> > (*b*)   the day on which a reasonable person with the the the abilities and in the circumstances of the person with the claim first ought to have known ...[23]

In the case of sexual assault, the law in Ontario has recently been changed and when it is proclaimed in January 2004 there will in effect be no Limitations Act defences in the case of sexual assault. The *Limitations Act, 2002* states, "a person with a claim based on sexual assault shall be deemed to have been incapable of commencing the action earlier than it was commenced".[24] This is similar to changes made in other provinces such as British Columbia.

Claims may therefore arise decades after the actual abuse. It may be that there is no time limitation on claims for damages arising from sexual misconduct within a school setting even if the misconduct did not amount to sexual abuse but was a form of sexual exploitation (see Chapter 4) or sexual harassment.

Although the application of the principle of vicarious liability to institutional abuse is a recent development, there is a strong likelihood that courts will find vicarious liability even in historical cases. A British Columbia court recently found the Government of Canada and the United Church vicariously liable for sexual and physical abuse that occurred in the 1940s. Neither defendant was aware of the abuse at the time nor was either found to be negligent.[25]

School boards, churches, the federal government and other school authorities have been flooded with historical claims, some going as far back as the 1960s. The federal Government has tried to establish a mediated settlement of all aboriginal residential schools cases. Other institutions are also settling long before trial. In school boards historical cases are handled by senior board staff in cooperation with the insurance companies.

Principals should ensure that good records are kept of contemporary situations even if the student does not pursue a complaint. Such records should be forwarded to the director's office. Other pertinent data should be assembled by central board staff and filed in contemplation of future litigation. School board record retention policies should be amended to reflect the reality that traditional limitations do not protect boards from litigation for sexual misconduct. Central payroll records, for example, should be kept for as long as possible, since such records can confirm or deny that alleged abusers did in fact work for the board or at a particular school during the period covered by a lawsuit. Ontario Student Records (including the index card) must be kept for 55 years. They can be used to place the location of the plaintiff student with certainty during the period of alleged abuse and can often document dramatic changes in grades or attendance that reflect the impact of sexual misconduct.[26] One record problem facing many school boards is that expired insurance policies were often discarded after seven years. In order to claim coverage under an expired policy for historical abuse claims, the insured school board is required to produce a copy of the insurance policy documents.

Principals often receive the original complaint of historical abuse from former students. Such complaints should be immediately reported to the Director of Education. If the complainant was under 16 years of age at the time of the alleged events, the appropriate Children's Aid Society must be notified, although any investigation of the allegations would be undertaken by the police.

When a principal suspects unprofessional behaviour between a board employee and a student over 16 years of age that is apparently consensual, and a formal investigation of the situation may have been frustrated, the principal may feel powerless to stop the misconduct. The Crown cannot successfully prosecute a case without the evidence of the student. The employee cannot be disciplined in such circumstances because a grievance would be filed and there would be no evidence to support the discipline. In such cases the employee should be made aware of the law. Specifically the employee should be told that there is no statute of limitations on criminal acts and apparently no limitation on civil actions for sexual misconduct. The student may at a later date decide to complain to the police or sue for damages. This may have the desired effect of discouraging the employee from continuing an exploitative relationship. In any event it may still be possible to impose discipline based on corroborative evidence by others within the school who may be aware of improprieties or breach of duty.

In the past, a board's best protection against civil liability was a lack of fore-knowledge and no contribution either by omission or commission to the abuse of a student. Now the only defence open to a board is to prevent abuse from happening by creating an environment that discourages abusers and encourages staff and students to report misconduct.

ENDNOTES

[1] *National Post*, March 11, 2002, p. A6.

[2] Brown and Zuker, *Education Law*, 3rd ed. (Toronto: Carswell, 2002), p. 124.

[3] *McIntyre Estate v. Ontario (Attorney General)* (2002), 218 D.L.R. (4th) 193 (Ont. C.A.).

[4] R.S.O. 1990, c. S.15.

[5] S.O. 2002, c. 24.

[6] [1999] 2 S.C.R. 534; [1999] 2 S.C.R. 570.

[7] *H. (S.G.) v. Gorsline*, [2001] 6 W.W.R. 132 (Alta. Q.B.).

[8] *A. (C.) v. Critchley* (1998), 166 D.L.R. (4th) 475 (B.C.C.A.).

[9] *M. (F.S.) v. Clarke*, [1999] 11 W.W.R. 301 (B.C.S.C.).

[10] [1999] 2 S.C.R. 534.

[11] *Bazley v. Curry*, *ibid.*, at 563.

[12] [1999] 2 S.C.R. 570.

[13] R.S.O. 1990, c. E.2.

[14] *G. (E.D.) v. Hammer* (2001), 197 D.L.R. (4th) 454 (B.C.C.A.), decision pending Supreme Court of Canada.

[15] David Finkelhor, "The Trauma of Child Sexual Abuse", in Gail E. Wyatt and Gloria J. Powell, *Lasting Effects of Child Sexual Abuse* (Newbury Park, CA: Sage Publications, 1988), pp. 61-62.

[16] *Ibid.*, p. 62.

[17] *Ibid.*, pp. 65-72.

[18] The actual wording of the section of the *Limitations Act*, R.S.O. 1990, c. L.15 was as follows:

> 45.(1) The following actions shall be commenced within and not after the times respectively hereinafter mentioned,
>
> …(j) an action for assault, battery, wounding or imprisonment, within four years after the cause of action arose.

[19] *Limitations Act, 2002*, S.O. 2002, c. 24, Schedule B, s. 4 (coming into force January 1, 2004).

[20] *Ibid.*, s. 6.

[21] [1992] 3 S.C.R. 6 at 35.

[22] *C. (H.) v. C. (G.C.)* (1998), 80 A.C.W.S. (3d) 557 (Ont. Gen. Div.).

[23] *Limitations Act, 2002*, S.O. 2002, c. 24, Schedule B, s. 5 (coming into force January 1, 2004).

[24] *Limitations Act, 2002*, S.O. 2002, c. 24, Schedule B, s. 10 (coming into force January 1, 2004).

[25] *B. (W.R.) v. Plint* (2001), 93 B.C.L.R. (3d) 228 (S.C.), currently under appeal.

[26] *Ontario Student Record Guideline*, issued December 1989, revised March 2000, Queen's Printer for Ontario, 1989.

CHAPTER 3

CHILDREN UNDER SIXTEEN — THE ROLE OF THE CHILDREN'S AID SOCIETY

INTRODUCTION

Allegations of sexual misconduct involving children under 16 present many challenges to a school. As described previously, there are criminal laws that create special offences investigated by the police, and there is overlapping jurisdiction under the *Child and Family Services Act*,[1] a provincial law administered by Children's Aid Societies. Chapter 3 will present the detailed legal obligations under this Act. It will also describe the Child Abuse Register, the Joint Protocols that have been developed to coordinate the activities of agencies, police and school boards dealing with abuse, and finally the need for detailed board policies that are consistent with the complex legal obligations assumed when reporting and investigating abuse.

PROTECTION OF CHILDREN

Children's Aid Societies were created by statute in order to protect children. In Ontario there are three Children's Aid Societies that have the power to investigate abuse: the Children's Aid Society, the Catholic Children's Aid Society and Jewish Child and Family Services. The religious affiliation of the family determines the jurisdiction of the society. In addition, there is Native Child and Family Services, which as of publication date does not have investigative authority. These agencies are usually organized on a county or regional basis.

The procedures for the identification of children who require protection and for the protection of children are set out in the *Child and Family Services Act* (the Act). Section 1 of the Act states: "The paramount purpose of this Act is to promote the best interests, protection and well being of children."[2] There are additional purposes to the Act that have to do with respecting parents and providing the appropriate services to children and families, but these must all be consistent with the paramount purpose of the Act. The role of the Children's Aid Societies is to investigate child abuse and then address the abuse through various means. The means vary from least intrusive to most intrusive. The means may or may not involve the court process.

If matters proceed to court, the courts of first instance that have jurisdiction in Ontario are the Ontario Court of Justice and the Unified Family Court. The Unified Family Court is technically a Superior Court; the Ontario Court of Justice is not. The Unified Family Court is considered a federal court. Both types of courts have judges presiding alone. There are no juries that assist in decision-making. At present there is no Unified Family Court in Toronto. Both courts derive their jurisdiction from the *Courts of Justice Act.*[3] The *Courts of Justice Act* sets out the parameters of judicial authority. Part Three of the *Child and Family Services Act* is the sole statutory authority for child protection matters.

The Act applies for the most part to children who are under 16 years of age, unless the children who are 16 years and older are subject to a court order. The definition of a child in s. 37(1) of the Act is as follows:

> ..."child" does not include a child as defined in subsection 3(1) [under the age of eighteen] who is apparently sixteen years or older, unless the child is the subject of an order under this Part.

In order to protect a child from harm, either actual or potential, the court must find that a "child is in need of protection" as defined in s. 37(2) of the Act. If it does find the child in need of protection, the court must determine whether or not a court order is necessary in order to protect the child. The types of court orders available, or the dispositions available if a child is found in need of protection, are found in s. 57 of the Act. Applications that initiate the court process are called protection applications. They are brought when an agency believes that parents and/or guardians actively cause harm, or are likely to cause harm, or fail to take actions to prevent harm to their children. Section 57 orders are available to a Children's Aid Society (CAS) once a child is found to be in need of protection. These orders depend upon what the court determines is in the best interests of children. The remedies available range from least intrusive to most intrusive: leav-ing a child in the parents' home with Society supervision, placing the children with someone else with supervision by the Society; placing a child in the care of the Society as a Society ward, and finally placing the child in the care of the Society as part of a more permanent placement plan, as a ward of the Crown, with or without access to the parents or guardians. Section 57 remedies are not possible if the abuser is a third party having charge of the child and the child's parent has not been in-volved in the harm. Therefore protection applications will not be initiated when the alleged sexual abuse involves an educational employee and a student.

Although protection proceedings will not involve school-based allegations of abuse, the wording of the Act does cover school-based abuse to the extent that the Children's Aid Societies are required to become involved. The same sections that define a child in need of protection set out categories of abuse and the criteria that must be satisfied in order to trigger Children's Aid Societies investigating abuse allegations involving third parties, such as teachers, whose actions have not been as a conse-quence of the failure of the parents and guardians to protect the children.

ABUSE

"Abuse" as defined by the Act may be physical, emotional, developmental, medical and/or sexual in nature. It also may involve leaving a child inappropriately supervised or unattended, or generally neglected. This is set out in s. 37 of the Act,[4] the original language for protection proceedings, and is replicated in s. 72, the duty to report section.[5] Though there are many headings for finding a child in need of protection for the purpose of triggering an abuse investigation conducted by the Children's Aid Socie-ties and the police, the sections of the Act that refer specifically to the behaviour that would be recognized as sexual abuse and sexual misconduct warranting CAS involvement appear and are defined in the *Education Act*[6] and the *Ontario College of Teachers Act, 1996,*[7] which states:

> 1. In this Act,
>
> . . . . .
>
> "sexual abuse" by a student of a member means,
>
> (*a*) sexual intercourse or other forms of sexual relations between the member and the student,
>
> (*b*) touching, of a sexual nature, of the student by the member, or
>
> (*c*) behaviour or remarks of a sexual nature by the member towards the student.
>
> . . . . .
>
> 40(1.1) The definition of "professional misconduct" under paragraph 31 of sub-section (1) shall be deemed to include sexual abuse of a student by a member.

This definition is not as inclusive as the definition envisioned by Sydney Robins in *Protecting Our Students* (the Robins report).[8] Robins had hoped that the words "sexual misconduct" would be utilized and defined specifically in the professional misconduct regulation under the *Ontario College of Teachers Act, 1996.*[9] He stated:

> In summary, the *Education Act*, the *Teaching Profession Act*, and the *Ontario College of Teachers Act, 1996* or regulations thereunder all establish conduct for school teachers violation of which may result in disciplinary proceedings affecting employment or professional status. Though sexual misconduct would clearly constitute "just cause" for discipline as well as professional misconduct, the standards, as presently stated provide little or no insight as to what sexual misconduct is. Only the regulation to the *Ontario College of Teachers Act, 1996*, specifically addresses the issue. The term sexual abuse is ill suited to embrace the full range of sexual activity that should constitute sexual misconduct. ...[10]

Recommendations six to eight in the Robins Report define sexual misconduct. In Recommendation 6.1, he argued that "... sexual misconduct should be amended to provide that professional misconduct includes sexual misconduct".[11] In Recommendation 6.2 he argued that sexual misconduct should be defined as "offensive conduct of a sexual nature which may affect the personal integrity or security of any student or school environment".[12] This does, however, appear in the Ontario College of Teachers Professional Advisory, which is discussed in more detail in Chapters 5 and 6, which deal with incidents involving students age 16 and over.

There is no specific definition of sexual abuse in s. 37(2)(*c*) or 37(2)(*d*) of the *Child and Family Services Act*, or in their parallel section (s. 72(1), (2) and (3)). The Act merely identifies sexual abuse as sexual molestation or sexual exploitation:

> [s. 37(2)] (*c*) the child has been sexually molested or sexually exploited, by the person having charge of the child or by another person where the person having charge of the child knows or should know the possibility of sexual molestation, or sexual exploitation and fails to protect the child;

> [s. 37(2)](*d*) there is a risk that the child is likely to be sexually molested or sexually exploited as described in clause (*c*);

This clearly has presented a problem both in the context of finding a child in need of protection and for the purposes of reporting the sexual abuse as per s. 72 of the Act. This has been remarked upon in some court decisions such as *R. v. Stachula* and *R. v. Cook*:

> There is much to be said about the fact that there is no definition of sexual abuse in the Act. ... Oxford's defines molestation as annoyance, hostile or vexatious interference. Webster defines it as a cause or state of harassment. ... Obviously there are a

number of definitions of "molestation" and of "condition" and of "sexual", but unfortunately none in the Act to help us as to just exactly what the legal test is …[13]

Sections 79 and 81 of the Act make efforts to define abuse. The definitions are vague. Section 79(1) of the Act defines abuse as "… a state or condition of being physically harmed, sexually molested or sexually exploited". Section 79(1), 79(2)(*a*) and 79(2)(*b*) are prohibitive. Any person having charge of child who inflicts abuse on child is guilty of a provincial offence, and may be charged accordingly under the *Provincial Offences Act.*[14]

Section 81 of the *Child and Family Services Act* defines the phrase to "suffer abuse": "In this section, 'to suffer abuse', when used in reference to a child, means to be in need of protection within the meaning of s. 37(2)".

Courts have found that the sexual abuse of a child is emotionally detrimental to the child.[15] Situations in which there may be behaviour that falls short of sexual molestation or exploitation may result in a finding that a child has suffered emotional harm of the sort that is set out in s. 37(2)(*f*) of the Act.

Sexual harassment may result in a finding that a child has suffered emotional harm. "Objectionable comments or conduct of a sexual nature that may affect a person's personal integrity or security in the school environment" may fall into that category, if the child has suffered emotional harm and the criteria of 37(2)(*f*) have been met.[16]

In s. 37(2)(*f*) the criteria for determining emotional harm are: anxiety, depression and withdrawal, self-destructive or aggressive behaviour, or delayed development *and* reasonable grounds to believe that the emotional harm suffered by the child results from the actions, failure to act or pattern of neglect on the part of the child's parent or a person having charge of the child.

It is a provincial offence for a person having charge of a child to inflict abuse and/or to permit someone to abuse, or to continue to abuse a child, or fail to prevent the harm.[17] Charges may be laid under the Act, and on conviction a fine and/or a term of imprisonment are imposed. These offences are strict liability offences. This means that the accused will be convicted upon proof of the act itself and the onus is on the accused to prove that he or she took reasonable care to avoid criminal conduct.[18] Words like "permit" or "cause" are used when dealing with strict liability offences. In *R. v. Sault Ste. Marie (City)*, the Supreme Court of Canada ruled on the nature of the onus to prove the strict liability offence.[19] The Crown's burden was beyond a reasonable doubt, but *mens rea* need not be established. The onus was on the accused to prove on a balance of probabilities that the violation was through no fault of his own — "that all reasonable care had been taken …".[20]

Section 85 of the Act sets out the penalty if the person having charge of the child inflicts the abuse or permits a child to suffer harm. The penalty if there is a conviction is a fine of not more than $2,000, or imprisonment of not more than two years or both.

The school board may be charged for the actions of its employees if the employee had charge of the child. Section 85(2) states, "A person who contravenes subsection 79(2) (child abuse), and a director, officer, or employee of a corporation who authorizes, permits or concurs in such contravention by the corporation is guilty of an offence …". Section 58.5(1) of the *Education Act* defines a school board as a corporation, as follows: "Every district school board is a corporation and has all the powers and shall perform all the duties that are imposed on it under this or any other Act".[21]

It is rare for cases to be dealt with under these sections. As Sydney Robins observed, "cases which are properly prosecutable as sexual abuse crimes will normally generally be dealt with under the *Criminal Code*, and not under the CFSA".[22]

In child protection cases, courts have generally relied on certain provisions of the *Criminal Code*[23] for the definitions of sexual exploitation, namely, ss. 151, 152 and 153. The standard of proof in criminal cases is different from the standard of proof required in child protection cases proceeding in the Ontario Court of Justice or, as stated above, when the offences are strict liability offences. The criminal law requires that sexual intent be established beyond a reasonable doubt. When a person is charged with a provincial offence, the standard of proof *on the Crown* is beyond a reasonable doubt to establish all the elements of the offence, but the standard of proof *on the defendant* to establish the defence of taking reasonable care is a lesser test on a balance of probabilities. This means that the facts establish a high probability but not absolute certainty. The onus in child protection cases rests on the Children's Aid Society. The standard of proof, however, is not a criminal standard but is on the balance of probabilities that a child is in need of protection and subsequently that it is in the child's best interests for an order to be made. As outlined above, this proceeding will not involve a third party, such as a teacher, who has charge of the child and has permitted or caused sexual abuse as defined in the Act. However, if charges are laid pursuant to the *Provincial Offences Act*, that the educational employee has permitted or caused sexual abuse, such employee would appear in Provincial Offences Court.

The question of who has charge of a child has also been the subject of case law. It was thought as late as 1984 that only guardians and/or parents could be considered as having charge of the child. One case held that neither bus drivers nor teachers who had temporary control over a child could be said to "have charge of the child".[24] This decision was appealed and on appeal the District Court held that having temporary control was equated with having charge of the child, and therefore bus drivers and teachers who had temporary control were considered to have charge of the child.[25] Subsequently, courts have suggested a person "having charge of the child" is defined as any adult exercising authority with the consent or acquiescence of the parent.[26] The Robins report makes it abundantly clear that teachers and principals would be characterized as having charge of the child.[27]

Reporting Abuse

The *Child and Family Services Act* mandates that Children's Aid Societies investigate suspected sexual abuse (with the police). For this reason the Act sets out a statutory duty to report. Section 72(1) of the Act sets out that duty. The threshold for reporting is a low one: reasonable grounds to suspect that a child is or may be in need of protection. The low threshold was designed to encourage reporting. In fact, for reporting purposes, the sexual abuse may be actual but if there is a risk of future sexual abuse, then the duty to report is activated as well. The wording of the section has been amended. Previously, the test for reporting abuse was "reasonable grounds to believe". That wording reflected a higher threshold. It has been suggested that the reason for the lower threshold was to encourage early identification of suspected sexual abuse. Early identification and early intervention were viewed as effective methods for ending the abuse and were ways of "putting children's safety first".[28]

Protecting Our Students acknowledged that the low threshold for intervention would result in reporting situations that would not warrant criminal, civil or disciplinary proceedings".[29] Members of the Ontario Legislative Assembly who debated recent amendments to the *Education Act* and other statutes that deal with the sexual abuse of students were concerned with over-reporting and false reporting. A fear of witch hunts was articulated.[30] Members of the Legislative Assembly suggested that certain mechanisms be put in place to protect teachers who were found to be not guilty. They included reimbursing teachers for legal bills and restoring the good name of the teacher. One member stated, "We need to protect our teachers from false allegations".[31]

Sydney Robins found this to be a valid concern as well. Chapter 5 of his report, "Avoiding False Allegations", analyzes and addresses this concern. Most common among the teachers' fears was the fact that allegations of sexual abuse, even when proved to be false, were remembered while the fact that the allegations were false had little significance. The reputation of the teacher had been ruined by the allegation. Teaching was described as "... a high risk job; for a man being a teacher is playing with fire".[32] There is belief among teachers that the number of men training to become primary school teachers has declined due to the fear of false allegations of sexual misconduct. There also is a climate of paranoia in the schools among teachers due to "a wave of unfounded sexual abuse allegations".[33] Notwithstanding the validity of the concerns expressed by teachers, the Robins report "... was unable to conclude that there is a plethora of false allegations of sexual impropriety made against teachers".[34] Though the report could not conclude that false allegations against teachers are completely rare, it has been suggested, albeit in another context, that "it [is] unlikely that any stable person in education would maliciously and falsely accuse a parent of abuse or use the reporting system to retaliate against or harass a parent".[35] It can be assumed a similar reasoning can be applied to a teacher who reports suspected sexual abuse of a student by another teacher or school staff member.

The Act sets out what is reportable based upon "reasonable grounds to suspect" in s. 72(1). The threshold is very low. It is unclear just what constitutes a "reasonable suspicion". Many teachers and other educational workers are reluctant to make a report that would trigger an investigation of a colleague without some "hard evidence". However, it is totally inappropriate for anyone other than the police or the Children's Aid Society to investigate a suspected sexual misconduct situation. Aside from possibly prejudicing a subsequent investigation by contaminating evidence, the investigation may alert the suspected employee, who could destroy evidence or attempt to intimidate witnesses and victims. When in doubt the Children's Aid Society should be contacted for advice. It is not necessary to reveal any names unless the Children's Aid Society worker believes there are sufficient grounds to make a report.

Sexual offences against children are serious criminal matters requiring professional expertise. A professional investigation, undertaken promptly in utmost confidence, can quickly exonerate an innocent implicated staff member and dispel any suspicions.

It should be noted that sexual exploitation, molestation, emotional harm or risk of these being caused by educational employees are also reportable. Section 72(1)3. deals with the sexual exploitation and sexual molestation that has occurred and/or was caused in some way by the action or inaction of a person having charge of the child, such as a teacher. Section 72(1)4. deals with the risk to the child that either is likely to occur due to that person's actions or failure to protect. Paragraphs 6 and 8 deal with the emotional harm that has occurred or is likely to occur as a result of the actions or inaction of a parent or a person having charge of the child. The words having "charge of the child" are designed to capture third parties such as teachers or educational assistants.

The duty to report is universal. Section 72 uses the word "person". However, though the duty to report suspected abuse is imposed on all persons, the penalty for failing to report falls upon specific persons. Included in the category of "any person" is "... a person who performs professional or official duties with respect to children". Although the statutory duty to report suspected abuse is imposed on all persons, the Act singles out those professionals whose failure to report a suspicion results in an offence. Section 72(4) of the Act sets out the offence. The Act singles out teachers, principals, social workers, counsellors, day nursery workers, and youth and recreation workers, among others.

The definition of professional duties will be interpreted broadly. For example, a police constable was technically not performing "professional or official duties with respect to children".[36] He was on duty at the police station on another matter and overheard a conversation that gave him reasonable grounds to suspect that there was a risk of sexual abuse. He reported his suspicions, based on what he overheard and a conversation that he had with police officers, to the local Children's Aid Society. The court found that although he was not the officer in charge of the investigation, he met the criteria for the test, as he was "an active duty police officer who gained information in the course of his 'professional or official' duties".[37] The court elaborated on the liberal interpretation of those words and how they applied to the reporting duty under the Act when it stated that "...all police officers have a primary duty to prevent the commission of a crime".[38]

Teachers, like police officers, have a duty to protect children. Theirs is a statutory duty that is set out in the *Education Act,* the *Teaching Profession Act*[39] and the *Ontario College of Teachers Act, 1996.* They are required to "intervene to protect a student from being victimized by any sexual misconduct in the school environment".[40] That duty may involve reporting to a principal or supervisory officer. It should also be noted that failure to comply with the Act is also professional misconduct as described in Chapters 3, 5 and 6.

There is some difference of opinion as to whether a volunteer working with children is a professional and has the same reporting duty as any of those professionals listed in s. 72(5)(*b*). The Robins report claims that volunteers are subject to that duty to report in the same way as teachers are.[41] Children's law expert Jeffrey Wilson disagrees and says that "volunteers are not such persons". He cites s. 72(5)(*b*), wherein it states "youth and recreation worker does not include volunteer".[42] If this is the case, it may be that because volunteers are not paid for their services, they are not considered to perform professional duties. This could present a problem for school boards. There are many volunteers in the school system, and they work closely with children. They may be persons to whom disclosures of sexual abuse are made and are persons who may have reasonable grounds to suspect that there has been sexual abuse. If they do not report abuse to the Children's Aid Society, they cannot be charged under the Act for failure to report. They can, however, be compelled to give evidence as witnesses at different proceedings under the Act. These proceedings could be to protect a child from parental abuse or neglect or an expunction hearing where a person can appeal being put on the Abuse Registry. In the event a volunteer makes a report to a school employee, that employee may be subject to charges if they fail in turn to report this information to the Children's Aid Society.

The offence of failure to report a suspicion of sexual abuse, just like the offence of abuse itself, is a strict liability offence that has also been described as "quasi criminal in nature".[43] The only defence to this charge is for the accused to prove he took reasonable steps to fulfil his duty to report.[44] This defence may be proved on the balance of probabilities. The Crown, however, has to prove all the essential elements of the offence beyond a reasonable doubt.[45]

Another defence may be the lack of definition for the words "sexual molestation" or "exploitation". "The inadequacy of ... definition of 'abuse', and more particularly 'sexual molestation' is most apparent and most unfortunate for those who are charged with identifying and reporting it".[46]

The penalty for failing to report suspected abuse is a fine of not more than $1,000. There is no term of imprisonment if convicted. Notwithstanding the importance of the reporting duty, the fine is relatively light.[47]

School Boards are vicariously liable for the failure of their employees to report in the same way as they are liable when employees abuse children.[48] Supervisory officers of the school board may be convicted for a teacher's failure to report suspicions of abuse to the Children's Aid Society.[49] A supervisory officer may be suspended or even dismissed for a teacher's failure to report.[50]

Courts in the United States have addressed vicarious liability based on failure to report. In New York, where a statutory duty to report exists, victims can sue the school teacher and also the school district for the teacher's and the school district's failure to report. A parent of a victim cannot sue.[51]

Not only must the suspicion be reported, but all the information upon which the suspicion is based must also be provided without a search warrant being required.[52] Written information such as a copy of a police victim statement in a separate case was given to the Children's Aid Society without a court order.[53] If confidential police records can be given to a Children's Aid Society then it could be argued that school board records pertaining to an employee regarding whom suspected sexual abuse has been disclosed may also be provided to a Children's Aid Society without a court order.

Generally speaking, however, the Children Aid Societies bring motions before a court to obtain confidential records. Section 74 of the Act establishes the threshold for disclosure of records that might otherwise be considered confidential or privileged. In s. 74(1) a record is defined as recorded information regardless of the physical form or the characteristics. Section 74(3) provides the means by which a Children's Aid Society may obtain records pursuant to a court order from a school board with respect to information concerning either a current or former school board employee about whom a suspicion (based upon reasonable grounds to believe) has been disclosed.[54]

The difficulty that Children's Aid Societies encounter when they bring disclosure motions for employee personnel records is that employee records that are released to the Society pursuant to a court order may not contain the material facts. This is true even where this documentation is a disciplinary letter. Sometimes disciplinary materials have been removed from the file. Thus, even if the file were summonsed to court and the order for the release of the records were granted, there might be nothing in the records confirming or denying past sexual misconduct or abuse, or allegations or complaints regarding a teacher's actions. The Robins report noted this problem. One of its recommendations is that detailed records be made and retained pertaining to complaints of sexual misconduct by teachers.[55] Another recommendation states that proper documentation should include details respecting any initial complaint or disclosure.[56] Reports made to the Children's Aid Society, police, the school board and the College of Teachers should also be retained, as should any notes of interviews, audiotapes, or videotapes that relate to internal investigations, legal proceedings or disciplinary measures taken by the board.[57] The notes taken during interviews should be factual and detailed.[58]

The Robins report also points out that the privacy legislation, the *Municipal Freedom of Information and Protection of Privacy Act*[59] has been perceived as preventing the disclosure of material facts if the material is personal information of the employee.[60] This is not the case. Sections 72 and 74 of the Act have been described by the court to "… have been legislated so that Societies could prosecute protection cases with the best possible evidence".[61] The Unified Family Court has stated, "… the protection of children under these sections is given priority over the privilege accorded to the police and other individuals under the exemptions provided for under the *Freedom of Information Act*".[62]

The duty to report is ongoing. If a person has additional reasonable grounds to suspect, he or she must report again even if she or he has made previous reports with respect to the same child.[63]

The person who has reasonable grounds to suspect must make the report directly to the appropriate Children's Aid Society. The person cannot rely on anyone else to report on his or her behalf.[64] There can be no delegation of that duty. This may be a particularly relevant section for teachers to whom abuse has been disclosed by children. The procedure in the past had been to bring the information to the attention of the principal, who would probably have been the one to report it to the Society. Furthermore, it is not correct to suppose that these laws require a person to report only when he or she has first-hand knowledge. The duty exists even when a suspicion is formed on the basis of third party reports, hearsay or overheard conversations.[65]

The report to the Children's Aid Society must be made "forthwith" according to s. 72(1). This word has been defined by the courts to mean "immediately", but with the provision that the context be carefully examined. The word was thoroughly analyzed in two Supreme Court of Canada cases involving breathalyzer tests. In one case, because the test is supposed to be administered forthwith, a delay of 30 minutes was not acceptable in order to set up the equipment.[66] In another case, the word "forthwith" was defined as "as soon as possible" in the circumstances as it can take 15 minutes for a machine to give an accurate reading.[67] With respect to teachers, principals and other school board employees who are mandated to report forthwith, it would be prudent to consider forthwith to mean immediately.

If there is to be a delay in reporting, steps should be taken to protect students without delay. In one case, a principal and superintendent were charged with failure to report forthwith as they had waited seven days to report. In the interim, they removed the "abusing" teacher from the classroom while they investigated the complaint. They were acquitted, despite their taking days to report. In the circumstances it was determined that the delay was reasonable, insofar as both the teacher and the super-intendent placed the child's safety first by removing the alleged abuser from the classroom.[68] In another case, a three-hour and forty-five-minute reporting delay was found to be well within the confines of the word forthwith. For the court, the issue was whether or not the purpose of the legislation had been carried out. It found that the child was safely ensconced in hospital prior to the abuse being reported by hospital staff. Thus the purpose of the legislation had been adhered to.[69]

Is there scope within the boundaries of the term forthwith that would permit teachers, principals, or school superintendents to begin their own investigation regarding the suspected abuse, prior to a report being made to a Children's Aid Society? While courts have found that in certain cases it is acceptable to make inquires to determine reasonable grounds to suspect that the abuse had occurred,[70] such a delay will be more acceptable where the complaint is of a less serious nature, or is vague, particularly if the alleged abuser is removed from the classroom.[71] Generally speaking it is the role of the police to conduct criminal investigations and the role of the police and the appropriate Children's Aid Society to conduct child protec-tion investigations; it is not that of the school board.

Principals must be cautioned that the duty of a principal to give assiduous attention to the health and comfort of pupils[72] and the authority of a principal to manage the affairs of the school,[73] which would normally require an immediate investigation of threats to student safety, are overridden by the *Child and Family Services Act*. The duty to report is paramount.

Reporting suspected abuse overrides the concept of confidentiality of information. Furthermore, there can be no prosecution of the reporter of the abuse as long as the reporter acts in good faith.[74] For example, a police officer who provided the Children's Aid Society with a copy of a victim's statement regarding her past sexual abuse given in another investigation was found by the courts not to be guilty of professional misconduct even though this was privileged police information.[75] Teachers and guidance counsellors are often provided with abuse disclosure that a child asks to keep confidential. Disclosing this information does not violate privacy rights because the reporting duty overrides the duty of confidentiality. There is no liability for reporting.[76]

The overriding principle of s. 72 of the *Child and Family Services Act* is that the duty to report is paramount. This is set out explicitly in the wording of s. 72(1) and expressed specifically by a court: "I am of the view that the duty imposed by section 72 is paramount."[77]

The Perspective of the Children's Aid Societies and Teachers

The relationship between the Children's Aid Societies and teachers appears to be inextricably linked to the manner in which the reporting duty is fulfilled, or not fulfilled, despite the legislative imperatives. The relationship between teachers and their representatives and Children's Aid Societies and their representatives has been described by the stakeholders as strained. The Robins report acknowledges, "there is a level of distrust between some children's aid workers and counsel for suspected teachers".[78] According to the Robins report, counsel for the suspected teachers have complained that they are given no information regarding the disclosures made by children, and thus are not able to respond to the allegations that are made. "They are too often kept in the dark as to what is said about them."[79] The workers have been criticized for being too inexperienced and for "uncritically evaluating the accounts of children".[80] The Children's Aid workers have mentioned that they utilize appropriate interviewing techniques.[81] They also mention that premature disclosure to the teacher and his or her counsel of the reported suspicion and the information upon which it is based compromises the investigation and has resulted in the student complainant being humiliated.[82] Most particularly worrisome for Children's Aid Society workers was their claim that teachers' unions "… thwart investigations by delaying the investigative process and disciplinary process, by causing teachers (all of whom are members of the same unions) to close ranks and not cooperate in the investigation".[83]

The Child Abuse Register

Children's Aid Societies have their own reporting duty in regards to the Child Abuse Register. The Children's Aid Societies must forthwith verify the reported suspected abuse and if the report is verified they are directed to report it in the prescribed form to the Director, who is then required to place the information, along with the name of the suspected sexual abuser, on a child abuse register.[84]

The duty to report the abuse to the Director, once the abuse is verified, is not discretionary.[85] Section 75(5) of the Act directs the Director to maintain a Child Abuse Register that has in it the verified information regarding child abuse.[86] The Act directs against the placing of the name of the person or any identifying information regarding the person who reported the suspected abuse to the society and who is not the subject of the complaint. Thus a teacher or school staff employee who makes a report to the society need not fear that his or her identity will be revealed on the register.

The register is confidential and its accessibility is limited to certain persons, as set out in the Act. This of course is problematic. Neither the police nor any member of the school board may examine the register to ascertain whether or not one of the teachers, for example, in a school board had been previously reported to the Children's Aid Society. Even the person reporting the suspected abuse under s. 72 may not inspect the register. By virtue of s. 75(6) of the Act, only the following have access to the register: a Children's Aid Society, the Children's Lawyer's Office, a coroner or a delegate acting under the *Coroners Act*[87] and a therapist and/or physician, or a researcher, given authorization by the Director, or Minister, or a registered person.[88]

This confidentiality applies to legal proceedings as well. The register and its contents are inadmissible except in limited circumstances, in particular, in the circumstances of an inquest or an expunction hearing or a hearing designed to ascertain whether or not the registered person may remove his or her name from the register. The register cannot be used in child protection proceedings.

What constitutes verified abuse for the purpose of the register? The Ministry of Community and Social Services has set out guidelines.[89] The minimum steps include searching the society's existing records as well as other Children's Aid Society records for relevant information, and to ascertain if there was former involvement with the victim, the parents or the alleged abuser who had charge of the child; interviewing the person who made the allegation or reported the suspected abuse; interviewing the victim; considering involving the police; contacting the Child Abuse Register to ascertain whether the child, alleged abuser or parent were previously registered. Section 2(1) of R.R.O. 1990, Reg. 71 directs the society to apply to review the register within three days of receiving the report of suspected child abuse.[90] Once the abuse is registered, the society has a duty to file follow-up reports with the register. There has been controversy over the phrase "verified abuse". It has been noted that the phrase is really subjective and discretionary.[91]

Where a person challenges his or her placement on the register an expunction hearing is held.[92] If teachers and other school employees or volunteers who have been found to have charge of the child, have had their names placed on the register, they would be entitled to a hearing under this section.

Once the verified information is placed on the register, the information and name of the alleged abuser stay on the register for at least 25 years, unless it has been expunged or amended by the Director.[93] Notice must be given to the registered person. He or she and/or his or her solicitor may inspect the register, and may request that the name be removed.[94] If the Director refuses to grant an administrative expunction of the name from the register, then a hearing will be conducted, by the Director or by a hearing officer authorized to hold the hearing who exercises the rights and duties of the Director.[95] The parties to the hearing are the registered person and the society generally.[96] The Director or his or her delegate must determine after holding the hearing that the information with respect to the identified person in the register is in error or should not be in the register, before he or she has the name expunged.[97] Ministry guidelines indicate that that the Director or hearing officer must be satisfied that the alleged abuse is sufficiently serious or there is a clearly established pattern or condition of abuse for the name to remain on the register.[98] The evidentiary burden is on the society to establish that the person identified on the register had charge of the child and caused the child to suffer abuse, or failed to prevent the abuse based on credible evidence[99] pursuant to the *Statutory Powers Procedure Act*.[100]

Hearing officers and courts have taken different positions on the issue of what constitutes credible evidence. Hearsay evidence may be permitted if the hearing officer determines it is credible. "The director's determination must be made on the totality of the evidence adduced before him. Having regard to the purpose and object of the registry and the social policy underlying the Act, the burden of proof in my view should not be too onerous."[101] The registered person is entitled to a full-fledged hearing. This means that the registered person, like the society, may call witnesses. The registered person may be entitled to cross-examine the child witness where courts are concerned about ensuring the registered person has a right to natural justice.[102] Generally speaking, as a result of the decision in *R. v. Khan*,[103] children may not be required to testify. Their out-of-court statements may be accepted into evidence through a third party if the requirements are met. There are two tests that have to be met.

The reliability test can be met if it can be shown through a third party in court that the child's statements were truthful, credible and reliable, and that the manner in which they were made demonstrated their truthfulness or credibility, *i.e.* they were spontaneous utterances, the child demonstrated that he or she knew the difference between the truth and a lie, and there was no reason to fabricate.

The test of necessity can be met if it can be demonstrated to the court that it is reasonably necessary that the statement be received, that there is no good reason for the child to testify and that, in fact, the child will likely be harmed emotionally if he or she testifies, and the information can only come to the court's attention through a third person to whom the child related the incident or events.[104] To demonstrate necessity, a court generally requires an expert psychologist, therapist or psychiatrist's report delineating the harm.

The hearings are private. Section 76(10) of the Act directs that the general public and the media shall not be permitted to attend.[105]

INVESTIGATION POLICIES, PROCEDURES AND PROTOCOLS

The investigation of suspected cases of sexual abuse is conducted by the police and Children's Aid Societies. The process of the investigation and management of the sexual abuse cases within the schools requires cooperation between the school and the investigating agencies.

Justice Robins in *Protecting Our Students* recognized the importance of developing protocols and policies on sexual misconduct and sexual abuse throughout the province of Ontario. Such protocols should govern the internal operations of the board and the relationship with outside agencies.

Protocols and policies are considered to be important tools for the prevention and early identification of sexual misconduct, and for protecting those already victimized by such misconduct.[106] The report stresses the urgency of a board developing a policy "on how complaints of sexual abuse should be acted upon, ... that is clear, fair, and known to all ...".[107] Most important, the absence of protocol "produces uneven or inappropriate treatment of students and teachers, unnecessary uncertainty, speculation, gossip and innuendo, heightened trauma to interested parties, particularly children and overall, a process that is seen to be arbitrary and unfair".[108]

The report uses the terms "policy", "protocol guidelines" and "procedures" interchangeably though it acknowledges that the Toronto District School Board distinguishes between them. The policy is the general statement of principles and goals adopted by the board. The procedures operationalize the policy. The protocol sets out rules of interaction between the board and outside agencies. The Societies and the police are such outside agencies, which play an integral part in the investigation and management of suspected sexual abuse.

The report acknowledged that various Ontario school boards had produced policies and procedures. A review of these policies revealed that there was no consistent interpretation of the duty to report under the *Child and Family Services Act.*[109] This was a concern of both Children's Aid Societies and the police, as many disclosures were not reported. Various school board procedures delegated the reporting duty to the principal, making the individual duty to report discretionary rather than mandated. Moreover, it was discovered that in certain school boards principals were expected to make a preliminary investigation and then determine whether the abuse was reportable.

Another area of concern for investigating agencies was that in some boards the procedures directed that a board employee suspected of sexual misconduct or abuse be informed of the allegation prior to the onset of the investigation, prior to contacting the Children's Aid Society or police. This process, of course, was said by Children's Aid Societies and the police to interfere with and undermine the investigative process, and the management of the investigative process.

Protocols with the Police and the Children's Aid Society

It is a policy direction of the Ministry of Education and the Ministry of the Solicitor General, that police services and school boards establish a protocol for the investigation of school-related occurrences. The purpose of the preparation of a police-school board protocol is to ensure that schools are safe, secure and are places of respect and tolerance. To that end procedures must be developed and put into place that reflect provincial expectations. The protocol is designed to provide a vehicle for communication between the schools and the police, and it appears though not stated explicitly, also children's aid societies. The protocol will serve to ensure the consistency of approach in the local protocols developed by the school boards and police services across the province.[110] It is not clear from the model that the signatories include Children's Aid Societies. The model only refers to school boards, band councils and the police.[111] The model provides for 23 elements that must be included in the local protocols. Throughout, the model emphasizes the reporting duty where a child is in need of protection and the role to be played by Children's Aid Societies with respect to the investigation of reports of suspected abuse and procedures for the sharing of information with the police and the boards.

In Toronto, the public and Catholic school boards and the Children's Aid Societies are partners to a detailed Sexual Abuse Protocol. Other partners include the Ministry of the Attorney General, the Ministry of

Community and Social Services and Young Offender Services Toronto Area Office. This protocol has a specific section on investigations on school premises and allegations against school employees.

The Ministry of Education has announced a Provincial Model for a local Police/School Board Protocol for the investigation of school-related occurrences that it wishes to have uniformly implemented. The Sexual Abuse Protocol and the Policy of the Toronto District School Board will be discussed briefly below with respect to the integration of the three systems when dealing with sexual abuse disclosures that involve teachers and other school staff and that trigger the involvement of the Children's Aid Societies.

In Toronto the need for integration of response has been long recognized. A Special Committee on Child Abuse was established in 1981 with the mandate to "improve coordination and delivery of services to abused children and their families".[112] Traditionally the police and the Children's Aid Societies "... operated in relative isolation, with frequently different philosophies and practices which often inadvertently left child victims in limbo, sometimes at serious risk".[113] In 1982 the Special Committee convened a multi-disciplinary group of professionals as the Protocol Development Committee to develop guidelines for the coordination of the investigation and management of all child abuse cases. This committee produced the *Child Sexual Abuse Protocol* in 1983. Since November 1983, the protocol has gone through two more editions: June 1986, and March 1995. Another edition is in the works.

A key element of the protocol is the agreed-upon team approach taken with respect to the investigation, prosecution and case management of sexual abuse cases. This was particularly essential insofar as one of the impediments to successful investigation, management and prosecution of child abuse cases was the multiple interviews of the child by different professionals of different systems. Not only did this approach traumatize the child, it also created a risk of contamination of the evidence. The child may have disclosed abuse and then been questioned many times by different professionals: teachers, principals, police, doctors, etc. The consequence of multiple examinations was often that defence lawyers could point out serious inconsistencies in the different interviews or argue that words or thoughts had been put in the child witness's mouth by the interviewer. In addition, potentially relevant details were often missed by untrained investigators.

Another significant difficulty noted by the developers of the protocol was the "... lack of a statutory legal definition of sexual abuse ...", which created a situation where the different definitions in the mandated systems actually increase the potential for inconsistent levels of reporting from the community, including professionals, and the potential for varying responses from the CAS and the Police.[114]

The Toronto Child Sexual Abuse Protocol is a "how to" manual for the coordinated response to sexual abuse in Toronto. It outlines how to conduct an investigation of child sexual abuse from the initial stage of reporting that is designed to ensure the protection of children, the provision of support to victims and families and the successful prosecution of the offender and the possible reintegration of the offender into the family. The signatories to it are committed to the implementation of the protocol as the means for responding to a sexual abuse disclosure in a uniform manner across the city of Toronto. It is described in some detail below to indicate the issues that should be addressed in any protocol that is developed with investigating agencies.

The Sexual Abuse Protocol is composed of 15 parts and five appendices. Each part is composed of guidelines and commentary that explains the reasoning behind the development of the guidelines. Part One deals with some key concepts, including the concept of the team and the challenge presented by the lack of a legal/statutory or formal definition of sexual abuse. Part Two is the introduction. Some of the significant parts of the protocol are outlined below.

The Investigative Team

The investigation of sexual abuse complaints is a joint investigation by the police and the Children's Aid Society using only designated personnel. Protocol requires the resources of a large urban police force. In smaller or more remote areas dependent upon local police or provincial police, it may not be possible to have specially trained officers who specialize in such investigations.

For the purposes of the protocol, designated personnel are Children's Aid Society workers (members of the intake teams), police officers (those who have taken specialized training), Crown Attorneys (assigned to sexual abuse cases) and probation officer (assigned to handle convicted sex offenders). These designated personnel receive specialized education and training and possess the advanced skills in investigating and prosecuting cases or in working with convicted offenders. The designated police officer shall have responsibility for the criminal investigation, while the designated social worker shall have responsibility for child protection investigation and the protection of the child. The rationale for the concept of a joint investigation is to assess whether there are any protection concerns regarding the child, ensure his or her safety and determine whether a criminal offence has occurred. The appropriate Children's Aid Society social worker is involved when the abuse relates to someone who has charge of the child. The police and Children's Aid Societies must ensure either that the designated workers and officers are available or that alternative qualified designated personnel are available to investigate. Furthermore, the joint aspect of the investigation will ensure that no relevant information gets lost. There shall be full verbal disclosure between the designated police officer and social worker at all times.

The Response to the Initial Report

The police and CAS constitute the team that responds to the initial report of sexual abuse or assault. Whichever agency receives the initial report should contact the other agency prior to an investigation commencing. In all reports of child sexual abuse "Mutual reporting is fundamental to the success of the Protocol."[115] Both the Children's Aid Society and the police must be involved to discuss the report and determine whether or not to conduct a joint investigation before arriving on the scene. Reports of sexual abuse received by either the police or the CAS shall be reported to the other organization and documents of the report shall be exchanged between the police and the CAS. When the CAS receives a report of suspected sexual abuse that involves an adult who does not have charge of the child (*i.e.* not a parent or a teacher), the CAS worker shall ascertain whether there are potential child protection concerns and then shall contact the police to discuss what their role shall be, if any. If the police are the first to receive the report, the uniformed officer who responds to the call should confirm the complaint, secure the situation and then ensure that a designated CAS worker is notified to discuss any potential or actual protection concerns and to discuss the role of the CAS in the investigation. The CAS and police should work as a team.[116]

Where the abuse is alleged to be at the hands of a parent, relative or babysitter, a team composed of the police and the CAS will cooperate to investigate the abuse. There are situations, however, where the police might conduct the investigation without Children's Aid Society involvement. The decision as to whether or not the joint investigation is appropriate is made once a report is made, prior to an investigation and based upon the facts of the case, the risk of further abuse, the alleged offender's position with other children, the needs of the victim and family, and the resources that are available.[117] Generally speaking, however, where the "accused does not have charge of the child nor is in a position of trust" and there are no potential child protection concerns, the role of the Children's Aid Society is short-lived.[118] The police proceed with the criminal investigation. This is the case in most investigations involving school board employees.

The First Stages of the Investigation

The protocol directs the Children's Aid Societies and the police to proceed on the assumption that the child's report or disclosure warrants a full investigation.[119] Children who have special language needs, who are hearing impaired, who are under age five or who have developmental delays also have more difficulty communicating. Subsequent recanting should not negate the investigation. It should not be taken as proof that the abuse did not occur. Children who cannot verbalize or who are unable to communicate effectively may provide disclosures and information through their actions and behaviour. In those circumstances the team should seek the assistance of specialized resource persons in the community, who serve as professional interpreters. These should be provided.

In some cases a child may have contracted a sexually transmitted disease or been physically harmed. The SCAN Team at the Hospital for Sick Children and the Public Health Officials become involved in these circumstances. In some cases testing is done to ascertain whether a pregnancy occurred as a result of sexual abuse or assault.

The Joint Interview of the Child

The members of the team introduce themselves to the child at the first contact and describe their roles. The designated social worker assesses whether the child is in need of protection and the police officer determines whether a criminal offence has occurred and whether or not to charge the offender. The purpose of the interview is to minimize the trauma for the child and secure as much detailed information as possible about the alleged disclosure, to minimize the contamination of the evidence and to maintain the integrity of the investigative process.[120]

The child should be interviewed by the team member who develops a rapport with the child and who has more experience in interviewing children who have made disclosures. There is also a discussion of the necessity of and method of providing augmentative devices to assist the child, particularly if the child is a special needs child. A computer is one such device. The protocol cautions the interviewer to only utilize secondary aids such as anatomical dolls after an initial verbal disclosure has been made, and only for clarification purposes. In order to ensure that no suggestion is made later that the child has been verbally prompted or led by the interviewers, the child should also be encouraged to verbally disclose or describe the events the child is depicting or trying to depict through the play with the dolls.[121] The child and the allied parents should be referred to a crisis support program to assist in dealing with the trauma that the child experiences through the disclosure process.[122]

Videotaping Interviews

All initial interviews of children should be videotaped. While this was not always possible in the earlier years, since the third edition of the *Child Sexual Abuse Protocol* was printed in 1995 the police and the societies have been videotaping interviews with children. The procedure for videotaping is delineated in this part of the protocol. The videotaping should be the rule of the interview process unless circumstances dictate otherwise, and if they do those circumstances should be documented. Videotaping should not be done if videotaping is part of the sexual abuse that the child disclosed. Rules on the duplicating of videotapes, and the ownership and retention of the videotape are set out in this part as well. In general, a sealed master copy of the interview is retaind and owned by the police. The police will make two additional copies and provide one to the society. The society shall have ownership of its copy and can destroy it or retain it according to proper Children's Aid Society procedures.

Multiple Victims

Often in school settings the abuser may be one adult in charge of many students and in a position of trust and authority over them. There may be a number of investigators depending upon the scope and size of the investigation. The team is made up of police and CAS workers. What is important to note is that team leaders will coordinate the police investigations and the investigations of Children's Aid Societies. A Crown Attorney should be assigned as well. The victims are interviewed separately. The team approach means that the team leaders have to be in constant communication with each other regarding the disclosures and the results of each interview. They have to ensure that their respective senior staff is informed of the results of their interviews and their plans. If the abuse occurred within a school then the school officials should also be informed. They should not be investigating however.

Investigations on School Premises

The current *Sexual Abuse Protocol* will most likely be updated to include the recent amendments to the *Education Act*. It recognizes four situations in which investigations take place on school property. These include situations where:

1. the abuse is disclosed at school and reported immediately by the school personnel to the society;
2. the abuse is disclosed outside the school and the police and society worker team wish to interview the child at school;
3. the abuse disclosure involves another child as an alleged offender; or
4. the abuse disclosure involves a school employee as the alleged offender.[123]

The protocol specifically states: "School personnel shall not conduct an investigation regarding the suspicion or disclosure, and shall question the child only to clarify the nature of the complaint."[124] The investigative team in consultation with the principal and any school social worker should develop a plan that addresses the immediate needs of the victim and that takes into account the whereabouts of the alleged offender.[125]

Generally, the investigative team should seek prior parental consent to the interview unless the best interests of the child require that the interview take place without the consent of the parent. The principal has the discretion to permit an interview.[126] The investigative team should request that the parent or guardian or child, if he or she is 12 years old or older, sign a consent to release of information form to allow for communication between the investigative team and the school principal. There is a commentary that underscores the reporting duty set out under s. 72 of the *Child and Family Services Act*. School staff are reminded to refrain from carrying out investigations particularly in light of the possibility that this could jeopardize the criminal investigation. The commentary asserts that at times the exploration of a suspicion of abuse can be done without leading the child victim and contaminating the future investigation by the police and the society. It is acknowledged that school staff will be the recipients of disclosures and should thus attempt to record general details (including the report maker's identifying information) and more specific details of the sexual abuse.

The signatory school boards must ensure that their internal policies are consistent with their reporting duties under the *Child and Family Services Act*. This becomes particularly crucial in situations where an employee of the school board is accused of sexually abusing a child. The internal school board policies should have clear reporting procedures as well as procedures regarding employee access to children during the investigation, and procedures for dealing with an employee who has been acquitted.

The protocol anticipated the changes to the adverse reporting requirement of the *Teaching Profession Act* Regulation, in particular s. 18(1)(b).[127] The protocol states that under no circumstances, despite the Act, should an alleged offender (a school board employee) be notified before the criminal investigation has begun. The protocol points out that the police considered that when teachers carried out what they thought was their s. 18(1)(b) duty they were interfering in the conduct of a criminal investigation.[128] The Robins report commented on the fact that the adverse report provision "… does not and should not apply to reports of suspected sexual misconduct".[129]

Interviewing the Alleged Offender

It is the designated police officer who determines the procedure for interviewing the alleged abuser. The police conduct the interview and the police disclose the results to the society's designated worker.

Potential Witnesses and Evidence at Trial

If criminal charges are laid, Children's Aid Society workers conducting investigations and working with child victims may be called as witnesses and files may be subpoenaed by the Crown or by defence counsel, if the contents are seen to be relevant. Teachers to whom sexual abuse has been disclosed may also be subpoenaed as witnesses to give evidence. The alleged offender's school personnel files may also be subpoenaed.

SCHOOL BOARD POLICIES AND PROCEDURES

It is essential that all incidents of sexual misconduct that could amount to abuse or a criminal offence be dealt with consistently and uniformly across the district. There should be a minimum of discretion permitted at the local school level. The Toronto District School Board Policy manual is entitled *Dealing with Abuse and Neglect of Students*.[130] It provides detailed direction on how to deal with all types of alleged abuse and sexual misconduct. In particular, it contains separate specific guide procedures that must be followed when allegations are made against staff or volunteers.

One section is devoted to situations involving victims under 16 when a board employee or a volunteer is the perpetrator of sexual abuse or sexual assault. This section prohibits board staff and volunteers from entering into sexual relationships with students of any age in their professional capacity, and for one year thereafter in the case of former students.[131] In a subcategory, it sets out the reporting duty with respect to suspected sexual assault or sexual abuse. Reports must be made immediately and directly to the Children's Aid Society. It is emphasized that the duty to report cannot be delegated, though the principal must be told of the suspicion and he or she should inform the superintendent.

Section 4.3.1 of the policy manual states that there should be no notification of "the implicated staff" until specific instructions are received from the police.[132] This section also stresses the importance not only of reporting the suspected abuse to the Children's Aid Societies, but also of providing the required information as set out in the appropriate form "Record of Report of Abuse/Neglect".[133] It is the responsibility of the person reporting to ensure that the time element is taken into consideration. The report has to be made "forthwith". The victim may have to be detained at school while the investigative team (the police and the Children's Aid worker) arrives. The child may also require support services.

The procedure requires the removal of an implicated staff member as soon as possible from an assignment that involves having contact with students once the police have begun their investigation.[134] In the case of a teacher or union member, he or she must be notified of the right to contact the union or federation representative.[135] The procedure deals with the necessity of documenting suspect abuse/neglect cases and the manner in which the documentation must be prepared and requires following up with the police and the Children's Aid Societies when it is not apparent that the investigation has commenced within 24 hours. It is the responsibility of the principal or designate to follow up with the Children's Aid Society and the police. The Children's Aid Society should also be notified when the child has been found to be in need of protection, or is known to be at risk and has transferred to another school or board.[136] It is also the responsibility of the principal or the designate to notify the Children's Aid Society worker so that supportive counselling can be provided, if deemed appropriate.[137] It is clear from the summary of the procedures set out in the Toronto District School Board's policy manual and in the Sexual Abuse Protocol that every effort is being made to carry out the legally mandated reporting obligations, to ensure the safety of the victim(s), to ensure that the investigative process is unimpeded, that the evidence remains uncontaminated, and that the alleged offender, if guilty, is convicted and taken out of the school environment.

ENDNOTES

[1]   R.S.O. 1990, c. C.11.

[2]   *Ibid.*, s. 1(1).

[3]   R.S.O. 1990, c. C.43.

[4]   *Child and Family Services Act*, R.S.O. 1990, c. C.11, s. 37(2)(*f*).

[5]   *Ibid.*, s. 72(1).

[6]   R.S.O. 1990, c. E.2.

[7]   S.O. 1996, c. 12, as amended by the *Student Protection Act, 2002*, S.O. 2002, c. 7, s. 2 [in force September 3, 2002].

[8]   Sydney Robins, *Protecting Our Students: A Review to Identify and Prevent Sexual Misconduct in Ontario Schools* (Toronto: Ministry of the Attorney General (Milner Graphics), 2002), p. 201.

[9]   O. Reg. 437/97 (see Appendix 5).

[10]   Robins, *Protecting Our Students*, p. 201.

[11]   *Ibid.*

[12]   *Ibid.*, p. 202.

[13]   *R. v. Stachula* (1984), 40 R.F.L. (2d) 184 (Ont. Prov. Ct. [Fam. Div.]), at 187, citing *R. v. Cook* (1983), 37 R.F.L. (2d) 93 (Ont. Prov. Ct.) at 98 (subsequently appealed (1985), 46 R.F.L. (2d) 174 (Ont. C.A.)).

[14]   R.S.O. 1990, c. P.33.

[15]   *Re S.* (1980), 15 R.F.L. (2d) 167 at 170 (Alta. Fam. Ct).

[16]   Robins, *Protecting Our Students*, at pp. 185, 202.

[17]   Jeffrey Wilson, *Wilson on Children and the Law* (Toronto: Butterworths, 1994), p. 3.14; *Child and Family Services Act*, R.S.O. 1990, c. C.11, s. 79.

[18]   *R. v. I. (B.F.)* November 1, 1989, Lennox Ont. Family Court, Kirkland J., as cited in Marvin M. Bernstein, Lynn Kirwin and Helen Bernstein, *Child Protection Law in Canada*, Vol. 2 (Toronto: Carswell, 1996), p. 11-8.

[19]   [1998] 2 S.C.R. 1299.

[20]   *Ibid.*, p. 1315.

[21]   *Education Act*, R.S.O. 1990, c. E.2, s. 58.5 (added 1997, c. 31, s. 32).

[22]   Robins, *Protecting Our Students*, p. 178.

[23]   R.S.C. 1985, c. C-46.

[24]   Bernstein, Kirwin, Bernstein, *Child Protection Law in Canada*, Vol. 2, p.11-7, citing *R. v. Kates*, [1987] O.J. No. 2032 (QL) (Ont. Dist. Ct.).

[25]   *Ibid.*

[26]   *R. v. Stachula* (1984), 40 R.F.L. (2d) 184 (Ont. Prov. Ct.), p. 174.

[27]   Robins, *Protecting Our Students*, p. 186.

[28]   *Ibid.*, p. 182, citing *Protecting Vulnerable Children: Report of the Panel of Experts on Child Protection* (Toronto: Ministry of Community and Social Services, 1998) (Chair: Justice Mary Jane Hatten).

[29]   *Ibid.*, p. 183.

[30]   Ontario Legislative Assembly Debate on Bill 101, October 3, 2001, p. 2373.

[31]   *Ibid.*, p. 2374.

[32]   Robins, *Protecting Our Students*, p. 279.

[33]   *Ibid.*

[34]   *Ibid.*

[35]   *Ibid.*, p. 280, citing Anthony F. Brown and Marvin A. Zuker, *Education Law*, 2nd edition (Toronto: Carswell, 1998), p. 139.

[36]   *Police Complaints Commissioner v. Dunlop* (1996), 26 O.R. (3d) 582 (Div. Ct.).

[37] *Ibid.*, p. 586.

[38] *Ibid.*

[39] R.S.O. 1990, c. T.2.

[40] Marvin A. Zuker, unpublished paper, "Bill 101" (August 28, 2002), p. 13.

[41] Robins, *Protecting Our Students*, p. 182.

[42] Wilson, *Wilson on Children and the Law*, p. 3.15.1.

[43] *R. v. Stachula* (1989), 40 R.F.L. (2d) 184 (Ont. Prov. Ct.), p. 186.

[44] *R. v. Kates*, [1987] O.J. No. 2032 (QL) (Ont. Dist. Ct.).

[45] *R. v. Stachula* (1984), 40 R.F.L. (2d) 184 (Ont. Prov. Ct.), p. 186.

[46] *Ibid.*, p. 187.

[47] *Child and Family Services Act*, R.S.O. 1990, c. C.11, s. 72(6.2).

[48] *Ibid.*, s. 72(6.1).

[49] *Ibid.*

[50] Marvin A. Zuker, unpublished paper, "Bill 101" (August 28, 2002), p. 6.

[51] *Lurene v. Olsson*, 740 N.Y.S.2d 797 (Sup. Ct. 2002).

[52] *Child and Family Services Act*, R.S.O. 1990, c. C.11, s. 72(1).

[53] *Police Complaints Commissioner v. Dunlop* (1996), 26 O.R. (3d) 582 (Div. Ct.), p. 587.

[54] *Ibid.*, s. 74(3). Note that s. 74.1 of the *Child and Family Services Act* is new (added 1999, c. 2, s. 25) and permits the court or the justice of peace to issue a warrant for access to a record prior to the initiating of an application, on the condition that there are reasonable grounds to believe that the record is relevant to an allegation that a child is or may be in need of protection. Section 74.2(1) should also be noted for it permits the obtaining of a warrant under s. 74.1 by telephone or other means of tele-communication if there are reasonable grounds for the issuance of the warrant and if it can be demonstrated that it would be "impracticable" to appear personally before the court or a justice of the peace.

[55] Robins, *Protecting Our Students*, p. 340.

[56] *Ibid.*

[57] *Ibid.*

[58] *Ibid.*

[59] R.S.O. 1990, c. M.56; Robins, *ibid.*, p. 338.

[60] *Ibid.*

[61] Bernstein, Kirwin, Bernstein, *Child Protection Law in Canada*, p. 10-6.1, citing *Children's Aid Society of Hamilton-Wentworth v. M. (T.)*, [1995] O.J. No. 4317 (QL) (Ont. U.F.C.).

[62] *Ibid.*

[63] *Child and Family Services Act*, R.S.O. 1990, c. C.11, s. 72(2).

[64] *Ibid.*

[65] William Foster, "The Statutory Common Law Obligations In Educators", in 4 Ed. L. J. (1993), p. 22.

[66] *R. v. Grant* (1991), 67 C.C.C. (3d) 268 (S.C.C.).

[67] *R. v. Brenshaw* (1995), 95 C.C.C. (3d) 193 (S.C.C.).

[68] *R. v. Papai* (January 20, 1993) (Ont. Ct. Prov. Div.).

[69] Bernstein, Kirwin, Bernstein, *Child Protection Law in Canada*, p. 10-6, citing *R. v. Shubat* (March 29, 1996) (Ont. Prov. Ct.), Gale J.; reversed (July 27, 1996), (Ont. Prov. Div.), Hunter J.

[70] *R. v. Papai* (January 20, 1993) (Ont. Ct. Prov. Div.).

[71] Robins, *Protecting Our Students*, p. 183.

[72] *Education Act*, R.S.O. 1990, c. E.2, s. 265.

[73] Operation of Schools — General, R.R.O. 1990, Reg. 298, s. 11.

[74] *Child and Family Services Act*, R.S.O. 1990, c. C.11, s. 72(7).

[75] *Police Complaints Commissioner v. Dunlop* (1995), 26 O.R. (3d) 582 (Div. Ct.).

[76] Brown, Zuker, *Education Law*, 2nd ed., p. 41.

[77] *Police Complaints Commissioner v. Dunlop* (1995), 26 O.R. (3d) 582 (Div. Ct.), p. 587.

[78] Robins, *Protecting Our Students*, p. 282.

[79] *Ibid.*

[80] *Ibid.*

[81] *Ibid.*

[82] *Ibid.*

[83] *Ibid.*

[84] *Child and Family Services Act*, R.S.O. 1990, c. C.11, s. 75(3).

[85] *Ibid.*, s. 75(5).

[86] *Ibid.*

[87] R.S.O. 1990, c. C.37.

[88] *Ibid.*, s. 75(6), (7), (8), (11).

[89] Ministry of Community and Social Services, Interim Guidelines for Reporting to the Child Abuse Register (1987).

[90] R.R.O. 1990, Reg. 71 under the *Child and Family Services Act*.

[91] Wilson, *Wilson on Children and the Law*, p. 3.23, citing *M. v. Ontario (Ministry of Community and Social Services)*, [1986] O.J. No. 1256 (QL) (Ont. H.C.).

[92] *Child and Family Services Act*, R.S.O. 1990, c. C.11, s. 76.

[93] R.R.O. 1990, Reg. 71, s. 3(2).

[94] *Child and Family Services Act*, R.S.O. 1990, c. C.11, s. 76(2), (3).

[95] *Ibid.*, s. 76(4), (5).

[96] *Ibid.*, s. 76(7).

[97] *Ibid.*, s. 76(8).

[98] Interim Guidelines for Expunction Hearing: The Register, *supra*, p. 4.

[99] *Child and Family Services Act*, R.S.O. 1990, c. C.11, s. 76(6).

[100] R.S.O. 1990, c. S.22.

[101] Wilson, *Wilson on Children and the Law*, p. 3.17, citing *Re Ridely and the Children's Aid Society for the County of Hastings* (April 30, 1981) (Ont. Div. Ct.), summarized in 8 A.C.W.S. (2d) 296.

[102] *Ibid.*, citing *B. (J.) v. Catholic Children's Aid Society of Metropolitan Toronto* (1987), 59 O.R. (2d) 417, 38 D.L.R. (4th) 106, 27 Admin. L.R. 295, 7 R.F.L. (3d) 441 (Div. Ct.).

[103] [1990] 2 S.C.R. 531.

[104] *Ibid.*, at 542, 546.

[105] *Child and Family Services Act*, R.S.O. 1990, c. C.11, s. 76(10).

[106] Robins, *Protecting Our Students*, p. 287.

[107] *Ibid.*, p. 114.

[108] *Ibid.*, pp. 287-88.

[109] *Ibid.*, p. 289.

[110] Ministry of Education and Ministry of Training Colleges and Universities, *Provincial Model for a Local Police/School Board Protocol*, July 11, 2002, p. 1.

[111] *Ibid.*, p. 12.

[112] *Child Sexual Abuse Protocol*, rev. ed. (1986), p. 1.

[113] *Ibid.*, p. ii.

[114]   *Child Sexual Abuse Protocol*, 3rd ed. (1995), p. 1.
[115]   *Ibid.*, p. 12.
[116]   *Ibid.*
[117]   *Ibid.*
[118]   *Ibid.*, p. 13.
[119]   *Ibid.*
[120]   *Ibid.*, p. 35.
[121]   *Ibid.*, p. 42.
[122]   *Ibid.*
[123]   *Ibid.*, p. 63.
[124]   *Ibid.*
[125]   *Ibid.*
[126]   *Ibid.*
[127]   *Ibid.*, p. 68. See Appendix 11.
[128]   *Child Sexual Abuse Protocol*, 3rd ed., p. 68.
[129]   Robins, *Protecting Our Students*, p. 212.
[130]   See Appendix 8.
[131]   *Ibid.*, p. 15.
[132]   *Ibid.*, p. 16.
[133]   *Ibid.*, p. 17.
[134]   *Ibid.*, p. 19.
[135]   *Ibid.*
[136]   *Ibid.*, p. 20.
[137]   *Ibid.*

CHAPTER 4

INITIAL REPORTING: THREE TYPES OF SEXUAL MISCONDUCT, THREE TYPES OF RESPONSE

A principal must ensure that the intervention in an alleged incident of sexual misconduct in a school is done in a manner that not only protects students but also respects the legal rights of the all the affected parties including the alleged victim and the alleged offender. In order to do this the principal must have a solid understanding of the duties and responsibilities of school officials when dealing with suspected or alleged misbehaviours by teachers and other school employees that lie within the legal and policy frameworks of sexual misconduct.

The laws and policies around sexual misconduct are complicated, and often overlap or appear contradictory. It becomes easier for the principal if it is understood that are three different legal contexts depending on the age of the alleged victim and there is a particular response to each:

- victims under the age of 16;
- victims age 16 to 17, or who are physically and mentally disabled; and
- victims 18 years of age and older or who are physically and mentally disabled.

Therefore, when a principal encounters a misconduct situation, the very first step is to determine the exact age of the alleged victim(s).

The following sections detail the legal and policy framework around sexual misconduct with students by a teacher, school support employee or volunteer. Please note, however, that while the decisions around reporting may vary in the circumstances, it is recommended that the following procedures *should be the same* in all three situations:

- reporting processes internal to the school board;

- procedures dealing with employees and volunteers who are alleged to have committed such misconduct; and
- procedures for internal investigation of situations where no crime is proven.

WHAT IS LAW AND WHAT IS NOT?

Principals should note that the *Criminal Code*, the *Child and Family Services Act*, the *Education Act* and the *Ontario College of Teachers Act, 1996* all contain mandatory procedures.[1] As with all legislation, there are penalties, fines and even imprisonment, enforceable at law, for failure to comply.

Many procedures and protocols will be stipulated by board policy. To the extent that such policies go beyond legislative minimums, they are enforeceable only by the employer school board as a matter of internal disicipline. Nevertheless, failure to comply could have serious consequences up to and including dismissal.

The Ontario College of Teachers created a *Professional Advisory* in September 2002 that covers many aspects of sexual misconduct and creates professional responsibilites for all members of the college. The legal status of this document is unclear. Unlike some other professional bodies such as the Law Society of Upper Canada or the Ontario College of Physicians and Surgeons, the College of Teachers is not a semi-autonomous regulatory body. It must seek ministerial approval for all professional rules that it creates. The *Advisory* has not received such approval. The *Advisory* states: "It may be taken into consideration by the Disciplinary Committee of the College".[2] However, in some cases the behaviour of members that is considered professional misconduct goes beyond the statutory definitions in the *Ontario College of Teachers Act, 1996*. An example is the list of so-called "grooming behaviours" contained in the *Advisory*. In addition, there are reporting requirements of members described as "professional responsibilites". The expectations of members to report suspicions of misconduct or disclosures of misconduct by another member are in excess of those imposed by either the *Ontario College of Teachers Act, 1996* or the *Child and Family Services Act*. It is strongly recommended that the provisions of the *Advisory* be followed by principals, since they are members, but it is not clear how enforceable these rules may be. A finding by the Discipline Committee based solely on criteria in the *Advisory* could be subject to legal challenge based on an argument that that the college has exceeded its legal authority.

SITUATION ONE

Sexual Misconduct with a Student under 16 Years of Age (Criminal Offence and Child Protection Issue)

Incidents of sexual misconduct involving children fall within the ambit of two separate pieces of legislation, a federal law that is the same across the country — the *Criminal Code* — and laws particular to each province and territory regarding child welfare. In Ontario the relevant law is the *Child and Family Services Act.*

The *Criminal Code* creates specific sexual offences investigated by the police, and the provincial laws require the reporting of suspicions of these offences and other types of defined abuse to Children's Aid Societies.

Principals should always remember that when a student is under the age of 16, all allegations or suspicions of sexual misconduct, even though they are criminal offences, must first be reported to the appropriate Children's Aid Society (see Chapter 3). The actual investigation of the allegations will be usually undertaken by the police, usually in partnership or cooperation with the appropriate Children's Aid Society. The result of the investigation may be a criminal charge being laid by the police and/or a finding of child abuse by the court.

Principals and teachers in Ontario are also governed by their professional responsibilities as defined by the College of Teachers, which requires that when a member "has reasonable grounds to suspect sexual abuse of students or sexual misconduct, a member has a responsibility to report suspected or alleged cases to appropriate authorities. This includes one or more or all of the following: child and family services, police, the employer *and the Ontario College of Teachers*". (Emphasis added.)[3]

In the following section some of the more common sexual offences involving children are described. All of these are considered serious and may result in imprisonment of the offender upon conviction. As a result, it is extremely important that nothing is done by the principal or other school employees that might later have the effect of impeding or interfering with the police investigation. This is best accomplished by not undertaking any internal investigations of complaints, allegations or suspicions before making a report to the Children's Aid Society. In order to collect evidence that will sustain a conviction at trial, police must conduct the first interview of all relevant witnesses. This will prevent such evidence from being tainted or corrupted by well-meaning interrogators who may put words in a witness's mouth or cause inconsistencies that will later create a reasonable doubt at trial. Reviewing the duty to report described later in this chapter should assure a principal that prompt reporting, rather than investigating, is the preferred response.

Sexual Offences Involving Students under 16

The most basic sexual offence is "sexual assault". An "assault" is generally defined in s. 265(1) of the *Criminal Code*. A person commits assault when he or she applies force intentionally to another person directly or indirectly, without consent, or attempts or threatens to do so.

A sexual assault is defined in s. 271(1) as an assault that is committed in circumstances of a sexual nature such that the sexual integrity of the victim is violated. While often referred to as "rape", sexual assault actually includes a much wider range of intrusive behaviours than just sexual penetration of a victim.

The police and/or the Children's Aid Society must determine whether the impugned conduct has the requisite sexual nature in order to support a charge and a court must confirm this to result in a conviction. Relevant considerations are what part of the body is touched, what is said by the assailant, gestures, threats or the use of force.[4]

The intent of the person committing the act is very important, and practically speaking is a major consideration of the police in determining whether a charge will even be laid. There must be an indication that the motive of the accused is sexual gratification. For example, it may be that the evidence supports an allegation that a child was touched on the buttocks but after a thorough investigation one of three different conclusions could be drawn based on context.

- The buttocks were slapped in a congratulatory way in an athletic context (inappropriate perhaps but not criminal);
- The buttocks were smacked in anger (assault); or
- The buttocks were touched for the sexual gratification of the assailant (sexual assault).

Another example involves the alleged close holding or hugging of a student. It could turn out to be any one of four situations based on context:

- a hug of reassurance or joy for a young student (appropriate);
- an age-inappropriate hug of non-sexual affection for a senior student (inappropriate);
- an act of restraint in a situation of classroom violence (inappropriate); or

- an unwanted romantic embrace (criminal).

These distinctions demonstrate that the simplistic direction to teachers not to touch children (often supported by teacher federations) is misguided. Touch can represent a basic form of human communication of love, sympathy or support. Teachers and other school staff should be directed more specifically, not to touch students in anger or for a sexual purpose.

Principals should remember that the task of determining whether an assault is sexual in nature lies with the police and/or the Children's Aid Society and the courts, and any suspicion or allegation should be immediately reported so that a thorough professional investigation can be undertaken.

In any assault, the lack of consent of the victim is a key ingredient of the offence. In sexual assaults involving children there is an age threshold, below which a child is deemed not to be able to consent. This is set out in the *Criminal Code* at s. 150.1.

It often comes as a surprise to principals that the threshold for consent in Canada is age 14. That means that a child of 14 can consent to sex with an adult of any age. Even more surprising, if the sexual act is with another child under the age of 16, and the complainant is less than two years younger, the age of consent may be as low as 12.

The one exception to the consent threshold is when a person is in a position of trust or authority towards a "young person", or the "young person" is in a position of dependency *vis-à-vis* the person. The *Code*, at s. 153(2), defines a young person as a person 14 years of age or more but under the age of 18 years. A position of trust or authority has generally been held to include: a parent, step-parent, adoptive parent, legal guardian, grandparent, uncle, aunt, boarder in the young person's home, baby-sitter, group home worker, youth group worker, employer and teacher.

Principals should note that sexual relations between a student and a school employee would likely be subject to this exception and that students under 18 cannot consent to sex with a teacher. This constitutes the offence of sexual exploitation under s. 153(1) (discussed in detail at pages 85-90).

It is irrelevant whether an accused believed the child to be of age unless the accused took all reasonable steps to ascertain the age of the victim.

In addition to consent not being a defence to a charge of sexual assault when the victim is under 14, this threshold of consent has resulted in the creation of other offences particular to children under this age — "sexual interference", s. 151 of the *Code*, and "invitation to sexual touching", s. 152 of the *Code*.

"Sexual interference" occurs when a person, for a sexual purpose, touches, directly or indirectly, with a part of the body or an object, any part of the body of a person under the age of 14. "Invitation to sexual touching" occurs when a person, for a sexual purpose, "invites, counsels or incites" a child under 14 to touch the body of another person including the person doing the inviting.

The Duty to Report Abuse

In Ontario, if a person who performs professional or official duties with respect to children, has reasonable grounds to suspect that a child under 16 is being or has been abused, that person shall forthwith report the suspicion and the information on which it is based to the appropriate Children's Aid Society. A more detailed explanation of the role of the Children's Aid Societies in investigating sexual misconduct can be found in Chapter 3. The duty to report expands to include children aged 17 or 18 if those children are in the care of a Children's Aid Society either in a foster home or in a group home.

The duty to report is contained in s. 72(1) of the *Child and Family Services Act*. Most principals will have reported various types of abuse (usually within a family context). The same rules apply when there has been an allegation of sexual misconduct by staff. It is a mandatory duty to report when there is a suspicion that "(t)he child has been sexually molested or sexually exploited, by the person having charge of the child or another person where the person having charge of the child knows or should know of the possibility of sexual molestation or sexual exploitation and fails to protect the child".

In addition, the Act also requires reporting a risk that a child is likely to be sexually molested or sexually exploited.

If there is no response from the agency or there are subsequent incidents involving the same child, there is a continuing duty to report (s. 72(2)).

The Act clearly defines who is considered to be performing professional or official duties in s. 72(5). The list includes the following occupations relevant to schools: teacher, school principal, social worker, employee of a day nursery, youth and recreation worker and nurse. There is *no* distinction between public and private school obligations under s. 72.

It is recommended practice to consider all school staff working with students, including educational assistants, paraprofessionals, office and secretarial workers, to have this duty. This should be clearly stated in any board protocol.

Principals may receive reports of suspicions by school employees or reports of student disclosures to school staff. In the past the principal made a report to the appropriate Children's Aid Society on behalf of the teacher or other staff member. Recent amendments to the Act make it clear that the duty to report crystallizes with the staff person forming the suspicion or hearing the disclosure. Section 72(3) clearly states that such a person must not rely on any other person to report on his or her behalf. This may not be congruent with the policies and practices of many school boards, which have used the principal as a pipeline to child welfare agencies and the police. Such protocols should be amended. The principal can facilitate such reporting.

A principal must ensure that the school staff know and understand the personal responsibility to report child abuse (including sexual misconduct). The principal should only be the primary reporting agent when the principal has formed the suspicion. It is recommended practice, however, to advise staff to report any suspicions to the principal so that the principal can invoke other procedures mandated by board protocols.

School employees are often confused about what constitutes a "reasonable suspicion" that would trigger the duty to report. Many confuse reasonable suspicion with reasonable belief. A suspicion can be based on conjecture, on speculation, on third-party reports, consistent rumours, gossip and observations of inappropriate student or staff behaviour. A suspicion does not require proof or independently verifiable evidence as would reasonable belief.

Many teachers and other educational workers are reluctant to make a report that would trigger an investigation of a colleague without some "hard evidence". However, it is totally inappropriate for anyone to investigate a potential sexual misconduct situation. Aside from possibly prejudicing a subsequent police investigation by contaminating evidence, the investigation may alert the suspected employee, who could destroy evidence or attempt to intimidate witnesses and victims.

Sexual offences against children are serious criminal matters requiring professional expertise. A professional investigation, undertaken promptly in utmost confidence, can quickly exonerate an innocent implicated staff person and dispel any suspicions. The investigation may result in criminal charges being laid and/or result in placing the alleged abuser's name on the Child Abuse Registry (see Chapter 3).

A safe rule of thumb for educators is that any disclosure of sexual misconduct by a student be believed for the purpose of forming a reasonable suspicion. If there is a cloud of doubt about the appropriateness of a staff member's conduct of a sexual nature towards students then a suspicion has been formed. Exceptions to this are rare and would generally be limited to situations where there has been a history of mistaken allegations regarding the victim or there is a psychiatric disorder that can involve the making of false allegations.

Disclosures of abuse by children can often be indirect. Experts in the field often describe disclosure as a process rather than a single event. Many children will even deny abuse has occurred when confronted by an adult. In fact one study involving over 600 children revealed that in cases where abuse was proven, 75 per cent of the victims initially denied the abuse. Sometimes an original disclosure is later recanted. In cases where the abuse was proven, 93 per cent of victims in a study then reconfirmed the abuse. Other common behaviours are forgetting, distancing, minimizing, dissociating and discounting. Sometimes full disclosure will occur over a period of months. This same study also demonstrated that preschool-aged children normally disclosed by accident while adolescents usually disclosed purposefully.[5]

Failure to report a reasonable suspicion of abuse is a provincial offence, which upon conviction can result in a fine or imprisonment (s. 81(1) of the *Child and Family Services Act*).

Principals and teachers in Ontario are also governed by their professional responsibilities as defined by the College of Teachers, which requires that when a member "has reasonable grounds to suspect sexual abuse of students or sexual misconduct, a member has a responsibility to report suspected or alleged cases to appropriate authorities. This includes one or more or all of the following: child and family services, police, the employer *and the Ontario College of Teachers*". (Emphasis added.)[6]

Principals and teachers should also be aware that s. 1, para. 27 of O. Reg. 437/97 states that "professional misconduct" for the purpose of the *Ontario College of Teachers Act, 1996* includes: "failing to comply with the member's duties under the *Child and Family Services Act*". The Discipline Committee of the Ontario College of Teachers has already heard a case filed by a parent against a principal that alleged failure to promptly report a disclosure of abuse.[7]

In summary, any reasonable suspicion, or any allegation, or any complaint of sexual misconduct involving a child less than 16 years of age by a teacher, board employee or volunteer must be reported to a Children's Aid Society. For procedures for dealing with employees who are subject to the allegation, please see "Dealing with the Employee after Reporting Suspicions and Allegations," at page 102.

SITUATION TWO

Sexual Misconduct with a Student Age 16 or 17
Sexual Misconduct with a Student with a Disability — All Ages
(Criminal Offence and Professional Misconduct)

Students Age 16 or 17

The duties of a principal when faced with suspicions of sexual misconduct involving a child under age 16 are clear and form part of the federal and provincial law as well as being professional standards. However, when sexual misconduct is alleged involving an adolescent 16 or 17 years of age, or a student with a mental or physical disability of any age, the responsibilities of a principal are not so clear. (For the definition of sexual assault and a discussion of intent, see pages 80-81.)

Principals are often concerned about the privacy rights of adolescent students. This is part of the greater ambiguity that surrounds the status of students of this age. School attendance is not manadatory, nor is residing at home, so they appear adult-like. On the other hand, students of this age cannot legally enter into a contract or a lease, they cannot vote and they cannot smoke or drink. In all of these respects they are still children. Principals should remember that a student under the age of 18 is still a "child". A teacher (and therefore the principal) is under a very strong duty, similar to that of a parent in regard to the child. This principle of *in loco parentis* has long been known and understood by teachers. Just as a parent would override the wishes of the child when the parent believes he or she is acting in the best interests of a child, so too, the teacher or principal must intervene when a situation that could amount to sexual assault or sexual exploitation is discovered.

When a complaint of sexual assault of a student by a board employee or volunteer is received it is expected that the principal will ensure that the police are immediately notified so that the child can be protected and risk of further abuse to the student or to other students can be eliminated.

The criminal law involving sexual acts hinges, as was described in the previous sections, on the concept of consent. No child under 14 is considered to have the capacity to consent to sex with another person. The law also deems that consent cannot occur when one partner is in a position of authority or trust and the other party is a "young person", which is defined in s. 152(2) of the *Criminal Code* as a person under the age of 18 but over the age of consent.

Section 153(1) of the *Criminal Code* defines "sexual exploitation" as follows:

Every person who is in a position of trust and authority towards a young person or is a person with whom the young person is in a relationship of dependency and who

(*a*) for a sexual purpose, touches, directly or indirectly, with a part of the body with an object, any part of the body of a young person, or

(*b*) for a sexual purpose, invites, counsels or incites a young person to touch, directly or indirectly, a part of the body or with an object, the body of any person, including the body of the person who so invites, counsels or incites and the body of the young person,

is guilty of an … offence.

A "position of trust or authority" has generally been held to include: a parent, step-parent, adoptive parent, legal guardian, grandparent, uncle, aunt, boarder in the young person's home, baby-sitter, group home worker, youth group worker, employer and teacher.

The case law indicates that whether someone is a person in a position of authority or trust is not determined by the accused person's role but by the nature of the relationship between the accused and the alleged victim. Considerations include the age differential, the evolution of the relationship and the status of the accused. A teacher is by definition in a position of trust.

The situation is less clear when there is no direct pedagogical relationship between the teacher and the child. When the teacher does not teach the student, the teacher may be able to argue that there is no position of authority and trust. It can be argued that the teacher by law is responsible for supervising the students of a school, not just the students in his or her particular classroom, and that therefore the relationship of trust exists between every teacher in a school and every student of that school.

Where the teacher is from a different school or school system, the teacher may deny any professional relationship of authority or trust with respect to the student. There is an argument that the student trusted the teacher because of his or her professional status even if the teacher is from another school.

A teacher may also be guilty of exploitation where that teacher, irrespective of professional responsibilities or authority, takes a child into his or her home, or provides food or money. It is likely that a position of dependency will have been created.

In the case of alleged sexual assault or exploitation involving adolescents in this age group, there is no legal duty to report by a teacher or the principal. This is because the *Child and Family Services Act* provisions on abuse do not cover this age group unless the adolescent is the subject of a protective order under the Act. In addition, there is no requirement under the *Criminal Code* for citizens to report crimes, of any kind. In some European countries there are so-called "Good Samaritan Laws" that do require citizens to report crimes, but in Canada this is not the case.

In circumstances where the sexual activity has been apparently consensual, not only is the principal not under any legislative imperative to report the alleged crime, the student who is subject to the sexual misconduct is often unwilling to complain to the police. Where a student is unwilling to complain the principal must ensure that the student is immediately advised of the *Criminal Code* provisions regarding sexual exploitation, the professional standards regarding sexual relationships between teachers and students (if appropriate) and any board policy on sexual relationships between board employees and students. If the student still insists that the relationship is consensual or does not wish to "get the staff member in trouble", the principal is faced with a dilemma.

The situation may be further complicated when the parent of the child does not wish the matter to be reported. It cannot be assumed by the principal that the parent is an objective arbiter of the best interests of the student. A parent may wish to avoid embarrassment or may object on religious or cultural grounds. The police will usually respect these concerns by conducting discreet inquiries and protecting the identity of the student. In one case, a 17-year-old female Muslim student was allegedly assaulted by a school support employee. The student was afraid she would be shunned by her parents or her community. A complete investigation and a criminal trial were held and the parents never found out.[8] In another Toronto board case, a parent wanted no involvement with the police in the abuse of her child because her spouse, who was living at home, was being sought by the police on serious criminal charges. In all these cases the principal must consider the interests of the child and the welfare of the school population as a whole.

The issue of sexual misconduct involving students over age 16 was considered by Justice Robins. He states:

> Some students are reluctant to involve the police. It is clear that a school is not bound by a student's own decision to decline to make a police complaint. Having said that, there are often larger issues of school safety that should prevail. It must be recognized that the failure of a student complainant to cooperate with the police may effectively prevent or hamper a full police investigation on the merits. Schools may be well situated to support students in a decision to cooperate with police.[9]

Justice Robins recommended that "every person who has reasonable grounds to suspect that a student sixteen years of age or older has suffered or is at risk of likely suffering ... sexual exploitation or sexual molestation by a teacher or another person having charge of the student" must report those suspicions to the police.[10]

In addition to criminal liability for sexual relationships with students under 18, there is a professional requirement that teachers not have sex with students of any age. The *Ontario College of Teachers Act, 1996* creates a self-regulating body for the teaching profession that is empowered to certify the qualifications of teachers and police teachers who do not perform or who engage in "professional misconduct". This Act only covers certified teachers who are members of the College of Teachers. Some private schools do not employ fully certified members of the college.

Under the *Ontario College of Teachers Act, 1996* a teacher may be disciplined for professional misconduct which, since September 2002, is deemed to include "sexual abuse" by s. 40(1). Sexual abuse is in turn defined in s. 1 of the Act as sexual intercourse and other forms of sexual relations between the member and the student, touching of a sexual nature or behaviour or remarks of a sexual nature towards a student. Thus any suspicion of such behaviour will at the very least require an internal investigation to determine whether there is professional misconduct that must be reported to the college. (This is discussed in more detail in Situation Three, at page 90.)

The Ontario College of Teachers has advised its members that:

Professional misconduct includes but is not limited to any sexual relationship with

   (i)   a student, regardless of the student's age
   (ii) a former student under the age of 18
   (iii) a former student who suffers from a disability affecting his or her ability to consent to a relationship.[11]

In addition, it should be remembered that the College of Teachers requires that when a member "has reasonable grounds to suspect sexual abuse of students or sexual misconduct, a member has a responsibility to report suspected or alleged cases to appropriate authorities. This includes one or more or all of the following: child and family services, police, the employer *and the Ontario College of Teachers*". (Emphasis added).[12]

In summary, although there is no formal mandatory duty to report situations involving students 16 and 17 years of age, nevertheless, it is strongly recommended that principals immediately report suspicions, disclosure or allegations of sexual activity between a teacher, board employee or volunteer and a student 16 or 17 years of age to the police and to the Director of Education.

In the event a police investigation is frustrated, and/or no charges result, the school board will probably have to commence its own investigation (see Chapter 6). For procedures for dealing with employees who are subject to the allegation, please see "Dealing with the Employee after Reporting Suspicions and Allegations" at page 102.

Sexual Exploitation of a Person with a Disability

In addition to students under the age of majority, all persons with a disability of any age are protected from sexual exploitation. This is of particular importance where schools provide special education programs for students up to age 21. Such students would be protected by the law regarding sexual exploitation of students between the ages of 14 and 18, but this protection is continued after age 18 in a slightly more limited form until the students leave the school system.

Section 153.1 of the *Criminal Code* creates the offence of "sexual exploitation of person with disability". This crime can occur when a person is in a position of trust toward the disabled person or the disabled person is in a relationship of dependency with the accused. In such a situation, if it is proved that for a sexual purpose, the accused has incited or counselled the disabled person to touch any person's body directly or indirectly, the accused will be found guilty of sexual exploitation.

Unlike the offence of "sexual exploitation", in which consent is not a defence where the complainant is under 18 years of age, it must be demonstrated that the touching of a disabled person 18 years of age or over occurred without voluntary agreement of the complainant. Lack of consent is not deemed just because the person is disabled. The nature of the disability must be such that the victim is incapable of consent (due to mental incapacity, for example).

Offences also occur when the accused incites the activity by "abusing a position of trust, power or authority" or where a complainant expresses, by words or conduct, a lack of agreement to sexual activity or, having consented, then expresses lack of agreement to continue the sexual activity.

A principal is not under any legislative imperative to report the alleged crime when the student is aged 16 and over unless the student is the subject of a protection order by a Children's Aid Society. The student and the parents or guardians of the student may be unwilling to complain to the police. In such cases the principal must ensure that the parent is immediately advised of the *Criminal Code* provisions regarding sexual exploitation of disabled persons, the professional standards regarding sexual relationships between teachers and students and any board policy on sexual relationships between board employees and students. If the parent still insists that the relationship is consensual or does not wish to "get the staff member in trouble", the principal is faced with a dilemma. In such cases principals must consider the best interests of the student as well as the greater good of the student population as a whole. Therefore a report to the police should always be made.

See page 88 for the Ontario College of Teachers' reporting requirements and definition of "professional misconduct".

In summary, although there is no formal mandatory duty to report situations involving disabled students 16 years of age and over, nevertheless, it is strongly recommended that principals immediately report suspicions of sexual activity between a teacher, board employee or volunteer and a disabled student of the age of majority to the police and report the allegation to the Director of Education.

In the event a police investigation is frustrated, and/or no charges result, the school board will probably have to commence its own investigation (see Chapter 6). For procedures dealing with employees who are subject to allegations, please see "Dealing with the Employee after Reporting Suspicions and Allegations" at page 102.

SITUATION THREE

Sexual Misconduct with a Student over the Age of 18 (Professional Misconduct/Breach of Board Policy)

Sexual Assault

There is no *Criminal Code* prohibition against consensual sexual relations between a teacher, or any other school employee, and a student who has reached the age of majority, unless the student is suffering from a mental or physical disability. (See pages 80-81 for the definition of sexual assault and a discussion of intent.)

The intent of the person committing the act is very important, and practically speaking is a major consideration of the police in determining whether a charge will even be laid. There must be an indication that the motive of the accused is sexual gratification.

Any suspicion or allegation of sexual assault of a student by a teacher or other school employee should be reported to the police. As described below, in Ontario there is also a responsibility to report suspected teacher misconduct to the College of Teachers.

Professional Misconduct

While there is no criminal criminal liability for sexual relationships with students 18 or over, there is a professional requirement that teachers not have sex with students of any age.

The *Ontario College of Teachers Act, 1996* creates a self-regulating body for the teaching profession that is empowered to certify the qualifications of teachers and to police teachers who do not perform or who engage in "professional misconduct". This Act only covers certified teachers who are members of the College of Teachers, principals, vice-principals and superintendents. Some private schools do not employ fully certified members of the college and are not subject to the Act or the rules of the college.

Since September 2002, there has been a professional prohibition against sexual relations between teachers and students. Section 40(1.1) of the *Ontario College of Teachers Act, 1996* defines "professional misconduct" as including sexual abuse of a student by a member. "Sexual abuse" of a student by a teacher means:

- sexual intercourse or other forms of physical sexual relations between the teacher and the student;
- touching, of a sexual nature, of the student by the teacher; or
- behaviour or remarks of a sexual nature by the teacher towards the student.

The Ontario College of Teachers has added detail to the statutory definition in a "Professional Advisory" issued on September 27, 2002. This advisory states:

Professional misconduct includes but is not limited to any sexual relationship with

(i) a student, regardless of the student's age
(ii) a former student under the age of 18
(iii) a former student who suffers from a disability affecting his or her ability to consent to a relationship.[13]

The College of Teachers also requires that when a member "has reasonable grounds to suspect sexual abuse of students or sexual misconduct, a member has a responsibility to report suspected or alleged cases to appropriate authorities. This includes one or more or all of the following: child and family services, police, the employer *and the Ontario College of Teachers*". (Emphasis added.)[14]

Section 30 of the Act states that the Discipline Committee of the College of Teachers upon making a finding of "professional misconduct" may revoke or suspend the Ontario Teaching Certificate of the offending member.

The Disciplinary Committee can only make a determination if a complaint is filed with the College of Teachers and a subsequent hearing confirms the misconduct. Complaints are voluntary and can be filed by any person.

Since principals and vice-principals in public school boards are members of the college, while there is no statutory duty to report sexual assault or sexual misconduct by teachers, there is a College of Teachers imposed "responsibility" to do so. It is anticipated that failure to report by a principal could result in a professional misconduct disciplinary proceeding by the college.

The statutory reporting duties for sexual misconduct with adult students appears to apply only to Boards of Education and not individual principals. In addition, a board is only required to report substantiated findings. The responsibility for all of the reporting lies with the senior administration of the board, not the staff member who first forms the suspicion or the principal who coordinates the school response. In addition, the report is only required if the teacher is employed to teach a person who is under 19 years of age or, in the case of special needs students, under 22 years of age.[15] Finally, the Act, by definition, only applies to teachers and does not apply to other employees and volunteers.

The College of Teachers in a Professional Advisory has tried to bring some clarity to this picture for principals and teachers and has apparently broadened its definition of sexual or professional misconduct beyond the statutory definition and created a "responsibility" that individual members report such conduct.

The *Ontario College of Teachers Act, 1996* is of no help in giving a principal direction when sexual misconduct involving adult students is first suspected or alleged. If the teacher is only employed to teach adults, there are apparently no mandatory reporting provisions even where the conduct has been proven.

There is no regime in place to assist with allegations of sexual misconduct by other board employees and volunteers. In the private school context principals must be provided with direction through policies and procedures established by the school itself.

Outside of Ontario there is little guidance for principals dealing with sexual misconduct by school employees involving adult students. Boards of education must provide clear policy direction.

Beyond Assault and Sexual Relationships

In *Protecting Our Students*, Justice Robins recommended that all boards establish a comprehensive policy on sexual misconduct covering all school board employees and volunteers that outlines sexual abuse and exploitation, sexual harassment and sexual relationships generally.[16] This broad stroke approach would make such conduct subject to internal discipline, up to and including dismissal, and would require internal reporting and internal formal investigations into all complaints, disclosures or observations in the case of non-criminal behaviours.

Most school boards in Ontario already have policies regarding discrimination under the *Human Rights Code*.[17] Included in such policies is harassment based on grounds of discrimination prohibited under the *Human Rights Code*. This includes sexual harassment of other staff and students. Justice Robins recommended that boards go beyond the traditional definition of sexual discrimination and include behaviour that is incompatible with the role of a teacher, regardless of whether students regard the behaviour as "unwelcome". Examples may be teasing, telling off-colour jokes, asking students on dates or to go on trips. These may be types of "flirting" or similar social behaviours that adolescent students might welcome or enjoy but that are not appropriate in a learning environment.

Justice Robins suggested the following behaviour be deemed to be sexual misconduct:

> objectionable comments or conduct of a sexual nature that may affect a student's personal integrity or security or the school environment. These may not be overtly sexual but nonetheless demean or cause personal embarrassment to a student based on a student's gender.[18]

Sexual relationships with adult students have presented a problem for educators, particularly when the age gap is relatively small, or the adult student is actually older than the teacher. There are many examples of students in such relationships actually marrying their teachers. Because both parties to the relationship are adults, it is often assumed that if a student consents, there is no reason for concern. However, the relationship between a teacher and a student is a professional relationship very similar to that of a doctor with a patient or a lawyer with a client. That is reflected in the fact that most professional regulatory bodies prohibit sexual relations with patient/clients and the College of Teachers is no exception.

The teacher is in a powerful position *vis-à-vis* a student, since the teacher has the power to grant or withhold a credit. When a sexual relationship develops, the integrity of the credit-granting process is in question. In addition, the relative bargaining power of the parties is not equal and there is always a danger that the student is being exploited. It is possible that students will not feel secure and protected in an environment where a teacher is openly courting a student. It may also raise a suspicion of unequal treatment or favouritism. Some students may be reluctant to resist advances, fearing retribution. There is also a concern that a student who leaves school may return later. That is why Robins recommended a province-wide prohibition upon sexual activity between a teacher and a former student under the age of 18. "Responsibility for ensuring that a teacher-student relationship is appropriate rests with the teacher, and not the student. This remains the case even if it is the student who attempts to initiate the relationship".[19]

Justice Robins recommended that the definition of sexual misconduct include the following:

> any sexual relationship with a student, or with a former student under the age of 18, and any conduct directed to establishing such a relationship.[20]

While the Robins recommendations, if followed by a board, would provide good direction for principals, there are still areas of ambiguity. The definition of sexual misconduct regarding sexual relationships is much too broad for non-teaching employees. It also fails to deal with so-called grooming behaviours that result in full-blown sexual relationships that start immediately after the professional relationship has ended. The Toronto District School Board has a policy that attempts to close some of these gaps.

The Toronto District School Board will hold all employees and volunteers accountable for the following:

(i) Board staff and volunteers working directly with a student of any age in their professional capacity (see (iii) below) will not enter into a sexual relationship with that student during the course of the professional relationship or for a period of one year thereafter.

(ii) In the case of students and former students under the age of 18, any such relationship, in addition to being a serious breach of Board policy, is also a criminal offence of sexual exploitation or sexual assault.

(iii) Professional capacity shall mean working or volunteering in the same school as the student is enrolled or otherwise supervising, counselling, coaching or assisting in extra curricular activities in which the student is participating, regardless of which school the student is enrolled [at].[21]

The Ontario College of Teachers has adopted this approach in its "Professional Advisory". This document makes several statements that appear to broaden the meaning of professional misconduct. As described above, the college forbids sexual relationships by teachers with a student of any age.

The Advisory then goes on to state that "professional misconduct of a sexual nature could involve a member's own students, other students or children, or even adults …". It then says that

> [t]here may be forms of professional misconduct that do not fall within the definition of sexual abuse but which may be considered sexual misconduct. … These behaviours may include sexual harassment and sexual relationships with students or any conduct which may lead to an unprofessional and inappropriate relationship with a student. The latter is often called grooming behaviour.[22]

> Grooming behaviours can often be apparently innocuous, such as having lunch or meeting for coffee but are part of a planned seduction or "romancing" of a younger person. *The strategy is to increase the opportunities for intimate social interaction that can in turn lead to personal discussions, sexual dialogue, touching, kissing and ultimately sexual propositions by the older person.* There appears to be a dispute as to whether such conduct can be "abuse" since by definition it constitutes preparation for abuse rather than necessarily being abuse itself.[23]

Nevertheless, boards should take every precaution when such behaviour is discovered.

The college incorporates Justice Robins' concerns by including in sexual harassment conduct or comments that are "incompatible with the role of the member, regardless of whether the affected students appear to be offended". The advisory also clarifies grooming behaviours by giving a non-exhaustive list of examples:

- sending intimate letters to students
- making telephone calls of a personal nature to students
- engaging in sexualized dialogue through the Internet with students
- making suggestive comments to students
- dating students.[24]

Principals, and, in fact, all teachers who are members of the college have a responsibility to report all forms of sexual misconduct to appropriate authorities. "This includes one or more or all of the following: child and family services, police, the employer *and the Ontario College of Teachers*".[25] Presumably this responsibility is extended to reporting sexual harassment or grooming behaviours.

Principals are advised to report allegations or suspicions of harassment or grooming behaviours by school employees to the Director of Education and, where appropriate, to the police and the College of Teachers.

INTERNAL REPORTING AND DEALING WITH THE ACCUSED EMPLOYEE — THREE TYPES OF MISCONDUCT, ONE SET OF RULES

Board Internal Reporting Procedures

In all situations of suspected sexual misconduct involving a student, including sexual harassment, the principal needs to ensure prompt and clear internal reporting in accordance with any board protocol. Such protocols must be developed not only to ensure that child abuse is promptly reported to the Children's Aid Societies or that sexual offences are reported to the police. The *Ontario College of Teachers Act, 1996* requires the board to report sexual misconduct to the College of Teachers.

In response to the amendments of the *Ontario College of Teachers Act, 1996*, the Ontario Public School Boards Association developed a draft set of recommended guidelines for school boards for reporting to the College of Teachers.[26] Included in these guidelines is a section on the duty of employees. This section is quoted below with additional recommendations of the authors in italics.

4. Duty of Employees

4.1 It is the duty of every employee to promptly report to the Principal of the school in which he/she works, the Superintendent responsible (*for*) the school or the Superintendent/or Manager responsible for Human Resources, any situation of sexual abuse by a teacher, *or other educational employee,* towards a student. *If the employee has a duty to report the suspicion to a Children's Aid Society, the principal must facilitate such a report.*

NOTE: sexual abuse includes:

- *sexual intercourse or other forms of sexual relations between a teacher, or other educational employee, and a student;*

- *touching of a sexual nature of a student by a teacher or other educational employee; or*

- *behaviour or remarks of a sexual nature by a teacher or other educational employee towards a student.*

4.2 It is the duty of every employee of the Board to report to the Principal of the school in which he/she works, the Superintendent responsible (for) the school or the Superintendent /or Manager responsible for Human Resources where the employee becomes aware that any employee (including himself or herself) has been charged with or convicted of a Criminal Code offence involving sexual conduct with a person under 18 years of age, or any offence which involves drugs, violence or theft.

4.3   It is the duty of any Principal, Superintendent /or Manager of Human Resources who receives the information under 4.1 or 4.2 *(above)* to immediately report such information to the Director of Education or ('gnate.

4.4   It is the duty of every Principal who believes that a teacher ....'s engaged in conduct that the principal believes should be the subject of a review by the College *(of Teachers')* investigation, discipline or fitness to practice committee, to promptly consult with his/her Superintendent and, where the Superintendent agrees that the matter should be referred to the College, to so advise the Director of Education/or designate.

4.5   It is the duty of every principal who imposes restrictions on any teacher's duties for the reason that the teacher engaged in professional misconduct, including sexual abuse, to promptly report this to his/her Superintendent and the Director of Education and/or designate.

All school boards should have detailed communications plans included in a sexual misconduct protocol to deal with ongoing internal communications after the initial report is made and to ensure that the appropriate board resources are made available to the school. Such procedures are described in Chapter 5.

Mandatory Board Reports to the College of Teachers

This mandatory duty lies with the board of education and not the principal. Since September 2002, s. 43 of the *Ontario College of Teachers Act, 1996* requires reporting by the board after there has been an actual finding that professional misconduct occurred or where a teacher resigns during an investigation into allegations of professional misconduct. This act only covers certified teachers who are members of the College of Teachers. Some private schools do not employ fully certified members of the College.

The findings may be internal to the board or external to the board.

INTERNAL TO THE BOARD

Section 43.2 of the Act states:

43.2 (1) An employer of a member who terminates the member's employment or imposes restrictions on the member's duties for reasons of professional misconduct shall file with the Registrar within 30 days after the termination or restriction a written report setting out the reasons.

(2) If an employer of a member intended to terminate the member's employment or impose restrictions on the member's duties for reasons of professional misconduct but the employer did not do so because the member resigned, the employer shall file with the Registrar ... .

> (3) If a member resigns while his or her employer is engaged in an investigation into allegations of an act or omission by the member that would, if proven, have caused the employer to terminate the member's employment or to impose restrictions on the member's duties for reasons of professional misconduct, the employer shall file with the Registrar ....

Section 43.3 states:

> 43.3(1) An employer shall promptly report to the College in writing when the employer becomes aware that a member who is or has been employed by the employer,
>
> . . . . .
>
> (c) has engaged in conduct or taken action that, in the opinion of the employer, should be reviewed by a committee of the College.

EXTERNAL TO THE BOARD

Section 43.3(1) of the Act states that an employer shall promptly report to the College in writing upon becoming aware that a member

    (a)   has been charged with or convicted of an offence under the *Criminal Code* (Canada) involving sexual conduct and minors;

    (b)   has been charged with or convicted of an offence under the *Criminal Code* (Canada) that in the opinion of the employer indicates that students may be at risk of harm or injury ...

Teachers Reporting Conduct of Other Teachers — "Adverse Reports"

Teachers are often reluctant to come forward with reports on the conduct of other teachers. This has been a result of s. 18(1)(b) of the Regulation under the *Teaching Profession Act*, which states in the section "Duties of a Member", that "A member shall, ... (b) on making an adverse report on another member, furnish him with a written statement of the report at the earliest possible time and no later than three days after making the report."

This "Regulation" is not a normal law passed by the Cabinet of the provincial government, but instead was enacted by the Board of Governors of the Ontario Teachers' Federation to prescribe the duties and privileges of members of the public teacher federation affiliates. The rules surrounding the behaviour of members of teacher federations are subject to internal complaint to the Relations and Discipline Committee and can technically result in a recommendation to the Minister of Education that an Ontario Teaching Certificate be suspended or cancelled, or that the member be reprimanded. The Discipline Committee used to deal with all "professional misconduct" before the creation of the College of Teachers but now it has become somewhat vestigial. Nevertheless, it still deals with matters internal to the federations such as adverse reporting.

Principals are no longer bound by the *Teaching Profession Act* or its regulations such as s. 18(1)(b). No other school staff, even those that may be members of other professional colleges, are bound by such rules. Some support staff union locals may have by-laws governing situations where employees report other members of the bargaining unit to management but these are unlikely to interfere with the reporting of sexual misconduct.[27]

The effect of the section on reporting suspected sexual misconduct has been curtailed by amendments to s. 12 of the *Teaching Profession Act*. This will be discussed in detail later in the section. However, the amendments still may not go far enough to completely remove the ambiguity around this section or counteract its psychological effects. The history of the section may be instructive.

For many years the adverse reporting section has caused a great "chilling effect" and many teachers have been reluctant to report suspicions or even disclosures of sexual misconduct by other members because they felt obliged to tell the fellow teacher of the report. *It is only human nature that people are reluctant to declare themselves to be a witness or to otherwise be involved in disciplinary or criminal proceedings. This is especially true where their identity will be immediately revealed to the accused. In addition, there is a possible inference in s. 18(1)(b) that to make an adverse report is somehow wrong or a possible ethical breach.* In *Protecting Our Students* Justice Robins states, "there is evidence that some teachers believe that the 'adverse report' provision does apply to cases of suspected sexual misconduct, and as a result, are hesitant to report their suspicions … It is clear to me that section 18(1)(b) continues to inhibit teachers from reporting their suspicions of sexual misconduct".[28] In one well-documented case a principal did not inform the receiving principal of complaints against a teacher being transferred. The teacher was no other than Ken DeLuca, who was later convicted of sexual crimes against 12 female students and one female teacher! For more details on this case see Chapter 1.

In an effort to counteract any "chilling effect", the former Toronto Board of Education actually passed a policy in 1993 that directed that "under no circumstances shall the implicated staff member be contacted until specific instructions are received from the investigating police".[29]

Police and Children's Aid Societies were not only worried about the potential chilling effect of s. 18(1)(b) but were concerned because informing a member prematurely could prejudice a police investigation and/or allow an accused teacher to flee. In addition, there had been situations where potential witnesses, including the complainant, had been threatened by a teacher who found out about an investigation. As a result, the following provision was added to the Metropolitan Toronto Child Abuse Protocol (which binds school boards, child welfare agencies, government ministries and the police in Toronto):

> According to the police, under no circumstances should an alleged offender be notified before the criminal investigation has started. To do so could be construed as interfering with a criminal investigation.[30]

In 1994 students in a Toronto secondary school complained to a vice-principal about the conduct of a teacher. The vice-principal in turn reported these allegations to the Children's Aid Society and the police. No charges resulted but an internal investigation substantiated the serious sexual harassment complaint and the teacher was disciplined. The teacher then complained to his local branch affiliate teacher federation that the vice-principal had not filed a written report with him under s. 18(1)(b). At that time principals and vice-principals were also members of the federation. The complaint was not submitted to the Ontario Teacher Federation Discipline Committee for a formal hearing because an internal committee found that the Toronto vice-principal's reporting of suspected abuse of a student under 16 was only a "conduit" for the mandatory duty under the *Child and Family Services Act* and therefore did not constitute an adverse report.[31]

In 2000, Justice Robins recommended that s. 18(1)(b) not apply to reports of sexual misconduct. In response, the Government of Ontario amended s. 12 of the *Teaching Profession Act* in 2002. As a result subs. 12(2) states:

> Despite any regulation made under subsection (1), a member who makes an adverse report about another member respecting suspected sexual abuse of a student by that other member *need not provide* him or her with a copy of the report or with any information about the report. [emphasis added]

"Sexual abuse" of a student by teachers is defined by s. 12(3) of the Act as,

    (*a*)   sexual intercourse or other forms of physical sexual relations between the member and the student,

    (*b*)   touching, of a sexual nature, of the student by the member, or

    (*c*)   behaviour or remarks of a sexual nature by the member towards the student.

This reform is a major step forward but there are still problems for the principal. First of all, it confirms that reporting criminal behaviour or sexual misconduct is an "adverse report", something that was not completely clear before and may be a step backward. It therefore has serious implications for the reporting of other criminal behaviour that is not covered by the definition of sexual abuse, such as assault or drug trafficking. In addition, it does not cover all the behaviours identified by Justice Robins as "sexual harassment":

> objectionable comments or conduct of a sexual nature that may affect a student's personal integrity or security or the school environment. These may not be overtly sexual but nonetheless demean or cause personal embarrassment to a student based on a student's gender.[32]

The amendment simply makes s. 18(1)(b) inapplicable. It says the teacher "need not" report to the colleague. This raises the real possibility that teachers will continue to make such reports on a voluntary basis. There may even be strong pressure from federation leadership to do so. As outlined above, reporting to a suspected offender prior to a formal investigation may seriously compromise a police investigation. Evidence could be destroyed, witnesses could be silenced or the teacher under suspicion could flee. In such circumstances, a teacher who follows s. 18(1)(b) may be in jeopardy of being charged by the police with being an accessory. More important, a frustrated criminal investigation or an acquittal at trial caused by premature reporting will then result in the board having to take responsibility for the safety of its students by conducting its own investigation and may leave the board and reporting teacher civilly liable to the victim.

The Ontario College of Teachers Professional Advisory issued September 27, 2002, reiterates the adverse report amendments making such reports discretionary but goes on to state:

> Members of the College may not engage in, or threaten to engage in, reprisals against anyone who discloses, reports or otherwise provides information with respect to alleged or suspected professional misconduct of a sexual nature.[33]

In summary, teachers are no longer required to report in writing to a colleague when they report suspicions of "sexual abuse". It is essential therefore that school boards make it clear in protocols and procedures, that it is an expectation that teachers never follow s. 18(1)(b) when reporting suspicions of sexual misconduct. Language such as that cited earlier in the Toronto District School Board policy is recommended. In the absence of such a policy a principal would be wise to ensure that the teaching staff of the school are informed of s. 12, and that they are counselled that no report should ever be made in such circumstances.

Dealing with the Employee after Reporting Suspicions and Allegations

As outlined above, the expectations of principals as regards reporting sexual misconduct may change depending on the age of an alleged victim, which can create confusion and the possibility of error. Dealing with the alleged offender, however, need not be as complicated.

If a teacher is charged with a sexual offence, the *Education Act* requires that the teacher be removed from the classroom. Section 170(1)12.1 of the Act states that every board shall:

> on becoming aware that a teacher or temporary teacher who is employed by the board has been charged with or convicted of an offence under the *Criminal Code* (Canada) involving sexual conduct and minors, or of any offence under the *Criminal Code* (Canada) that in the opinion of the board indicates that pupils may be at risk, take prompt steps to ensure that the teacher or temporary teacher performs no duties in the classroom and no duties involving contact with pupils, pending withdrawal of the charge, discharge following preliminary inquiry, stay of the charge or acquittal, as the case may be.

It is clear therefore, that if a teacher is charged with a sexual offence against a minor the teacher must be removed from the classroom. A minor is any person under the age of 18 (situations 1 and 2, above). Also note that this duty to remove is created by any charge of a sexual nature regardless of where and when the sexual offence was alleged to have occurred.

When the alleged victim is 18 or over, the removal of the teacher is discretionary (situation 3, above). This places a principal in a difficult situation when the alleged victim is an adult and/or the circumstances around the alleged offence require an assessment of potential risk to other students. In practice this judgment would normally be expected to be exercised by a school superintendent or the Director of Education. It is recommended that a board policy and procedure be in place to provide criteria for such removal. Some boards require all persons charged with sexual misconduct offences to be removed regardless of the age of the victim.

This statutory removal of a teacher only occurs once charges are laid. What happens while a disclosure or suspicion is being investigated? Justice Robins, in *Protecting Our Students,* reviewed the practices of school boards dealing with investigations of employees. He found that some school boards provided that every teacher accused of sexual misconduct or abuse must be removed from the classroom, pending investigation, while other boards regarded this decision as discretionary. For example, the Toronto District School Board policy states that "[w]here a student/former student discloses sexual abuse/sexual assault by a staff member and the police have begun an investigation, that staff member will be assigned, as soon as possible, to suitable alternate duties outside the school".[34] By contrast, the Toronto District Catholic School Board policy states: "Upon notice of an allegation of abuse against an employee of the Board, which the Director believes is serious, the Director shall remove the employee from direct unsupervised contact with students".[35]

While it is obvious that removal of a suspected abuser potentially reduces risk to other students, such removal also protects the teacher by helping to ensure that the subsequent investigation is not complicated by the continued presence of the teacher at the alleged crime scene and that evidence is not tainted by the teacher continuing to interact with potential witnesses. In addition, as Justice Robins comments, "A mandatory policy of removal is said to reduce the speculation about the merits of each allegation as all teachers are treated equally. This is said to ensure fairness for teachers."[36]

The difficulty of a discretionary removal policy is that it forces board officials to make a determination about the relative merits of the allegation before an investigation has started. If the allegation is determined to be likely to be true, then students are at risk and the teacher must be removed. If the case against the teacher appears weak at first blush, then there is an apparent reduced risk. Teacher unions and civil libertarians would argue that the presumption of innocence that exists prior to conviction should be the determining factor and that a teacher should not be removed from the classroom on the basis of mere suspicion. However, careful analysis shows that in making this judgment prior to investigating the official will in fact be making a determination of likely guilt or innocence very prematurely. Another difficulty with a discretionary policy is that the status of the teacher must be constantly reviewed as the investigation proceeds in order to ensure that potential risk is carefully monitored. A policy that says all teachers are removed at the time an investigation is begun removes the need for ongoing and very subjective analysis and simply makes the fact of an investigation itself the sole criterion for removal. A mandate to remove all teachers pending investigation is a recommended best practice.

Not all investigations of sexual misconduct involve teachers of course. Other school support staff such as educational assistants, caretakers and paraprofessionals are subject to suspicion or complaint. In such cases the *Education Act* is of no assistance. Justice Robins recommended that all employees including teachers and volunteers be covered by a board policy and protocol. In addition, his recommendation also includes all formal investigations of sexual abuse and harassment, not just criminal investigations.[37]

Another area of concern is the actual placement of the teacher or other employee during the investigation and/or after charges have been laid. This is normally a decision of the superintendent or Director of Education and can include assignment to non-teaching duties, home assignment with pay, suspension with pay or suspension without pay depending on the circumstances. Considerations should include potential risk not just to students but to other employees, potential of embarrassment to the employee based on the extent to which the allegations are generally known within the board or the community and whether the employee is in fact doing useful work. Once charges are laid and become public domain the recommended best practice is home assignment. If the employer has no appropriate alternative work for a suspended employee and the trial process is going to be very lengthy, the suspension may be converted to a suspension without pay.[38]

Usually a school board has little direct knowledge of the content of a police investigation and must wait for the trial process to be completed before determining the consequences for an accused wrongdoer. However, if the employer has sufficient first-hand evidence of the allegations on which to make a determination of serious wrongdoing, the employer may proceed to dismiss the employee before the trial process is completed.

The removal provisions of the Huron-Superior Catholic District School Board Child Abuse Policy and Procedures are an example of discretionary protocol:

> Upon notification that a report has been made to the C.A.S. or Police Services alleging child abuse by an employee ... The Director will ensure that the employee's work location is reviewed and that an appropriate work location is determined in light of the preliminary investigation. Work locations may include:
>
> - The original work location,
> - home duty with pay,
> - alternative work location.
>
> The employee may also be:
>
> - suspended with pay,
> - suspended without pay,
> - terminated.[39]

The removal provisions of the Toronto District School Board Policy and Procedure Dealing with Abuse and Neglect of Students, developed in the early 1990s by the predecessor Toronto Board of Education and successfully implemented for almost 10 years, is an example of the objective blanket removal protocol for all employees. It states:

> Where a student/former student discloses sexual abuse/sexual assault by a staff member and police have begun an investigation, that staff member will be assigned, as soon as possible, to suitable alternative duties outside the school, not involving contact with students until the police investigation has been completed. In the case of a teacher or unionized employee, she/he must be notified of the right to contact her/his federation/union representative.[40]

One significant implementation concern for principals is determining when a formal investigation has actually begun. When a principal is in contact with the Children's Aid Society or police it is recommended to specifically ask, "Is an investigation going to be undertaken?". An affirmative reply from the intake worker at the Children's Aid Society or police officer should trigger a removal protocol.

Other Relevant Sections of this Book

For procedures dealing with accused employees, please see "Dealing with the Employee after Reporting Suspicions and Allegations" at page 102. For internal reporting, see "Internal Reporting and Dealing with the Accused Employee" at page 96. For internal investigation procedures, see Chapter 6.

ENDNOTES

[1] R.S.C. 1985, c. C-46; R.S.O. 1990, c. C.11; R.S.O. 1990, c. E.2; S.O. 1996, c. 12.

[2] Ontario College of Teachers, *Professional Advisory*, approved by Council, September 27, 2002, p. 1. (See Appendix 1.)

[3] *Ibid.*, p. 4.

[4] Greenspan and Rosenberg, *Martin's Criminal Code*, 2003 edition (Aurora, Ont.: Canada Law Book), s. 271, p. 532.

[5] "The Process of Disclosure", in *Child Welfare Journal* Vol. LXX, No. 1, pp. 3-15.

[6] Ontario College of Teachers, *Professional Advisory*, approved by Council, September 27, 2002, p. 4.

[7] *The Globe and Mail*, Tuesday, February 22, 2000.

[8] *R. v. Marshall*, Provincial Court, Criminal Division, unreported, January 27, 2000, Bigelow J.

[9] Sydney Robins, *Protecting Our Students: A Review to Identify and Prevent Sexual Misconduct in Ontario Schools* (Toronto: Ministry of the Attorney General (Milner Graphics), 2002), p. 323.

[10] *Ibid.*, p. 322.

[11] Ontario College of Teachers, *Professional Advisory*, approved by Council, September 27, 2002, p. 3.

[12] *Ibid.*, p. 4.

[13] *Ibid.*, p. 3.

[14] *Ibid.*, p. 4.

[15] *Ontario College of Teachers Act, 1996*, S.O. 1996, c. 12, as amended, s. 43.1 (see Appendix 6). Note that while it is professional misconduct to have sexual relations with a student of any age, it apparently is only reportable when the teacher works with minors or disabled students under age 22. Therefore a teacher working only with adult students would not appear to be subject to the discipline of the college. Boards of education should close this apparent loophole by having an internal policy as regards adult students.

[16] Robins, *Protecting Our Students*, p. 322, Recommendation 76.

[17] R.S.O. 1990, c. H.19.

[18] Robins, *Protecting Our Students*, pp. 311-313.

[19] *Ibid.*, p. 312.

[20] *Ibid.*, pp. 311-314, Recommendation 70.

[21] Toronto District School Board, *Procedures Dealing with Abuse and Neglect of Students*, para. 1(d), cited in Robins, *Protecting Our Students*, p. 482. (See Appendix 8.)

[22] Ontario College of Teachers, *Professional Advisory*, approved by Council, September 27, 2002, p. 2.

[23] Oral decision of Mr. Justice Blair on behalf of the Divisional Court on January 20, 2003, in *Markson v. Ontario College of Teachers*, Doc. 538/01, at para. 7.

[24] Ontario College of Teachers, *Professional Advisory*, approved by Council, September 27, 2002, p. 3.

[25] *Ibid.*, p. 4.

[26] *Protocol for Reporting Teacher Professional Misconduct*, publication of the Ontario Public School Boards Association — Labour Relations Services, September 2002. (See Appendix 7.)

[27] Some collective agreements bind employers to dismiss employees that are found to be not in good standing by the executive of the union local but such provisions are likely unenforceable in situations where an employee has a duty to report, either under law, or board policy.

[28] Robins, *Protecting Our Students*, pp. 212-213.

[29] *Standard Procedure 54*, para. 8(d), Toronto Board of Education, Minutes, June 24, 1993, also contained in *Procedures Dealing with Sexual Abuse and/or Sexual Assault*, Toronto District School Board, para. 4.3.1, cited in Robins, *Protecting Our Students*, p. 493. (See Appendix 9.)

[30] *Child Sexual Abuse Protocol, Third Edition*, March 1995, published by the Metropolitan Toronto Special Committee on Child Abuse, p. 68.

[31] Complaint of Jack Young to the PPP Committee, District 15, OSSTF 1995 (records internal to the bargaining unit).

[32] Robins, *Protecting Our Students*, p. 312.

[33] Ontario College of Teachers, *Professional Advisory*, approved by Council, September 27, 2002, p. 4.

[34] *Procedures Dealing with Sexual Abuse and/or Sexual Assault*, Toronto District School Board, para. 4.4.1, cited in Robins, *Protecting Our Students*, p. 495.

[35] *Suspected Child Abuse Reporting,* Toronto Catholic District School Board, s. 17, TCDSB Policy Register, approved March 2000.

[36]   Robins, *Protecting Our Students*, p. 336.

[37]   Robins, *Protecting Our Students*, p. 448.

[38]   *Re The Perth County Board of Education and Ontario Public School Teachers' Federation*, Grievance of Donald Currie, June 29, 1994, decision of arbitrator Gail Brent.

[39]   *Child Abuse Policy and Procedures*, Huron-Superior Catholic District School Board, para. 8(e), in Robins, *Protecting Our Students*, p. 488.

[40]   *Policy on Dealing with Abuse and Neglect of Students*, Toronto District School Board, Procedure 4.4.1, cited in Robins, *Protecting Our Students*, p. 495.

CHAPTER 5

AFTER THE INVESTIGATION

The completion of a police and/or the Children's Aid Society investigation may have a very significant impact upon the school. During an investigation every effort should be made to respect the privacy of all concerned. In addition, criminal investigations are most effective when conducted in secrecy or with discretion. Therefore nothing should be said to other staff, students or the broader school community. *Board policy should dictate total official silence by all school officials during investigations prior to charges being laid.*

Despite these rules and the best efforts of staff, rumours often start to circulate. As long as the investigation continues, it is necessary to contain the rumours without specifically denying or confirming the investigation. This places the principal, in particular, in a very difficult situation. However, once the process has been completed it is no longer possible to contain knowledge of the circumstances to the narrow circle of those directly involved, particularly when there has been rumour-fueled pressure from the school community to provide information. Nor is it possible to refuse comment because the matter "is a police matter".

It is essential that boards have a designated spokesperson to whom all press inquiries are directed. In large boards a communications department discharges this function. In smaller boards a senior official, preferably one who has received some media relations training, should be designated.

A social worker or senior staff member with training in child welfare issues should be designated as a resource person who can coordinate board responses to allegations of sexual misconduct. This resource person should also be charged with the responsibility of convening a response team that will assist the school in crisis.

It is imperative that a comprehensive strategy is in place in anticipation of the completion of the investigation that includes:

- placement of the alleged offender;
- communications to the entire school community;
- psychological or social work support to affected students;

- support for staff and all other students; and
- advice and support to parents.

Upon completion of an investigation there are several possible consequences. The police, in consultation with the Crown Attorney, may:

- lay charges;
- "caution" the alleged offender;
- not lay charges; or
- later withdraw the charges or have them stayed.

After an accused employee is arrested there are many other possible scenarios, including: a bail hearing, a preliminary inquiry, a guilty plea or a trial. At trial, the accused employee may be found guilty and sentenced, may be found guilty and discharged or may be acquitted. Each of these scenarios requires a different response and some general guidelines that form the basis of a detailed intervention strategy are provided below.

WHEN CHARGES ARE LAID

The police, after investigating the allegations of sexual misconduct, will assess the evidence and will determine whether the witnesses are credible or whether there is any corroborating physical evidence. If it is determined that a *prima facie* case has been made out, the alleged offender may be charged. This does not mean that the police or the Crown Attorney's office absolutely believes that a crime has been committed. It means that the elements of the offence, the physical act (*actus reus*) and the intent (*mens rea*) are sufficiently evident that a court could possibly convict. In a sexual offence, the *actus reus* could be the physical assault or the words of an inducement and the *mens rea* would be the sexual intent.

In Canada, the police and the Crown have "prosecutorial discretion" and are not required to charge in every case where a crime has been committed and an alleged offender has been apprehended. It is always a judgment call based on the experience of the officers and Crown lawyers involved. It is expected that they will act in good faith in the best interests of the community. The problem with sexual offences is that all too often there are few, if any, corroborating witnesses to the sexual misconduct and little corroborative evidence. It is often one person's word against another's. In such cases the decision to lay a charge may simply be a subjective evaluation that there is the "ring of truth" about the allegations. In one recent case police charged a Toronto school teacher on the basis of a videotaped interview of a female victim who earnestly and believably described assaults that took place 20 years before. After several weeks the charges were withdrawn when she continued to make the same earnest and believable charges about several other people, including her doctor and other professionals. It turned out that the complainant had experienced serious abuse by a family member in her childhood and had generalized this experience to all adults in authority at the time. The teacher sued the police for "malicious prosecution". This case was later settled.[1]

All sexual offences in Canada are called hybrid offences. This means that not only can the Crown decide whether or not to lay a charge, the Crown can choose to treat the alleged offence as a serious matter or a minor matter. If serious, the case proceeds by "indictment", which entitles the defendant to a jury trial in Superior Court and can upon conviction often result in a long prison sentence. If considered less serious the case proceeds in a "summary" manner in Provincial Court and often results in a short incarceration, probation or fine. In the United States there is a similar distinction between felonies and misdemeanours. At the "arraignment", a first court appearance on the charges, the Crown Attorney will usually elect to proceed by indictment or by summary proceedings. If an indictment is announced the accused in turn can elect trial by Superior Court jury, Superior Court judge alone or Provincial Court judge. The accused may later change the election "down" from jury to Superior Court judge or Superior Court judge or to Provincial Court judge, and the Crown may also resort to summary proceedings later. However, neither party can elect back "up" to a different option at a later date.

In the case of serious criminal charges the accused is entitled to a preliminary inquiry in front of a judge to determine if a *prima facie* case exists on which a properly directed jury could convict. In many cases, with the permission of the provincial Attorney General, an indictment can be "preferred" by the Crown Attorney and no preliminary inquiry is held.

Obviously, an allegation of a sexual offence in a school setting will almost always be treated seriously at first with the police requesting a warrant for the arrest of the accused from a judge, arresting the accused and detaining him or her until a bail hearing is scheduled before a justice of the peace. While a person charged with an offence can be released on a "promise to appear" by the police themselves, the *Criminal Code*[2] directs police not to release an accused where "detention is in the public interest", where the police believe on reasonable grounds that it may be necessary to secure or preserve evidence, prevent the continuation or repetition of the offence, or protect victims or witnesses, or where there is a risk of flight. In some cases the police may arrest without a warrant if they believe the accused may flee or that persons are at immediate risk of harm. If the accused is detained, where a justice of the peace is available the accused must be brought before the justice as soon as possible within 24 hours or as soon as possible thereafter if no justice is available. At this time a hearing is held to determine whether bail will be granted.

In Canada, bail is called "judicial interim release". In order to keep an accused in custody the prosecutor must satisfy the justice that the accused may attempt to flee, that the public needs to be protected or that there is a substantial likelihood that the accused will continue to commit crimes, or that the detention is necessary to maintain confidence in the administration of justice. As a rule a teacher or other educational employee will not present a flight risk and is unlikely to have a criminal record or violent history that would cause concern about public safety. Therefore teachers and other educational employees will not likely be detained but will be released on conditions such as keeping the peace and being of good behaviour, not communicating with the victim or witnesses and not attending at the school pending the outcome of the trial. In the case of a violent crime there may also be a restriction against the possession of firearms. Where conviction implies a serious likelihood of imprisonment, "sureties" may be required to ensure the accused's attendance at trial. Unlike the United States, where cash bail is required and forfeited upon failure to appear, cash deposit bail is quite rare in Canada. Usually a third person, often a friend or relative, is required to promise to pay a set amount of money if the accused misses any future court dates. Such a person is called a "surety". Once the accused is released, there is then a considerable delay (sometimes years) until the preliminary hearing or trial is convened.

It must be stressed that at no time during any of these legal proceedings can it be assumed that the accused is guilty of a criminal offence. The particulars of the offence are contained in either an "information" sworn by a police officer prior to an arrest or the indictment itself. The determination of guilt is a formal process of demonstrating to a court beyond a reasonable doubt that the crime as alleged was committed by the accused. This is a very high threshold of proof and many defences, often "technical" or procedural, are open to the accused. The principle of "innocent until proven guilty" remains paramount. That is why the accused is usually released from custody, for example, and why the incidents that are the basis of the criminal charges must always be referred to as "alleged incidents".

Placement of the Accused Employee

If a teacher is charged with a sexual offence, the Ontario *Education Act*[3] requires that the teacher be removed from the classroom. Section 170(1)12.1 of the Act states:

> on becoming aware that a teacher or temporary teacher who is employed by the board has been charged with or convicted of an offence under the *Criminal Code* (Canada) involving sexual conduct and minors, or of any other offence under the *Criminal Code* (Canada) that in the opinion of the board indicates that pupils may be at risk, take prompt steps to ensure that the teacher or temporary teacher performs no duties in the classroom and no duties involving contact with pupils, pending withdrawal of the charge, discharge following preliminary inquiry, stay of the charge or acquittal, as the case may be;

It is clear, therefore, that if a teacher is charged with a sexual offence against a minor the teacher must be removed from the classroom. A minor is any person under the age of 18. Also note that this duty to remove is created by any charge of a sexual nature regardless of where and when the sexual offence was alleged to have occurred.

When the alleged victim is 18 or over, the removal of the teacher is discretionary. This places a principal in a difficult situation when the alleged victim is an adult and/or the circumstances around the alleged offence require an assessment of potential risk to other students. In practice this judgment would normally be expected to be exercised by a school superintendent or the Director of Education. *It is recommended that a board policy and procedure be in place to provide criteria for such removal.* Some boards require all persons charged with sexual misconduct offences to be removed regardless of the age of the victim.

While it is obvious that removal of a accused employee potentially reduces risk to other students, such removal also protects the teacher by helping to ensure that the subsequent investigation is not complicated by the continued presence of the teacher at the alleged crime scene and that evidence is not tainted by the teacher continuing to interact with potential witnesses. In addition, as Justice Robins commented in *Protecting Our Students*, "A mandatory policy of removal is said to reduce the speculation about the merits of each allegation as all teachers are treated equally. This is said to ensure fairness for teachers".[4] There is a fuller discussion of this rationale in Chapter 4. In addition, examples of board policy statements can be found in that chapter at page 103.

Not all allegations of sexual offences in schools involve teachers of course. Other school support staff such as educational assistants, caretakers and paraprofessionals may also be charged. In such cases the *Education Act* is of no assistance. Justice Robins recommended that all employees, including teachers as well as volunteers, be covered by a board policy and protocol. In addition, his recommendation includes all formal investigations of sexual abuse and harassment, not just criminal investigations.[5] It is recommended that board policy dictate the removal from the school of any support staff employee or volunteer charged with a sexual offence pending the disposition of the charges by the court.

Another area of concern is the actual placement of the teacher or other employee during the investigation and/or after charges have been laid. This is normally a decision of the Superintendent or Director of Education and can include assignment to non-teaching duties, home assignment with pay, suspension with pay or suspension without pay depending on the circumstances. Considerations should include not just potential risk to students but to other employees, potential of embarrassment to the employee based on the extent to which the allegations are generally known within the board or the community and whether the employee is in fact doing useful work. There are other potential complications. In one instance a support staff union grieved the presence of a teacher assigned to central office duties. It was alleged that many of his temporary duties were clerical in nature and should have been undertaken by the support staff employees. Once charges are laid and become public domain, the recommended best practice is home assignment. In some instances other employees at the alternative work location may complain that they feel uneasy with the accused employee present in the workplace. If the employer has no appropriate alternative work for a suspended employee and the trial process is going to be very lengthy, the suspension may be converted to a suspension without pay.

During the period of absence the board should select a designated person, usually the superintendent or the principal, to convey to and receive information from the absent employee. The employee should be instructed not to contact the school directly. Usually a school board has little direct knowledge of the content of a police investigation and must wait for the trial process to be completed before determining the consequences for an accused wrongdoer. However, if the employer has sufficient first-hand evidence of the allegations on which to make a determination of serious wrongdoing, the employer may proceed to dismiss the employee before the trial process is completed.

It should also be remembered that once a teacher is charged with an offence involving sexual conduct and minors or is charged with an offence that in the opinion of the employer indicates that students may be "at risk" the board must "promptly" report in writing to the College of Teachers.[6]

Informing and Supporting the School Community

Criminal Charges are Public

Once a charge is laid, the allegations are in the public domain. In Canada, the judicial system is a fundamental component of democratic governance and, therefore, must at all times be open to public scrutiny. When charges of a sexual nature are laid the general rule is that the identity of the accused is public information. The identity of the victim may not be revealed although an adult victim may waive the right to privacy.

Where a person under age 18 is the victim, the right to privacy is absolute. In some cases this requires that some of the circumstances around the allegations remain confidential to protect the privacy of the victim. For example, if a parent or relative of the victim is the accused, then the name of the accused will remain confidential because of the risk of identifying the victim. In a case where the accused is under the age of 18, s. 110 of the *Youth Criminal Justice Act*[7] requires that the identity of the accused not be disclosed except under court order, and s. 111(1) protects the identity of the victim if he or she is under 18.

Once criminal charges are announced *it is essential that the senior administration of the board designate a single press spokesperson* so that correct information is provided and the privacy rights of all the affected individuals can be protected. Larger boards will have a communications department or a staff member with responsibility for dealing with the media. In smaller boards the Director's office or a Superintendent should assume this responsibility. The principal of the affected school should *instruct all staff to make no comments to the press and to refer all inquiries to the central spokesperson.*

Principals and other school board officials are often concerned about the "privacy rights of the accused" and are reluctant to publicly discuss the laying of criminal charges or to name the accused. Unions will also protest any public discussion, claiming that the professional reputation of the member will be permanently destroyed on the basis of allegations that have not been proven in court. In fact the *former* Federation of Women Teachers Federations prepared a video and resource kit for teachers called "A Teacher's Worst Nightmare" that focused on the negative impact on teachers in the relatively rare situation of false allegations being publicized. These materials are no longer in circulation and the Elementary Teachers Federation of Ontario has produced a new video and resource materials on the topic.[8]

However unpleasant it may be and however prejudicial to the reputation of the teacher or educational worker, the fact remains that the laying of criminal charges is public information.

The police often meet on a regular basis with the "police beat" reporters and disclose the latest charges that have been laid. In most large communities the laying of a criminal charge is not widely broadcast simply because of the volume of such charges. In smaller communities, however, local newspapers often feature a "police blotter" that contains a verbatim list of charges provided by the police. This can even include relatively minor criminal matters such as impaired driving.

When a teacher or other educational worker is charged with a sexual offence, particularly when it involves a student, the matter is not only public in principle, it is considered "newsworthy" and once brought to the attention of the media will in most cases be widely reported.

The press will likely be informed by the police at the regularly scheduled beat reporter conference. Sometimes the police will issue a special media release, particularly if the investigating officer thinks that the accused may have committed other crimes involving other unknown victims. The police hope that the publicity may bring other witnesses or victims forward to permit more charges to be laid or to solidify the evidence in the existing cases. Even where no deliberate action is formally taken by the police, reporters may find out about the charges through contacts or informants within the force. Often the press covers bail hearings or even overhears conversations amongst police at the police station. No matter how it happens, it is wise to assume that sooner or later the charges will be reported.

The school community will always feel betrayed when allegations of institutional abuse are made. However, this sense of betrayal will be compounded if there is a perception that somehow the institution is hiding something or engaging in cover-ups. The parents and many of the older students will naturally be curious about the incident and will want to be assured that the institution is doing everything it can to protect students. It is the authors' experience that when a school community finds out about sexual charges being laid in the media first, before being told by the school, there are feelings of anger and suspicion. When the parents and students have first been informed by the school there is a sense that the institution is taking responsibility and doing everything it can to protect students.

It is essential that the school maintain close contact with the police during the investigation and secure the agreement of the police to receive at least 24 hours' prior notice of the laying of charges or arrest of the accused. This will not only allow the school time to inform the school community before the local television station or newspaper but will allow the facts to be reported in context and not as a sensational headline or a story containing inaccuracies, rumours or speculation.

The Toronto District School Board has a practice of giving advance notice to students, parents and the greater school community. This is accomplished by a response team that helps the school with all of the issues that arise when sexual charges are laid against staff. The team comprises the principal (and vice-principal) along with the school social worker, school psychologist, school Superintendent, a representative of the Director's office and a centrally assigned sexual abuse response worker. This team assembles at the school as soon as the investigation has begun and should be in place by the time the police decide to lay charges.

Not all school boards have the internal resources to deal with sexual misconduct allegations. In such cases it is recommended that a social worker or psychologist in private practice be placed on a retainer for such situations. In addition, legal advice should be immediately provided to the principal and any other official directly involved. These resources should also be used for developing and implementing a communication plan for the school community. *In larger boards the communications department can spearhead this initiative. Smaller boards should consider retaining a media consultant.*

Justice Robins recommends that school boards have such a communication plan for these situations. He states that "where school staff have been accused of sexual misconduct, particularly abuse of multiple students, other students and school staff, parents and the community may be deeply shaken. As well, speculation, gossip and innuendo may circulate, adversely affecting students and the school staff directly involved. A communication plan avoids or reduces the adverse affects on the school and its community and promotes fairness to all parties."[9]

Any time a teacher or educational employee is charged with sexual offences involving students, there will be intense news media attention on the case. Often the media will want to visit the school and interview students and staff. In a large school board the communications department can ensure that the press are directed to a senior official and that media releases are prepared. In smaller boards principals may have to deal with the media on their own. All press inquiries should be re-directed to the designated spokesperson.

It is advisable to request that the press not interview students or staff on school property. Despite best efforts, however, persistent reporters may wait just off board property and approach students or staff for comment.

As a precaution the principal should counsel staff not to speak to the press, but little can be done to prevent students or parents commenting. However, if staff, students and parents from understand the nature of the charges, the need to maintain neutrality and the concept of innocence until proven guilty the chance of rash or incendiary comments is reduced. In addition, if the school is seen to be supporting the students and keeping the community informed it is less likely that accusations of cover-up will be made.

Staff

Once alerted to the charges the response team convenes a meeting of all school staff. Whenever possible this is at the beginning of the day. In larger schools two meetings are convened so as to permit yard duty, safe arrival and/or bus supervision to occur uninterrupted. The assembled staff are informed of the charges and that the name of their accused colleague will be made public. They are assured that the union will retain the best legal counsel. It is also explained that while the accused is considered innocent until proven guilty the *Education Act* requires that teachers charged with such offences not have contact with students. In the case of non-teaching employees it can be explained that it is inappropriate to return a suspected offender back to the school since there is a potential risk to students. In most cases as a condition of bail, the accused is not permitted to return to the school in any event. The staff will also be advised that all students will be informed as well as their parents. A variety of emotional responses to the news will occur among staff. Some close friends of the accused will be in denial or want to blame the complainant. Others may believe the allegations and will feel betrayed or angry. The staff must be assured that counselling is available for them. One strategy is to set up a box located in a discreet setting into which staff members can drop requests to meet with a social worker or psychologist.

Students

Once the school staff has been informed the next task is to tell the students. In the Toronto District School Board the practice has been for response team members to attend each class, even junior and senior kindergarten. When interventions were first undertaken, the younger students were excluded. Response teams quickly found out that by lunchtime the youngest students had heard the news. Unfortunately, the second-hand information was often exaggerated and the main objective of the information sessions, the prevention of inaccurate rumours, had been defeated. Obviously the content of the presentation has to be age appropriate, but the essential message is always the same. The charges are explained, and the accused is identified. Students are reminded of the presumption of innocence and the basics of the criminal trial process are explained. Students should be urged not to jump to conclusions. Students will often want to offer support to the teacher and not believe the allegations. They should be cautioned against taking sides and reminded that while it is appropriate to express concern for the departed employee, the students who were allegedly victimized also need support. Students should also be reminded that the identity of the alleged victims must remain confidential and disclosures by students are taken seriously by the school and complainants are supported. As with staff, individual counselling should be offered and a box for such requests should be discreetly located. It is not unusual for other disclosures of abuse to be triggered in these situations. The disclosures may be about intra-familial abuse, other school-related incidents or may actually involve the accused. In larger boards there may be in-house psychological or psychiatric resources. In smaller boards serious consideration should be given to contracting with private social workers, psychologists or psychiatrists for short-term student counselling.

Parents

The next step is informing the parents. This is best accomplished in a two-step process, a letter sent home with the student, and a weekday evening meeting scheduled as soon as possible. The letter should contain the same information shared with the students. It will also advise the parents of the meeting.

The principal should chair the meeting. The trustee for the area will probably wish to participate. It is advisable to meet with the trustee before the meeting to ensure the board's policies and other legal restrictions are understood. In one case a trustee made statements at the time charges were laid comparing the situation with Mount Cashel. The teacher was later cleared and sued the trustee for defamation.[10] *It is preferable that a senior official or the school Superintendent explain the legalities of the situation and describe the board's policies and procedures.*

At the meeting information about the charges can be provided. It is helpful to have a police representative or the investigating officer present to speak about this. The board's policies and legal responsibilities should be explained, preferably by a senior board official. Parents should be informed about what the students have been told and what social work and psychological support is available. In addition, parents should be advised how to deal with the topics of sexual misconduct and abuse at home with their children.

While the meeting is public, the target group is the parent community. For this reason any media in attendance should be asked to identify themselves and leave the meeting. A representative of the board should be available to answer questions outside the meeting room.

The meeting can be very difficult to manage. If the accused staff member is popular and/or respected by parents the mood may be one of anger and denial. Often these emotions are directed towards the complainants. In such cases parents should be reminded that forming judgments that the accused is not blameworthy means that they are not believing their children. On the other hand, new or less popular staff may be assumed to be guilty. In both cases parents need to be reminded that it is up to the courts to decide guilt and that it is everyone's responsibility to maintain a neutral stance and focus on trying to maintain a normal classroom environment.

Note: Off-Duty Misconduct

Allegations of sexual abuse or assault committed by a board employee while off duty and involving persons other than students or other board employees also require action by the school. The behaviour of teachers is always under public scrutiny. Criminal charges against a teacher will always create anxiety in the community and a perception of risk to students.

The *Education Act*[11] requires that teachers "inculcate by precept and example" good behaviour for students. This duty is imposed on teachers, according to several court decisions, not just during work hours but in their public and private lives outside the school. This duty has been held to include, possession of stolen property,[12] the expression of extreme political beliefs,[13] threatening letters[14] and appearing nude in a magazine.[15]

Section 43.3(1)(*a*) of the *Ontario College of Teachers Act, 1996*[16] requires that sexual offences allegedly committed against a minor be reported to the college.

In addition, s. 43.3(1)(*b*) requires the school board to report a criminal charge "that in the opinion of the employer indicates that students may be at risk of harm or injury".

If a teacher is charged with a sexual offence involving young persons, the *Education Act* requires that the teacher be removed from the classroom. See page 113.

The duty to report and the duty to remove places the board in the same position with regards to off-duty conduct by a teacher as it does with misconduct alleged within the school. Therefore, it is recommended that the same responses be initiated for all sexual offences involving teachers even though they are not directly related to the school.

There is no clear legislative direction with regard to educational staff who are not members of the college. Nevertheless, those staff directly employed in schools must be treated in a fashion similar to teachers in order to prevent a risk to students or potential liability. Those employees in positions where there is no direct contact with students should have their status reviewed by the Director before returning to work.

THE POLICE ISSUE A CAUTION

At the completion of the investigation the police may, after consultation with the Crown Attorney's office, decide not to lay charges. This may be because the police believe that the suspect has not done anything wrong, because there is doubt that the evidence will be sufficient to support a conviction or because the evidence will not even support a *prima facie* case that could proceed to trial. Where the investigating officer believes that some misconduct took place but cannot lay a charge, the officer may schedule a meeting with the suspect. At such a meeting the suspect will be advised that no charges will be laid. The officer will then go on to explain the relevant *Criminal Code* provisions and "caution" the suspect that any reported breaches of these in the future may result in criminal charges being laid.

One scenario that might result in a caution would be where a teacher is "dating" a student and sexual relations are suspected but cannot be proved because the student refuses to give evidence. The investigating officer would explain the law of sexual exploitation (see Chapter 4) and warn the teacher that such behaviour could result in criminal charges being laid.

When police caution and release an education employee without charges the employer has a problem. A caution is a red flag that something inappropriate may be going on. It is certainly not a clear vindication of the employee. While there is no *Education Act* requirement to remove the employee from the school, there is a serious risk of liability should the employee be returned and the misconduct continue or occur again. The board should contact the investigating officer to determine the grounds for the caution. If there is any reasonable risk that misconduct may have occurred, an internal investigation by the board will have to be undertaken. In such circumstances it is advisable to remove or continue to remove the employee from the school until the investigation is complete. If this occurs, under the *Ontario College of Teachers Act, 1996*, s. 43.3(2) there is a duty to report in writing within 30 days a restriction on a teacher's duties involving sexual misconduct.

In Chapter 6 internal investigations are described in detail. For the purposes of this chapter it is sufficient to say that the purpose of an internal investigation is to determine whether the act complained of occurred using the civil liability threshold of proof based on "a balance of probabilities". This is significantly different than the criminal test of "beyond a reasonable doubt". The balance of probabilities means that there is a greater than 50 per cent chance that the event occurred. This is the test that is used in law suits, tribunals and labour arbitrations. As was demonstrated in the O.J. Simpson case, it is possible to be held not liable at a criminal trial and liable at a civil trial on the same facts.

In the case of the issuance of a caution the employee's privacy right must be respected and no public comments should be made by the principal or any other board official. Unfortunately, there are no such restrictions on the police or on the general public. Often the investigating officer will advise the alleged victim or their family of the caution. In such cases it is common for the rumour mill to start and for the principal and other board officials to be questioned by parents and members of the community. In most cases the investigation will have proceeded quietly up to this point and the interviewed witnesses will have been instructed not to talk about the case. Now, the cat will be out of the bag, but unlike in a situation where charges have been laid there is nothing that can be reported to parents or the community. The only safe answer is "that the matter is under review"… period.

An internal investigation will attempt to clear up the ambiguity created by the police caution by examining all the evidence applying the civil standard of proof. If vindicated the employee can return as described below under "Employee is Cleared of All Wrongdoing". If not, then discipline will result as described below under "Findings of Guilt".

NO CHARGES ARE LAID

At the completion of the investigation the police may, after consultation with the Crown Attorney's office, decide not to lay charges. This may be because the police believe that the suspect has not done anything wrong and the person is cleared of all wrongdoing, because there is doubt that the evidence will be sufficient to support a conviction or because the evidence will not even support a *prima facie* case that could proceed to trial. Before making any decisions about the employee the investigating officer should be contacted to determine the reasons that charges were not laid. In some cases this can be done by the principal, by the superintendent or by other central board officials.

EMPLOYEE IS CLEARED OF ALL WRONGDOING

In the best scenario, the original allegations have been kept in confidence and the police will have quickly and quietly completed the investigation. In such circumstances the return to work will occur without remark.

The first step in the re-entry process is to have a meeting with the employee and if appropriate any union or legal representative. It may be advisable to have the Superintendent for the school also participate. If there has been a quick and confidential investigation, the employee will probably wish to return to work immediately and with no fanfare. Since the official reason for the absence has been "personal business", other employees will be expected to respect the privacy of the returning employee. The suspected employee should be offered counselling and other emotional supports during the re-entry. It is advisable that the employee not talk to others in the school in detail about the experience. The principal should instruct the returning employee not to reveal the identity of the witnesses and/or the complainant. If the employee remains concerned he or she should be counselled to consult with a lawyer to determine any legal rights he or she may have.

Unfortunately, it is often difficult to keep sexual misconduct investigations completely secret. Sometimes a witness, a parent or the employee under investigation reveals the situation and rumours start. Until the investigation is complete it is impossible for the principal to comment. However, once the investigation has ended and police and senior board staff are confident nothing culpable occurred there is an opportunity to clear the air. Therefore during the re-entry meeting the employee should be consulted about his or her concerns and offered a variety of strategies. It may be that the employee wishes to be transferred even though there has been an undertaking to publicly support the employee's return. If possible such requests should be honoured, especially if there has been widespread knowledge of the allegations in the school community. Where the employee does wish to return to the school an offer should be made to inform the school community that the employee has been cleared and encourage that he or she be welcomed back. This can be done by a letter home to parents or a parents' meeting or both. The employee may prefer that nothing be said publicly and such a request for privacy should be honoured. Whatever strategy is employed, the principal should keep a close eye on the employee for the first few months as Post-traumatic Stress Syndrome or other serious emotional reactions may be slow to develop. Any serious changes in behaviour or performance should be noted and the appropriate support offered.

In these situations the issue of "false allegations" often arises. While rare in the author's experience, they can occur. The most common source of false allegations occurs in divorce or separation disputes, not in institutional settings. If the police believe that the allegations were deliberately false, a charge of mischief will be laid against the accuser. In the case of children below the age of criminal responsibility (age 12), counselling or treatment should be provided in such circumstances. The disclosure and the result of the investigation should be put in the documentation file of the Ontario Student Record so that in the event of a future complaint police and Children's Aid workers can be alerted. In one situation a sexual abuse complaint against a teacher was filed by the parent of a child who had recently transferred to the school from another jurisdiction. The same day, the Ontario Student Record arrived from the sending school. It contained several similar complaints by the child's mother from other schools, none of which had been substantiated. This record prevented a potentially embarrassing and costly intervention.

BETWEEN CHARGES AND TRIAL

Once charges have been laid against an employee the school and its community must wait for months, even years, before a trial is scheduled, held and concluded. During this time there is usually little news that can be reported, yet tensions may build and rumours may continue to spread. During this time the employee will be on an assignment away from students or will be home on leave with pay. During this time one person, usually the school Superintendent, should be designated as a contact person for the accused employee. All official communications should be made only through that designate.

The interregnum between the laying of charges and the trial may be interrupted if the charges are later dropped or "stayed", or if there is a preliminary inquiry.

WHEN CHARGES ARE SUBSEQUENTLY DROPPED

Occasionally developments subsequent to the laying of charges will result in the Crown Attorney reassessing the case. Sometimes a key witness will recant testimony, sometimes additional investigating leads to a different suspect or the Crown reappraises the merits and decides there is insufficient evidence to proceed.

In such cases it is natural for the suspect employee and his or her supporters to assume that the employee has been vindicated. While this might very well be the case, the board will wish to investigate why the charges were dropped and perhaps undertake its own investigation. Charges that are dropped can always be laid again later. Just as when police investigate and no charges are laid, the board must be assured that some form of sexual misconduct did not take place before returning the absent employee to duty. A principal should be careful to reserve any comment about the situation until direction has been received from senior board officials. If a return is contemplated the procedures on pages 123-124 should be followed.

The *Ontario College of Teachers Act, 1996* requires that the board "promptly" notify the Ontario College of Teachers in the event charges are withdrawn.[17]

WHEN CHARGES ARE STAYED

The Crown Attorney sometimes will go to court and ask that a judge "stay" the proceedings. This will occur for the same reason that charges are withdrawn. When a case is stayed, it remains active for one year and can be re-activated at the request of the Crown Attorney. Therefore, just as when charges are dropped, no assumptions can be made about the culpability of the employee. The board, usually through counsel, should investigate the circumstances around the stay before making any determinations about returning the employee. If return is contemplated, the procedures outlined in the previous section should be followed.

The *Ontario College of Teachers Act, 1996* requires that the board "promptly" notify the Ontario College of Teachers in the event charges are stayed.[18]

THE PRELIMINARY INQUIRY

In the case of serious criminal charges the accused is entitled to a preliminary inquiry in front of a judge to determine if a *prima facie* case exists on which a properly directed jury could convict. When an accused appears in front of a judge on an indictable offence, there is an opportunity to elect how the case will be tried: a trial in front of a Provincial Court judge, a preliminary inquiry and trial by District Court judge and jury, or a preliminary inquiry and trial by a District Court judge sitting alone without a jury (see page 111).[19]

In many cases, with the permission of the provincial Attorney General, an indictment can be "preferred" by the Crown Attorney and no preliminary inquiry is held.[20] However, in circumstances where the Crown wants to be assured that the evidence to support the charge is sufficient, a court will hear evidence and make the decision whether a trial will be held.

While the preliminary inquiry proceedings are conducted in a criminal court in front of a judge, there is no jury. The Crown examines witnesses under oath and the defence cross-examines these witnesses. It is unusual for a full defence to be mounted at the preliminary inquiry, although the defence counsel will try to cast doubt on the credibility of the witnesses and will submit that a *prima facie* case has not been made out.

The preliminary inquiry will occur many months after charges were laid. It is to be expected that there will be substantial publicity surrounding the hearing. The board would be best advised to monitor the proceedings. The principal should try to maintain an air of neutrality in the school during the proceeding. It is advisable that there be a communication plan in place that focuses on the emotional needs of the school community. It must be stressed at all times that the hearing is not about guilt or innocence but rather whether or not there will be a trial.

In many cases the defence will request a publication ban on the evidence presented at the hearing. School boards will likely monitor the inquiry, using a lawyer or senior staff member. While the proceedings will be reported to the board's senior staff, principals should be cautious when discussing the particulars with school staff, students or parents. Publication bans apply generally to the news media but a parent newsletter or a memo posted on a public notice board containing trial events subject to a ban might attract judicial criticism. In addition, in sexual offence cases, certain proceedings require exclusion of the public in order to protect child witnesses and sexual offence victims.[21]

If the judge decides that there is insufficient evidence the employee will be discharged. It must not be assumed, however, that the employee has been vindicated. It is still necessary to determine the reasons for the refusal to indict. As with charges being dropped or charges not being laid at all, the employee may still have engaged in sexual misconduct or other forms of culpable behaviour that present a potential risk to students. Once it is clear that no risk is presented, a re-entry plan as described in the earlier section is recommended.

If a teacher is discharged at the preliminary inquiry the *Ontario College of Teachers Act, 1996* requires that the board must "promptly" notify the Ontario College of Teachers.[22]

If the employee is indicted, there will be another long wait until the actual trial. A board communication strategy should be in place similar to that used when charges are first laid. Often the delay between charges and preliminary inquiry will straddle a school year. It is necessary that students and parents who were not involved when the charges were laid be informed of the board's policies and the facts of the case, and offered emotional support. It is important that these new parents be advised on how best to deal with these issues with their children. It may be necessary in serious cases where there has been a substantial lapse of time to have a second meeting with parents to accomplish these objectives.

A PLEA OF GUILTY

Any time after charges are laid, at arraignment, remand hearings, the preliminary inquiry or any time during the trial, the accused employee may choose to enter a guilty plea. The consequences for such an employee are discussed in the section Finding of Guilt, below.

A CRIMINAL TRIAL

The accused employee will eventually have to face a criminal trial. In the case of serious offences that are proceeded with under indictment the accused can elect a trial by Provincial Court judge, District Court judge and jury or District Court judge sitting alone. In less serious cases (summary offences) the trial will always held before a Provincial Court judge. Whatever the procedure the principal must ensure that students, staff and parents understand the need for neutrality and respect for the legal process.

Despite efforts to expedite criminal proceedings, trials can occur a year or two after the charges were laid. When this occurs the principal may require another communication plan in place to ensure that students and parents who are new to the school are informed of the facts of the case and provided with appropriate support. In addition, students who were in the school at the time of the charges (including the alleged victims) may have moved on to other schools. Where the offences are particularly serious or notorious, emotional and other support should be provided at the new schools for students who so request.

Trials of sexual offences involving child victims are unlike most other criminal trials. Child witnesses are prepared for court by specially trained court workers who make sure the children are familiar with the courtroom and understand the proceedings. Any witness under the age of 14 years or who has a physical or mental disability may have a support person with him or her during the giving of evidence.[23] The right of the accused to face his or her accuser has been determined to be outweighed by the need to get a full and candid account of events without risk of intimidation. Witnesses under the age of 18, or who are handicapped, may give evidence from behind a screen, so that they do not have to look at the accused, or may have their evidence taken outside the courtroom by closed circuit television.[24] The accused may be prohibited from personally cross-examining a witness under the age of 18.[25] The court may also prohibit the publishing or broadcasting of the identity of the victim or other witnesses.[26]

Just as when charges were laid, the media will want to visit the school and interview students and staff, often to provide a "backgrounder" for the trial coverage. Principals should refer the media to senior administration. The principal should remind staff that denying the charges and defending a colleague might have the effect of indirectly communicating a lack of belief in student complaints. They should also be reminded that the identity of the victim and other witnesses must not be revealed and that to do so is contempt of court or a criminal offence.[27] It should also be pointed out that publicly taking sides has a very divisive impact on the school community and alienates parents. Despite best efforts, however, persistent reporters may wait just off board property and approach students or staff for comment. As a precaution the principal should counsel staff not to speak to the press but little can be done to prevent students or parents from commenting.

It is natural that people will take sides during a criminal trial. Often accused teachers or educational employees are well respected and have roots in the community. It is hard to believe such people would harm students. At the same time others may know the alleged victims and be sympathetic. The trial may act as a catalyst for these conflicting opinions, causing a public confrontation between the factions. In one case, at Brown School in Toronto, a teacher, John Freestone, was charged with abusing a young boy 20 years prior. After the community was informed of these charges, three grade 5 and 6 female students came forward and complained that Freestone often hugged them and pressed his erect penis against them. He was then charged with sexual interference. A teacher called the young complainants "dirty liars".[28] The principal encouraged students and parents to contribute to a defence fund for the teacher. Public meetings called by the board turned into ugly shouting matches. At trial, the prosecution witnesses were forced to run a gauntlet of angry shouting Freestone supporters as they entered the court every day. Although the judge believed the girls, Freestone was acquitted because th re was reasonable doubt that what the children were feeling was a whistle Freestone claimed he carried in his pocket and not his penis. While the pro-Freestone faction believed they had been vindicated, a month later, Freestone pleaded guilty to the historical charges that had triggered the girls' disclosures. According to *Toronto Star* reporter Judy Steed, "the rancour of battle hung like toxic fog in the air". What went wrong? "The parents got caught up trying to sort out whether the teacher was guilty or not".[29]

A public debate on guilt or innocence not only alienates the school community and demoralizes staff, but also revictimizes the complainants. Other students learn the wrong lesson and there is a risk that future abuse may go unreported and that students will not be protected. The principal must do everything to prevent this polarization and stress that the court system will determine the truth.

FINDINGS OF GUILT

When an educational employee is found guilty of a sexual offence under the *Criminal Code*, there are three possible consequences at law. In the case of an indictable (serious) offence the court will consider incarceration. In rare cases where the guilty party is ill or there are mitigating factors the employee may be placed under "house arrest" or given a long period of probation. In less serious cases the employee may be placed on probation only.

The *Ontario College of Teachers Act, 1996* requires a board to "promptly" report a teacher convicted of an offence under the *Criminal Code* involving sexual conduct with minors or that in the opinion of the employer indicates students may be at risk.[30]

The status of the guilty employee will normally be the concern of the senior administration of the school board. Some board policies require the immediate dismissal from employment of an employee convicted of sexual abuse. For example, the Toronto District Board Policy states:

> If a Board employee is convicted of abusing a student, or if an internal investigation determines, on the balance of probabilities, that the employee abused a student, the employee will be dismissed from employment. Any volunteer found to have abused a student will no longer be permitted to volunteer.[31]

Other boards are less specific and refer the decision to the Director of Education:

Whether the Board employee is found guilty or not guilty of criminal charges, the Director will make a recommendation to the Board regarding continuance of employment, terms of employment and termination of employment.[32]

In some cases where a transgression is considered less serious a person can be "discharged". This means there is no record or criminal conviction. This can be either conditional or absolute. Conditions may be that the guilty person be of good behaviour for a specific period of time or undertake some form of community service or counselling. Upon successful compliance with the conditions, the record of conviction is expunged. When an absolute discharge is ordered there are no criminal consequences for the guilty person and no criminal record will result.

When a teacher has received an absolute or conditional discharge there is no specific duty under the *Ontario College of Teachers Act, 1996* to report to the College of Teachers. Interestingly, the duty to report only occurs when charges result in conviction. This is an oversight since the actual charges should have already been reported. If the teacher was discharged at the preliminary inquiry or if the charges were dropped or stayed, there remains a duty to report.[33]

However, some school board policies, such as that of the Algoma-Superior Catholic District Board, require that a finding of guilt triggers a review of the employment status of such an employee. In most cases, even where there is no mandatory review, a further internal investigation will occur to review the circumstances. It is highly unlikely that some form of discipline would not be imposed as well as a transfer of the employee and the imposition of work restrictions and conditions. Of course once that occurs, there is a duty to report the imposition of conditions in writing within 30 days under the *Ontario College of Teachers Act, 1996*.[34]

All boards should have a policy that outlines the consequences of a finding of sexual misconduct.

A guilty finding immediately has serious consequences for the school community. Friends and colleagues of the employee will be shocked, upset and devastated and the staff will require emotional support. The victim and his or her family and friends will feel vindicated but the let-down that accompanies the end of a long stressful process will require close attention to emotional needs. Parents will display a range of emotions from denial to anger. Care must be taken to use the moment to assure the school community that:

1. victims of misconduct are believed and supported;
2. this event will contribute to a greater sense security for students; and

3. a vigilant environment will be created that will be less likely to tolerate any form of sexual misconduct in the future.

ACQUITTAL

When an educational employee is acquitted of charges many people believe that the employee has been cleared and expect him or her to return immediately to the school. An acquittal means that a court did not find beyond a reasonable doubt that the accused committed the crime. Of course this can mean that nothing happened and the accused was entirely innocent. The court must find that the events occurred as charged and that the accused intended to commit the crime. Thus a court, for example, can find that a teacher touched a student but may not find that there was the requisite sexual intent. In one case the teacher claimed that the bump in his pants was not an erect penis (sexual intent) but possibly keys and a comb in his pocket.[35] In many cases there are only two eyewitnesses to a sexual crime, the alleged victim and the accused, and the court must believe one version or the other. Since teachers are often well-respected individuals and the victims are children or adolescents who may appear confused or unsure of events, the court will often give the benefit of the doubt to the teacher. In many cases an accused can be acquitted on technical defences. In one case the teacher was charged with asking to sexually touch his student when the facts proved he asked the student to touch him. He was therefore acquitted of the crime as charged.[36] In some cases, accused are acquitted because of delays that prejudice their right to a fair trial.

It should also be noted that the definition of professional misconduct casts a much wider net than the *Criminal Code*. An employee's behaviour may not be criminal but it may result in professional misconduct or culpable behaviour (see the next section). The first interest of the board is protecting students and the school must be confident that an employee can return without risk of harm to students.

In *Protecting Our Students*, Justice Robins notes the confusion about acquittal.

> Some existing policies and protocols provide for the termination of employment on the findings of guilt or upon a determination, in the employment context, to a lesser standard of proof, that sexual abuse occurred. More problematic is what transpires after an acquittal in criminal proceedings. The interested parties with whom I met all understood that acquittals do not bar subsequent disciplinary proceedings. However, there was evidence presented to me that this understanding is not shared by all board representatives in Ontario. Misunderstandings as to the meaning and effect of acquittals persist.[37]

For this reason Robins recommended that

> School board policies and protocols should specifically state that the board needs to make a determination whether the sexual misconduct has occurred, whether or not any criminal charges have resulted in findings of guilt.[38]

The policies of both the Toronto District School Board and the Algoma-Superior Catholic District School Board provide for internal review subsequent to acquittals prior to making any decision about the status of the employee.

An internal review will first require a thorough reading of court transcripts to determine why the employee was acquitted. Such transcripts can also provide evidence of other non-criminal culpability. If the transcripts are inconclusive, then an internal investigation will have to be undertaken. (See Chapter 6.)

Boards should have a policy requiring internal investigations upon acquittal of a board employee charged with sexual offences.

In the event that the subsequent review and/or investigation does clear the employee then a return to work strategy should be developed.

The first step in the re-entry process is to have a meeting with the employee and if appropriate a union or legal representative. It may also be advisable for the school Superintendent to participate.

Until the investigation is completed it is impossible for the principal to comment or discuss the situation with school staff, students or parents. However, once the investigation has ended and senior board staff are confident nothing culpable occurred, there is an opportunity to clear the air. Therefore during the re-entry meeting the employee's concerns should be heard and a variety of strategies offered. See the procedures outlined on pages 123-124.

WHEN CONDUCT MAY BE CULPABLE BUT NOT CRIMINAL

Just because criminal charges are not laid or an employee is acquitted does not mean the employee is "cleared". Many behaviours by teachers or other adults working with students may not constitute a sexual offence, but may be contrary to board policy (such as sexual harassment), may amount to professional misconduct as determined by a professional college or may simply be inappropriate. In some cases no charges may be laid because alleged victims refuse to cooperate with police or are reluctant to testify in court. Where no criminal charges are laid but there are still allegations or suspicions of sexual misconduct, it is not advisable to return the employee to a school setting until there has been an internal investigation. This is consistent with the recommendations of Justice Robins.[39]

Culpable behaviours that may constitute sexual misconduct or create a risk of sexual mistreatment for students are described in detail elsewhere in this book. Principals should remember that alleged incidents may occur in a non-school context. Off-duty conduct relating to venues and activities that involve students or other young people such as plays, concerts, sports teams, choirs, boy scouts or socializing in bars is subject to scrutiny.

The following is a list of behaviours that if alleged and not disproved by external investigation must be investigated internally:

- inviting an individual student to the employee's home or offering accommodation without parental consent;
- giving or offering illicit drugs to students;
- giving or offering alcohol or tobacco to under-age students;
- "dating" students or seeing students in private or isolated situations;
- exchanging personal notes, comments or e-mail that is sexually suggestive or contains sexually inappropriate comments or jokes;
- offering personal gifts or loans of money to students;
- phoning students at home about personal matters;
- gender-related comments about a student's physical attributes;
- repeated "compliments" regarding a student's appearance, hair or clothes;
- unwelcome or gratuitous physical contact;
- displaying sexually offensive pictures or other materials;
- sexual relationships with students aged 18 and over; and
- sexual relationships with former students.

In addition to these specific behaviours Justice Robins adopted a concern expressed by the Ontario Teachers Federation that school board standards for behaviour of coaches be established relating to locker room activity, behaviour on tournaments and driving students from games. In addition, the behaviour of teachers interacting with students outside the regular school day, such as in drama and music rehearsals, should be scrutinized.[40]

When an investigation reveals conduct such as that described above, discipline must be imposed. Depending on the seriousness of the situation and the perceived risk to students it may be advisable to transfer the employee. In any event, some clear directions must be given, in writing, to the employee. These directions should specifically make reference to the culpable behaviour. "You are to refrain from offering personal gifts or loans of money to students", for example. The directions could limit the role of the employee in extra-curricular events, or require an open office door at all times, no curtains on office windows, etc. Such directions must be accompanied by a warning that any repetition of the misconduct will likely result in termination. Care must be taken to ensure that there is a central board record of the discipline and/or written direction. This will ensure that new principals and Superintendents are aware of the conditions in the event the employee is transferred or a new principal arrives at the school.

Remember that the *Ontario College of Teachers Act, 1996* requires a board to file a written report within 30 days about any teacher when the board "imposes restrictions on the member's duties for reasons of professional misconduct".[41]

It is recommended that boards develop a code of conduct for employees that lists the types of behaviours that constitute non-criminal sexual misconduct.

ENDNOTES

[1] *Cox v. Metropolitan Toronto Police Services Board* (October 21, 1998), Doc. No. 97-CV-129371 (Ont. Ct. Gen. Div.).

[2] R.S.C. 1985, c. C-46.

[3] R.S.O. 1990, c. E.2.

[4] Robins, *Protecting Our Students: A Review to Identify and Prevent Sexual Misconduct in Ontario Schools* (Toronto: Ministry of Attorney General (Milner Graphics), 2002), p. 336.

[5] *Ibid.*, p. 337.

[6] *Ontario College of Teachers Act, 1996*, S.O. 1996, c. 12, as amended, s. 43.2(1).

[7] S.C. 2002, c. 1.

[8] The video package "It Can Happen to You — Preventing Allegations of Assault and Professional Misconduct" is available from "ShopETFO" at (416) 962-ETFO.

[9] Robins, *Protecting Our Students*, p. 337.

[10] *Cox v. Metropolitan Toronto Police Services Board* (October 21, 1998), Doc. No. 97-CV-129371 (Ont. Ct. Gen. Div.).

[11] *Education Act*, R.S.O. 1990, c. E.2, as amended, s. 264 (1)(c).

[12] *Re Etobicoke Board of Education and Ontario Secondary School Teachers' Federation, District 12* (1981), 2 L.A.C. (3d) 265, Ontario, decision of arbitrator K.P. Swan.

[13] *Ross v. New Brunswick School District No. 15*, [1996] 1 S.C.R. 825.

[14] *Toronto (City) Board of Education v. Ontario Secondary School Teachers Federation, (District 15)*, [1997] 1 S.C.R. 487.

[15] *Shewan v. Abbotsford School District No. 34* (1987), 47 D.L.R. (4th) 106 (B.C.C.A.).

[16] S.O. 1996, c. 12.

[17] *Ontario College of Teachers Act, 1996*, S.O. 1996, c. 12, as amended, s. 43.3(1).

[18] *Ibid.*, s. 43.3(2).

[19] *Criminal Code*, R.S.C. 1985, c. C-46, as amended, s. 536.

[20]   *Ibid.*, s. 577.

[21]   *Ibid.*, s. 487.

[22]   *Ontario College of Teachers Act, 1996*, S.O. 1996, c. 12, as amended, s. 43.3(2).

[23]   *Criminal Code*, R.S.C. 1985, c. C-46, s. 486(1.2), (1.3) and (1.4).

[24]   *Ibid.*, s. 486(2.1), (2.2).

[25]   *Ibid.*, s. 486(2.3).

[26]   *Ibid.*, s. 486(3).

[27]   *Ibid.*, s. 486(5).

[28]   Judy Steed, *Our Little Secret* (Toronto: Random House, 1994), p. 103.

[29]   *Ibid.*, p. 105.

[30]   *Ontario College of Teachers Act, 1996*, S.O. 1996, c. 12, as amended, s. 43.3(1)(*c*).

[31]   Policy Dealing With Abuse and Neglect of Students, Toronto District School Board, para. 2(f), cited in Robins, *Protecting Our Students* (Toronto: Ministry of the Attorney General (Milner Graphics), 2002) p. 483.

[32]   Child Abuse Policy and Procedures, Huron-Superior Catholic District School Board, para. 8(f), cited in Robins, *ibid.*, p. 449.

[33]   *Ontario College of Teachers Act, 1996*, S.O. 1996, c. 12, as amended, ss. 43.2(1), 43.3(1), (2).

[34]   *Ibid.*, s. 43.2(1).

[35]   *R. v. Freestone* (September 10, 1992) (Ont. Prov. Ct. Crim. Div.), Scullion Prov. Ct. J.

[36]   *R. v. Seymour*, [1995] O.J. No. 2700 (QL) (Prov. Ct.).

[37]   Robins, *Protecting Our Students*, p. 337.

[38]   *Ibid.*, p. 337, Recommendation 95.

[39]   *Ibid.*, p. 315.

[40]   *Ibid.*, pp. 336-37, Recommendations 93, 94.

[41]   *Ontario College of Teachers Act, 1996*, S.O. 1996, c. 12, as amended, s. 43.2(1).

CHAPTER 6

INTERNAL INVESTIGATION OF SEXUAL MISCONDUCT ALLEGATIONS

An internal investigation will be undertaken in the event that allegations of sexual misconduct are made about a school employee that do not amount to criminal offences or child abuse as described in Chapter 5. If the alleged victim is 18 years of age or older there will have been no outside investigation but in the case of a teacher a complaint may have been made to the College of Teachers. In such a case although the board will cooperate with the college, it is not relieved of the responsibility to investigate the conduct on its own. In most cases involving students under 18 an internal investigation of sexual misconduct will occur after an investigation by the police and/or a Children's Aid Society has concluded and no criminal charges have been laid. There may be situations, of course, where a report to a Children's Aid Society or the police has been made but no formal investigation has been undertaken for some reason.

The consequences of an affirmative finding will be serious, such as involuntary transfer or discipline including suspension without pay or dismissal from employment. In the case of teaching employees there may be professional sanctions by the college. In all cases an allegation of sexual misconduct can severely damage an employee's reputation. Many employees are concerned that they may be the victims of false or malicious allegations. Therefore it is essential that employees have confidence in the investigation procedures of the board. The suspicions, complaints or allegations should be investigated promptly, professionally and without bias.

In addition, once the employer has imposed a sanction, the employee has the right to challenge the findings by grievance and arbitration in the case of a unionized employee. If a non-unionized employee is dismissed, that employee can sue the board for wrongful dismissal. The investigation will then be subject to the scrutiny of a third party who is usually legally trained and who will apply the *Evidence Act* and basic standards common to courts and tribunals. In most cases the written investigation itself will not be the basis of any legal proceedings but the oral testimony of the investigator will be required at subsequent litigation.

WHO INVESTIGATES ALLEGATIONS OF SEXUAL MISCONDUCT?

In the ideal world the school board would have a trained investigator on staff. However, only the largest boards in Ontario have this luxury. Most boards will be required to consider hiring an outside investigator, often a lawyer. This achieves two goals; it provides a legal opinion that supports the subsequent actions of the board and it provides evidence that will be presentable at a court or tribunal. This can be expensive, however, and in cases that at first instance appear to be relatively minor, or constitute harassment or culpable behaviour, board officials may decide that the superintendent in partnership with the principal or the principal alone will investigate.

This chapter is designed to guide a principal who is assisting in or directing his or her own investigation.

THE DUTY OF FAIRNESS

While investigators of alleged sexual misconduct by employees are not limited by the restrictions of criminal law, such investigations must be conducted in a manner that allows any wrong to be detected, but protects the interest of the accused. In the event evidence is obtained in a manner that constitutes a breach of due process or fundamental fairness, it may not be accepted by a tribunal or court that later deals with the consequences of a finding of misconduct.

It should be kept in mind that interviews of complainants, witnesses and the accused employee are part of an investigative procedure that must be complete before any conclusions are drawn.

The accused employee must be presumed innocent until facts demonstrate the misconduct. There is a tendency, by investigators, to try to gather information to prove what they have already determined or suspect to be true rather than what actually happened. It is essential that investigators focus on the facts and avoid making conclusions at too early a stage. Get the "Who", "What", "Where", "How" and, if relevant, "Why". If the board does not have a policy requiring employees to be sent home pending internal investigations, notwithstanding the presumption of innocence, if in the judgment of a principal at any stage of the investigation, an employee may present a risk to students or other employees, the alleged wrongdoer may be suspended with pay.

RECEIVING A COMPLAINT OR ALLEGATION

The beginning point of any investigation is usually the receipt of a complaint. If the complaint involves a student victim aged 18 or over and no sexual assault is alleged, the principal may have to continue to investigate after advising the appropriate senior board official of the situation. In all other cases no further steps to investigate should be taken, until the advice of police and children's aid has been given and there is specific clearance to continue.

The matter to be inquired into must be defined and the issues identified, the sources of available information must be identified and the investigation must be initiated and continued through to some disposition.

Complaints or allegations about board employees may come from students, other employees, volunteers, parents and visitors, the general public or trustees. In most cases, the complaint should be received by a principal and immediately reported to the Superintendent or Director of Education.

Complainants or witnesses are usually concerned about possible personal ramifications of having made the complaint. The principal should be able to advise a complainant or witness about some of the following issues or, if in any doubt, should seek immediate assistance from the Superintendent or Director. Those issues are: fear of reprisal, confidentiality and adverse reports against teachers.

A complainant or witness should be immediately assured that an accused employee would be advised that, regardless of the truth of an allegation, any act of reprisal would result in disciplinary action.

It is not possible to guarantee anonymity or complete confidentiality to any complainant or witness, but every effort will be made to protect the privacy of individuals. Depending on the seriousness of the matter, other managerial or supervisory employees may have to be informed of the details. If subsequently it is determined that a crime has been committed or abuse has occurred, the witness will be questioned by the police or the Children's Aid Society. If any action is taken against a respondent that could be construed as discipline and the respondent files a grievance, the law requires full disclosure of the material facts on which the employer is acting. In some cases, complainants or witnesses will be required to give evidence under oath at a labour arbitration hearing.

The *Regulation under the Teaching Profession Act*[1] requires any member of the Ontario Teachers' Federation, on making an adverse report on another member, to furnish that member with a written statement of the report at the earliest possible time and not later than three days after making the report. Teachers should be advised that as of September 2002 there is no longer a requirement to file such a report if the teacher is reporting "sexual abuse", which is defined as:

- sexual intercourse or other forms of physical sexual relations between a member and a student (of any age);
- touching, of a sexual nature, of the student by a teacher; or
- behaviour or remarks of a sexual nature by the member towards a student.[2]

Non-teaching employees who report on a colleague are not legally required to inform that colleague of the report.

GATHERING EVIDENCE

After the complaint is received and an investigation appears warranted, it is important to act promptly. With the passage of time, facts become stale and memories fade.

Interview Techniques

When a scheduled interview is conducted, it is best to have two investigators present. This permits one person to question the subject while the other person takes down detailed notes. When receiving a complaint this is not always possible. Nevertheless, detailed notes are essential. If the principal receives verbal complaints about an employee, it is essential that complainants be told that, in order for the employer to act, there must be a documentary record. It is useful to get written statements signed by witnesses. Such persons should be told that, if the investigation results in disciplinary action, they might be required to give their evidence under oath at a labour arbitration hearing. When the statement is prepared by the investigator, the witness must read the statement. The witness may also keep a copy.

The witness may request a support person to be present at the interview. This is particularly advisable if the subject is an alleged victim or a child. Such persons should be advised that by being present they are witnesses to the interview or complaint and are therefore potentially liable to be subpoenaed in subsequent legal proceedings. In the case of child witnesses it is best that the support person be an adult who is trusted by the child. It is not advisable to involve a parent or relative as this presents a risk that the child witness will be influenced by the adult or may be reluctant to discuss "embarrassing" details.

In the case of young children it may be difficult to get a written statement. Nevertheless, they may later be called as witnesses in subsequent legal proceedings. Therefore it is important that they read and understand the investigators' notes. Children as young as six years old have given evidence in labour arbitrations involving employees dismissed for sexual misconduct. The arbitrator will accept such evidence if he or she is satisfied that the youngster understands the difference between the truth and a lie.

As with the initial complaint, there can be no promise of anonymity to a witness. Anonymous complaints or evidence that cannot be attributed to a person for the purpose of cross-examination in subsequent litigation cannot be the basis of disciplinary action by an employer. In addition, secret files and records on employees kept by a suspicious principal may not be used as evidence and will not be used as the basis of discipline. Under the Ontario *Municipal Freedom of Information and Protection of Privacy Act*,[3] an employee is entitled to know any personal information that is being kept on file and a violation of this right will preclude the evidence from being admitted.

Many people assume that by placing the word "confidential" on a document, it will not be disclosed or discoverable. This is not true in the public employment context. When preparing a document, it is wise to consider that it may eventually have to be disclosed to the person who is the subject of the document. At arbitration, for example, a grievor has the right to full disclosure of the board's case. Interviewed witnesses may be surprised when they are subpoenaed by the lawyers for the disciplined employee or when counsel for the employer calls to prepare for arbitration. While the employer will not release the names of interviewers early in the disciplinary process, if an arbitration is convened names will be revealed on agreement of the parties or under the order of the arbitrator.

Order of Interviews

In most investigations of suspected sexual misconduct, it is best to interview the implicated employee near or at the end of the investigation. It is best to start with the person who first came forward with the information, allegation or complaint, especially if no complete statement was taken at the time of the original report. If the source of the information was not the actual alleged victim or one of the alleged victims then the principal must next undertake a thorough interview, including obtaining a signed statement of the alleged victim(s).

If the original informant or the victim names any persons who were eyewitnesses or who could corroborate some element of the complaint then all such persons should be interviewed. The interviews should be conducted in the same manner as those of the victim or original informant. So too, if these witnesses mention other persons who could support or contradict the allegations, every reasonable effort should be made to interview these persons.

Interviewing Implicated Employees

Usually at some point in the process the investigator will begin to form a clear picture of what happened, despite the fact that there are several other potential witnesses. When this occurs, it is time to interview the implicated employee in order to present the complaints and the investigator's understanding of the events, and afford the employee an opportunity to present his or her version of the events as well as the names of corroborative witnesses (if any). The implicated employee should be notified, in advance, that she or he is being interviewed in order to investigate a possible incident of sexual misconduct.

Generally an implicated employee does not have the right to union or federation representation during an investigatory interview unless there is entitlement under a collective agreement. The right of representation usually only starts with the imposition of discipline that would normally occur after the investigation is complete. If, however, the investigator feels that the presence of a representative would be helpful, the union or federation may be invited to attend. Often the union will make its presence a condition of advising its member to consent to an interview. Representatives present at an investigation are there to support the employee, but should not be permitted to argue, cross-examine the investigator, confront, interfere or respond for the accused. In addition, union representatives have no right to be given full disclosure of the findings of the investigation or the names of any witnesses. This is essential to prevent possible intimidation of witnesses.

It is essential that meetings with implicated employees be clearly investigative and not inquisitory. The questions should be asked in a polite and professional manner. Answers that strike the investigator as unsatisfactory should not be challenged but simply recorded. It is not the time or place to confront the implicated employee. No conclusions should be drawn nor criticisms made which would turn the meeting into a disciplinary meeting.

Refusal to be Interviewed

An employee who is the subject of an investigation does not have the same right to remain silent as a criminal accused. The employer has the right to a full accounting by an employee of conduct while at work. As a result, the principal has the right to make negative presumptions when an employee refuses to attend an interview or answer specific questions. When an employee refuses to attend an interview or refuses to answer a specific question, he or she should be advised that in the absence of the subject employee's evidence, the principal would be forced to rely on the uncontradicted evidence of others.

Unions are often reluctant to allow implicated members to be interviewed in internal investigations of sexual misconduct. This is because lawyers will advise the union that if there is a subsequent criminal investigation, the police will have access to the interview notes and the employee will therefore have compromised his or her right of protection against self-incrimination. In addition, since sexual misconduct is also subject to discipline by the College of Teachers, counsel for the college prior to any hearing may subpoena the interview notes by the discipline committee.

ADMISSIBLE EVIDENCE

An investigation should be conducted bearing in mind that the findings, if they result in discipline, will be subjected to litigation. Therefore the evidence relied upon must conform to strict legal standards.

While the investigator's report should conform to legal standards, the document itself is unlikely to be relied upon by a third party. An arbitrator or judge will want to hear all of the evidence under oath, subject to cross-examination by counsel for the disciplined employee. However, the employee's lawyer will subpoena the report in order to prepare for cross-examination, and inaccurate reporting, ambiguities or obvious contradictions will undermine the credibility of the witness.

Circumstantial evidence can be used to prove "just cause" for discipline if it points to the employee in question *and* excludes any other person.

Evidence must be first-hand and provable by sensory facts. As a witness at arbitration, a principal will be asked what he or she personally saw, heard or smelled. Only witnesses qualified as experts can testify as to their opinion. As an example, you can say that you smelled alcohol on a person's breath, but you cannot conclude that she or he was drunk.

Evidence that comprises statements by persons other than the witness as to what the witness said is hearsay and is not generally admissible unless it is contained in a routine report made in the course of business or is an admission by the disciplined employee. A good example would be a situation where a student alleged that he was abused by a teacher behind a closed office door. A person who was outside the door could give evidence that he saw the student enter the office, or that he saw the teacher inside the office. This is useful corroborative evidence. However, that person would not be allowed to tell a tribunal what the alleged victim said happened inside the office. This would be hearsay, unless it could be characterized as a request for help and therefore an initial complaint.

WRITING A REPORT

At the conclusion of the investigation, it must be determined whether culpable behaviour occurred. The test for the investigator is the same as that used by civil courts and tribunals — "the balance of probabilities". If a preponderance of the evidence clearly points to culpable behaviour, then the investigator may reasonably conclude that it occurred. It is not necessary for the case to be made "beyond a reasonable doubt", which is the standard of proof required for a criminal conviction. A good example of the difference is the famous O.J. Simpson trial. On essentially similar evidence, a criminal court acquitted Simpson and a civil court found him responsible for two murders. The reason that criminal courts have a stricter test is that the liberty of the individual could be at stake. The loss of a job or the imposition of discipline does not warrant this same degree of protection for the individual. In addition, the potential risk to students requires taking reasonable precautions to remove or constrain the activities of individuals believed on reasonable grounds to have sexually abused or harassed a student.

The report should set out the original allegations or circumstances that prompted the investigation. It should then outline in narrative form the events that are believed to have occurred with a concluding section upholding or refuting the allegations. Concerns about credibility of witnesses and conflicts in evidence should be included. The actual names of all witnesses should be concealed, with initials or code words used instead. Original interview notes should be kept in a safe place but should not form part of the report itself.

The investigation may not support all or any of the original allegations, but may uncover other culpable behaviour or sexual misconduct. The investigator is not restricted to supporting or refuting the original allegations. The principal has a duty to act on any behaviour that puts students at risk, breaches policy or constitutes professional misconduct. Unions often protest this practice as unfair and an abuse of process, but the principal must remember that there is an overarching duty to protect children.

If an investigation has been undertaken by a principal or other board staff, it should be reviewed, first by senior staff and then by a lawyer to determine if the process was correct and the findings sustainable at law. The lawyer can also then give an opinion to senior staff of the board as to the appropriate discipline warranted by the misconduct.

If the employee is to be seriously disciplined or dismissed, it is advisable for the lawyer who has reviewed the report to compose or assist with the composition of a board report supporting the action. This summary can be provided to the implicated employee but it is not necessary or advisable to provide the investigation report to the implicated employee at this time. If the misconduct was relatively minor and a reprimand or transfer is contemplated, then the findings of the investigation can be given orally to the employee at a disciplinary meeting.

All parties to the investigation should be apprised of the fact that the investigation is closed.

In the event that there is insufficient evidence of wrongdoing or it is determined that no discipline is warranted, the documentary record of the investigation, including all interview notes and statements, should be destroyed. The accused employee is, of course, entitled to know if the allegations have not been substantiated.

A complainant is entitled to know whether the complaint was substantiated. If the employee has mistreated a child, the parent of the child is also entitled to know whether discipline was imposed, but should be cautioned that this is personal information about the culpable employee and the disposition should remain confidential. In most other cases the privacy of the culpable employee should be respected.

Witnesses will not generally be privy to personal information about the accused or the complainant. However, should the discipline be grieved, they are entitled to be fully informed as to their role in any subsequent proceedings.

Principals should be aware that many collective agreements require that disciplinary materials in an employee's file must be removed after a period of time if there are no intervening incidents. These are sometimes referred to as "sunset periods". When sexual misconduct has been proven, no matter how minor, there must be a report to the Ontario College of Teachers (see Chapter 5). Such a report and any subsequent college findings would not be subject to sunset provisions.

ENDNOTES

[1] *Regulation under the Teaching Profession Act*, updated to 2002 as included in A.F. Brown, *Consolidated Ontario Education Statutes and Regulations* (Toronto: Carswell, 2002), s. 18(1)(*b*).

[2] *Teaching Profession Act*, R.S.O. 1990, c. T.2, as amended, ss. 12(2) and (3).

[3] R.S.O. 1990, c. M.56.

CHAPTER 7

SEXUAL MISCONDUCT SCENARIOS

The following scenarios are presented as examples of the types of problems school administrators may face. The reader is encouraged to try to solve the problem on his or her own. An alternative is to use these scenarios as the basis for group discussion at training sessions or school staff meetings on the issue of sexual misconduct. At the end of the chapter are suggested responses and courses of action based on the appropriate legislation and the authors' opinion as to best practice. In real situations, to the extent that there is no board policy governing some aspect of a situation, a principal should always seek the counsel of senior staff to ensure compliance with the board's established practice and/or a lawyer to ensure compliance with the law.

These scenarios are not designed as statements of final authority on a specific issue. Only a court of law, guided by individual case facts, can be considered as an authority on a specific issue. These scenarios should be considered fictitious or hypothetical, and any resemblance to real people or to specific incidents is coincidental.

SCENARIO ONE

Frank is a 15-year-old grade 10 student at Red Brick Collegiate. Until recently his marks and attendance were above average. Lately, however, he has missed classes and his second semester results were disappointing except for an "A" in physical education taught by Mr. Peach. Another grade 10 student, Andy, asked for an interview with Mr. Brown, one of the guidance teachers. Andy reported to Mr. Brown that the basketball coach, Mr. Peach, often had Frank, who was an average player on the team, alone in his office with the door shut and often drove Frank home after practice. Mr. Peach regularly visits Frank at his home, and has stayed for dinner with Frank's family. Andy also reported that several of the other boys on the team were saying that Frank was Mr. Peach's "bum boy".

Mr. Peach has been a teacher for 20 years, is the Physical and Health Education Department Head, lives near the school and is very popular in the community as a successful basketball and soccer coach. Many students choose to come to Red Brick because of the sports program.

Mr. Brown has come to you, the principal, stating that he "suspects something is going on".

What is your advice to Mr. Brown?
What further actions should you take?

SCENARIO TWO

Sherry is a grade 12 student at Crimson High School. She turned 18 one month ago. She is a popular and attractive student and is very successful academically. Sherry's mother has phoned the principal and complained that Mr. Grant, a 30-year-old English and drama teacher at Crimson, has been "dating" her daughter and she "wants it stopped". The mother says she confronted her daughter and Sherry got angry and said, "I'm not a child any more. It's none of your business". Mr. Grant is not currently teaching Sherry but did teach Sherry in grade 9.

What should the principal do?

SCENARIO THREE

Jeremy is a 13-year-old grade 8 student at Mustard Junior High School. He is already an accomplished musician and is being mentored by a music teacher, Mr. James, after school. Mr. James has told the principal that Jeremy could be a successful professional musician. Jeremy has come to the office asking to speak to the principal. In the privacy of the principal's office Jeremy complains that Mr. James "makes him uncomfortable". The principal asks "in what way?" Jeremy responds, "he touches me here", pointing to his groin.

What should the principal do?

SCENARIO FOUR

Ms. Jones is a new teacher in the English department of St. Mary's Catholic High School. She has come to the principal with concerns about another teacher in the department, Mr. Smithers, who is 45 years old. Mr.

Smithers has on several occasions asked Ms. Jones out on a "date" and she has politely but firmly refused. He continues to "pester" her. She has overheard some of the female students talking to one another about Mr. Smithers, calling him an "old perv" and talking about how he stands very close to them and makes remarks about their anatomy. They also joke about the "cheesy" swimsuit calendar hanging over his desk which students can see. Ms. Jones' visit to the principal was prompted by a complaint from a grade 11 girl that Mr. Smithers has repeatedly asked her to "fly away south" with him.

What should the principal do?

SCENARIO FIVE

Mr. MacDonald is a special education classroom assistant in a self-contained class for developmentally delayed children. Mrs. Young, the Special Education Resource Teacher, returns to the class from the washroom and sees a 19-year-old girl, Ruth, sitting in Mr. MacDonald's lap, the fly of her jeans open, masturbating. Mr. MacDonald is stroking her back and whispering in her ear. Mrs. Young asks, "what's going on?" and Mr. MacDonald says, "You know Ruth, she's always playing with herself, I was trying to calm her down".

What should Mrs. Young do?

SCENARIO SIX

The principal of Juniper Grove Secondary School is walking through the library. As he passes a computer workstation, at which Jane, a 16-year-old student, is sitting, he sees a pornographic image on the screen. He asks Jane to stand up; she protests, but eventually moves away. The principal sits at the keyboard and quickly determines that the image was attached to an email addressed to Jane from Mr. Jackson, a Library Resource Teacher at Birch Glen Secondary School, where Jane used to be enrolled. The email message reads, "Wouldn't you like to try this?"

What should the principal do?

SCENARIO SEVEN

Naomi is a 13-year-old girl in grade 8 at Father Smith Catholic Elementary School. She is "big for her age" and very physically attractive. Her math teacher, Ms. Winters, is a young new teacher who is very popular with the female students. Naomi's father appears in the principal's office with a file of correspondence that he found in Naomi's bedroom. He claims the correspondence has been exchanged between Ms. Winters and Naomi. In the letters apparently written by Ms. Winters, Naomi is described as a little "hottie" and there are extensive lesbian sexual fantasies involving the teacher and the student in many of the notes. The father also claims that Naomi's sister has told him that Naomi is Ms. Winters' "pet" and often receives "counselling" alone in Ms. Winter's office.

What should the principal do?

SCENARIO ONE ANSWERS

Frank is under the age of 16. If Mr. Brown suspects any sexual misconduct then he has a duty to report a reasonable suspicion of child abuse to the appropriate Children's Aid Society. The fact that the report is by a third party, Andy, and not a disclosure by the student, Frank, is not a consideration. It is advisable to accept the report at face value for the purpose of determining whether there is a duty to report or a possible crime that has been committed. By law Mr. Brown must make the report personally, although the principal can facilitate the report. In determining whether there is a reasonable suspicion, the following indicators are relevant:

- the sudden change in academic performance and attendance;
- the fact that the only good grade is from Mr. Peach;
- that the behaviours alleged by Andy constitute elements of "grooming";
- that the amount of time Mr. Peach is spending with one child seems excessive and inappropriate.

The fact that Mr. Peach has a good reputation and is well liked should not cloud the judgment of either Mr. Brown or the principal. It is often a mistake to base decisions on reporting on personal judgments of character. It is essential that all complaints or disclosures be treated in the same manner and that no prejudgments be made before an investigation has been undertaken by the appropriate authority.

Mr. Brown may be reluctant to report on a fellow teacher and may also raise the issue of adverse reports. Section 18(1)(b) of the Regulation under the *Teaching Profession Act* apparently requires Mr. Brown to give a written copy of his report to Mr. Peach within three days. The principal must advise Mr. Brown that the *Teaching Profession Act* has been amended and Mr. Brown is under no such duty in these circumstances. In fact, under the College of Teachers Professional Advisory, Mr. Brown has a duty to report reasonable suspicions. In addition, it could be pointed out that both the *Child and Family Services Act* and the Professional Advisory prohibit any reprisal by Mr. Peach.

At this stage the Superintendent and the Director's office should be notified. In addition, preparations should begin to assemble a response team to help the principal with a communications strategy in the event charges are laid and to provide emotional and psychological support to the victim, other students and the staff.

Despite the duty of the teacher to report, many Children's Aid Societies will not investigate a report of sexual misconduct involving a person who is not a family member, caregiver or babysitter because they do not believe the "child is in need of protection".

In addition to a possible case of abuse, there is a strong risk, on the basis of these facts, that Mr. Peach is committing the crime of sexual exploitation as described in s. 151 of the *Criminal Code*. This crime is committed in a situation where a person (Mr. Peach) is in a position of authority over a victim and the victim is between the ages of 14 and 18 years. The sexual activity can be touching, inviting touch for a sexual purpose or actual sexual intercourse. Therefore, whether or not the Children's Aid Society is involved, the police should be notified.

If the Children's Aid Society and/or the police indicate that there will be an investigation, Mr. Peach should be told immediately that he is being placed on home assignment and that he should contact his union. Unless the investigating agency specifically permits, the principal should say nothing about the nature of the allegations. The principal should determine when the investigators will arrive and what plans they have for an in-school investigation. Instructions should be requested as to when Andy or Frank should be available for questioning, and whether their parents can be notified. Andy should be kept in the office until the investigators arrive unless the investigators will not be arriving that day.

Only if the Children's Aid Society and the police do not undertake an investigation should the principal or board staff make any further inquiries.

The Director's office and the responsible Superintendent should also be consulted. It is advisable to send Mr. Peach home until some facts are determined. This is because, even if no sexual impropriety is taking place, the alleged conduct of Mr. Peach would constitute "grooming" behaviour as defined by the College of Teachers Professional Advisory and may require internal discipline and a report to the College of Teachers of professional misconduct.

In such a case the best practice would be to take a signed statement from Andy as soon as possible. Then Frank should be interviewed and a signed statement taken. Based on this information, staff should consult with an abuse specialist or external consultant or lawyer about any future steps to be taken.

SCENARIO TWO ANSWERS

The principal should advise the mother about the *Teaching Profession Act* prohibition on sexual activity between teachers and students as well as any board policy about teacher conduct. He or she should reassure the mother that the complaint will be acted upon immediately.

Sherry is over the age of 16 and therefore not subject to the *Child and Family Services Act*. Since she is 18, consensual sexual activity between her and a teacher is not a criminal offence. However, at this point it is not clear whether sexual activity is involved and, if it is, whether it began before the age of 18, which would constitute the offence of sexual exploitation. Unfortunately there is not enough detail to determine whether "dating" includes sexual activity.

As long as there is a possibility of a criminal offence being committed it is best not to conduct an investigation even to determine the meaning of "dating" in this context. The police should be called. If the police agree to undertake an investigation then Mr. Grant should be told immediately that he is being placed on home assignment and that he should contact his union. Unless the police specifically permit, the principal should say nothing about the nature of the allegations. If the police investigate and Sherry refuses to cooperate, frustrating any criminal proceeding, or if the police do not investigate, the matter is not over. The principal must then notify the Superintendent and/or the Director's office and begin an internal investigation. At this stage it would be advisable to contact a social worker or other mental health professional to provide support or advice to Sherry.

The definition of "sexual abuse" under the *Teaching Profession Act* includes sexual intercourse or other forms of sexual relations between a teacher and a student *of any age*. Neither the Act nor the Advisory is clear as to whether the prohibition only includes a current student-teacher relationship. This might be a consideration of the disciplinary committee in the event of a complaint. Even if no sexual activity is taking place, the behaviour may still fall within "grooming" behaviour as defined by the College of Teachers Professional Advisory and may require internal discipline and a report of professional misconduct to the College of Teachers.

In the event that the principal undertakes an investigation, the principal should first talk to Sherry.

If Sherry admits to a sexual relationship the principal must advise the student that Mr. Grant has engaged in professional misconduct and the principal has a responsibility to report it, and that Mr. Grant will be subject to possible internal board discipline and a College of Teachers disciplinary hearing. Mr. Grant should be told immediately that he is being placed on home assignment pending a full investigation and that he should contact his union.

If Sherry denies any sexual activity, but admits seeing the teacher socially for meals, movie viewing or dancing, the principal must advise the student that Mr. Grant has engaged in professional misconduct "grooming behaviour" and the principal has a responsibility to report it, and that Mr. Grant will be subject to possible internal board discipline and a College of Teachers disciplinary hearing. Mr. Grant should be told immediately that he is being placed on home assignment pending a full investigation and that he should contact his union.

If Sherry refuses to cooperate, the ability to sustain discipline internally will be compromised. Nevertheless, the matter should be reported to the college even though a College Disciplinary Committee Hearing will be similarly compromised. Sherry should be so advised. In addition, the principal should immediately meet with Mr. Grant. At this meeting the law of sexual exploitation and the rules of the college should be explained. The teacher should be specifically instructed not to have sexual relations with students and should be given a list of other prohibited behaviours. In addition, the teacher should be advised that there is no limitation period on criminal or civil liability for sexual misconduct by a teacher.

SCENARIO THREE ANSWERS

As soon as the principal receives the disclosure, all further questioning should cease. The moment Jeremy points to his groin the principal has a reasonable suspicion of child abuse or sexual misconduct. If the touching has occurred and there was sexual intent on the part of Mr. James, it would constitute "sexual interference" under the *Criminal Code*, s. 151.

The principal must immediately call the appropriate Children's Aid Society. It is likely the society will not view this as a case of a "child in need of protection" and will defer any investigation to the police or will undertake a joint investigation with the police in order to determine whether the teacher should be placed on the Child Abuse Register. Although the society will notify the police, the principal should also immediately call the police to ensure that there is a rapid response.

In discussions with both the society and the police, the principal should ask when the investigators will arrive, whether Jeremy should be interviewed at the school or elsewhere and how and when Jeremy's parents are to be notified. In addition, the police should know when the child is expected to go home. The principal should clarify whether Jeremy is to go back to class or whether he can go home for lunch. If the investigation is not going to occur that day, the principal should also seek direction from the police as to what information can be shared with Jeremy's parents before the interview. Finally, the principal should get specific direction as to what, if anything, is to be said to Mr. James and whether the teacher should be sent home immediately.

If the police are going to undertake an investigation at the school, it is likely that the teacher will be sent home. Unless specific permission is given by the police, nothing should be said to Mr. James, other than that he should contact his union.

The principal should immediately notify the Superintendent and the Director's office so that preparations begin to assemble a response team to help the principal with a communications strategy in the event charges are laid and to provide emotional and psychological support to the victim, other students and the staff.

If the police will be interviewing Jeremy at the school, the principal should try to have himself or herself or a staff member that Jeremy trusts present. Usually the police will oblige. Such a person should be aware that he or she could become a witness in subsequent legal proceedings.

SCENARIO FOUR ANSWERS

Mr. Smithers is apparently engaging in behaviour that would constitute sexual harassment against his colleague Ms. Jones. This would normally be covered by a board policy, which would outline the procedures by which Ms. Jones could complain. Some policies have a "mandatory response" provision, which would require the principal to immediately investigate whether or not Ms. Jones formally complains. If there is no clear board policy the behaviour would constitute harassment within the meaning of the Ontario *Human Rights Code* and should be investigated, since Ms. Jones could file a complaint with the Human Rights Commission. The principal should advise Ms. Jones of any applicable board policy and assure her that he will undertake an investigation immediately.

In addition to harassment of a colleague, Mr. Smithers' actions (the comments, the requests to "fly away" and the objectification of women in the calendar) could constitute sexual harassment of students. While this would probably also be part of any board policy, the definition of sexual abuse in the *Ontario College of Teachers Act, 1996* and the *Teaching Profession Act* includes behaviour or remarks of a sexual nature by the teacher towards the student. In addition, the College of Teachers Practice Advisory lists behaviours such as sexual harassment and making suggestive comments to students as professional misconduct and requires the principal to report this alleged behaviour to the Director or designate (the appropriate Superintendent) an appropriate agency. It should be noted that Ms. Jones has discharged her duty by reporting to the principal.

Ms. Jones may raise the issue of adverse reports (s. 18(1)(b) of the Regulation under the *Teaching Profession Act*) that apparently requires Ms. Jones to give a written copy of her report to Mr. Smithers within three days. The principal must advise Ms. Jones that the *Teaching Profession Act* has been amended and Ms. Jones is under no such duty in these circumstances. In fact, under the College of Teachers Professional Advisory, Ms. Jones has a duty to report reasonable suspicions. In addition, it could be pointed out that and the Professional Advisory prohibit any reprisal by Mr. Smithers.

In either case the principal must immediately undertake an investigation of Mr. Smithers' behaviour. It is a judgment call whether Mr. Smithers will be sent home pending the results of an investigation, but unless there are strong program-related reasons to leave Mr. Smithers in the school it is advisable to send him home.

The behaviour towards students is not apparently a criminal offence unless there is evidence of actual touching or invitation to touching. If a subsequent investigation reveals complaints of such a nature, any ongoing investigation should immediately cease and the appropriate authorities should be contacted, depending on the age of the student.

A further consideration for the principal will be the possibility that spiritual or other counselling needs to be arranged for Mr. Smithers' students.

SCENARIO FIVE ANSWERS

Mrs. Young will have, on these facts, some concerns about the appropriateness of Mr. MacDonald's actions. Since Ruth is 19, there is no Child and Family Services obligation to report. However, s. 253.1 of the *Criminal Code* creates the offence of "sexual exploitation of a person with a disability" by a person in a position of trust with the disabled person. Mr. MacDonald would be a person in a position of trust.

While there is no duty to report a crime, other than child abuse, the Professional Advisory requires that when a member of the college has reasonable grounds to suspect "sexual abuse", there is a responsibility to report the suspicion to appropriate authorities, which include the employer, the police or the college. "Sexual abuse" includes "sexual intercourse or other forms of sexual relations" and "touching of a sexual nature" by a *member*. In this case the employee is a classroom assistant and not a teacher and is therefore not a member of the college. There may, however, be a board policy that requires reporting of suspected abuse by any board employee. If there is no policy, Mrs. Young should still report to the principal.

The principal in turn should report to the Superintendent, and in consultation with the Superintendent inform the police. If the police decide to investigate then Mr. MacDonald should be sent home.

In order to secure a conviction for this offence it must be demonstrated that the disabled person over the age of 18 did not consent in some manner or was incapable of consent. This might be a difficult case to prosecute as a sexual offence. However, as an assault, it would not be open to Mr. MacDonald to claim he was "correcting the child", which is a defence otherwise available to teachers under s. 43 of the *Criminal Code*.

In the event that no criminal charge is laid or conviction registered, the principal should investigate the matter and ensure that Mr. MacDonald is given explicit instructions about dealing more appropriately with disabled students that are acting in this manner. If the principal is satisfied that Mr. MacDonald was acting innocently or naïvely, a letter of reprimand (discipline) may be appropriate in such a case.

SCENARIO SIX ANSWERS

The sending of a suggestive email such as this, accompanied by a pornographic picture, is typical of the activities listed in the Ontario College of Teachers Professional Advisory as "grooming behaviours".

Such behaviours constitute professional misconduct and trigger reporting duties. However, other relevant considerations are:

- the age of the student;
- the fact that Mr. Jackson was a teacher at Jane's former school and may have been Jane's teacher;
- the familiar nature of the email; and
- Jane's apparently complicit behaviour.

It is possible that a relationship of some intimacy may already exist between Mr. Jackson and Jane. Therefore it is possible that Jackson has sexually exploited Jane within the meaning of the *Criminal Code*, s. 153. This includes touching or asking to touch for a sexual purpose. Therefore the principal should take Jane to the office and call the Superintendent and the principal. There should be no questioning of Jane or any further investigation undertaken until the police either decline to investigate or decide not to lay charges.

If the police decide to investigate, the principal should contact the principal of Birch Glen and the appropriate Superintendent. Unless specific permission is given by the police, nothing should be said to Mr. Jackson other than that he should contact his union.

Immediate social or other counselling should be arranged for Jane once the police interviews have been completed.

In the event there is no police investigation or no charges are laid, there must be an internal investigation. Aside from professional misconduct, Mr. Jackson may have also breached board policies on Internet use. Mr. Jackson must receive firm discipline appropriate to the circumstances and must receive specific directions in writing regarding conduct with female students and the board's computer system. This would constitute "conditions imposed on the member's duties for reasons of professional misconduct", which the board must report to the college.

SCENARIO SEVEN ANSWERS

The principal must consider the following factors:

- the age of the child (13);
- the explicit sexual content of the letters; and
- the other alleged behaviours of the teacher.

If the principal has a reasonable suspicion that Naomi was sexually abused there must be an immediate referral to the Catholic Children's Aid Society. In addition, the police should also be called to ensure a prompt response. There is an apparent risk that sexual touching or intercourse has occurred, which constitutes the offence of "sexual interference" under s. 151 of the *Criminal Code*.

Despite the duty to report, many Children's Aid Societies will not investigate a report of sexual misconduct involving a person who is not a family member, caregiver or babysitter because they do not believe the "child is in need of protection". In this situation the Children's Aid Society will be involved to the extent of determining whether Ms. Winters should be placed on the Child Abuse Register.

If the Children's Aid Society and/or the police indicate that there will be an investigation (which is very likely in these circumstances), Ms. Winters should be immediately told that she is being placed on home assignment and that she should contact her union. Unless the investigating agency specifically permits, the principal should say nothing about the nature of the allegations. The principal should determine when the investigators will arrive and what plans they have for an in-school investigation. Instructions should be requested as to when Naomi should be available for questioning, and whether her father should also stay. Clarification as to whether Naomi's father can be present for her interview should also be ascertained. If this is not the intention of the police, the principal should be present or try to have a staff member that Naomi trusts present. Usually the police will oblige. Such a person should be aware that he or she could be a witness in subsequent legal proceedings. Naomi should be kept in the office until the investigators arrive unless the investigators will not be arriving that day.

The principal should immediately notify the Superintendent and the Director's office so that a response team can be assembled to help the principal with a communications strategy in the event charges are laid and to provide emotional, spiritual and psychological support to the victim, other students and the staff.

If there is insufficient evidence of actual sexual relations to support a criminal charge then an internal investigation must be held. If such an investigation confirms Ms. Winters as the author of the letters, this will constitute a serious case of professional misconduct under the *Ontario College of Teachers Act, 1996*, and possibly board policy. There is no doubt that Ms. Winters would be dismissed from employment. While there may be strong feelings on the board regarding lesbianism, the grounds of professional misconduct will be sufficient to sustain the discipline and will not prejudice the board's case at a subsequent arbitration. The dismissal must be reported by the board to the College of Teachers, which would convene a disciplinary hearing.

APPENDIX 1

PROFESSIONAL ADVISORY

Ontario College of Teachers

PROFESSIONAL ADVISORY

*Professional Misconduct Related to
Sexual Abuse and Sexual Misconduct*

Approved by Council September 27, 2002

The Council of the Ontario College of Teachers has approved this Professional Advisory. The intent of this advisory is to help members of the College identify the legal, ethical and professional parameters that govern their behaviour and to prevent sexual abuse of students and sexual misconduct. This advisory is not to be construed as providing an exhaustive list of unacceptable behaviours, but rather is intended to provide examples and guidance.

The authority of the College to investigate complaints against members of the College and to deal with issues of professional misconduct is stated in the *Ontario College of Teachers Act*. The Investigation Committee and the Discipline Committee of the College may consider this advisory when reviewing allegations of professional misconduct. The Discipline Committee will determine, in each case, whether particular behaviour amounts to professional misconduct.

The term "sexual abuse" is defined by the *Student Protection Act*. That definition is set out below. The term "sexual misconduct" is used in this advisory to refer to any behaviour of a sexual nature which may constitute professional misconduct.

Members of the College should consult their employer's policies to ensure that they are familiar with all expectations and obligations that may exist in their particular workplaces and communities related to the contents of this professional advisory.

This advisory applies to all members of the Ontario College of Teachers, including but not limited to teachers, consultants, vice-principals, principals, supervisory officers, directors of education and those working in non-school board positions.

SEXUAL ABUSE AND MISCONDUCT 2002.09.27

Why an advisory on professional misconduct of a sexual nature?

Public and professional sensitivity to and awareness of sexual abuse and sexual misconduct has increased in recent years, not only in teaching but also in other professions, particularly where people are in positions of trust and moral authority. In April 2000, the provincial government released the report of former Justice Sydney L. Robins *Protecting Our Students: A review to identify and prevent sexual misconduct in Ontario schools*. This report made numerous recommendations for the teaching profession, including a recommendation for the College to clarify and elaborate on members' obligations and professional duties.

Student Protection Act

In June 2002, the Ontario legislature passed Bill 101, the *Student Protection Act*. This Act modified existing legislation and placed new obligations on members of the profession. The College has undertaken to issue this professional advisory as the *Student Protection Act* comes into force.

Building on the standards of practice and the ethical standards

Members of the College demonstrate care for and commitment to students that require them to act in students' best interests and report suspicious behaviour or allegations of professional misconduct of a sexual nature to appropriate authorities. Members must take a student's disclosure of abuse or exploitation seriously, even if some allegations prove to be unfounded. Dealing with victim disclosure requires professional judgement. This advisory provides some criteria to assist members in using their judgement.

Members maintain professional relationships with students and recognize the trust that the public places in them. They are aware of the negative impact of boundary violations on students. They respond professionally to victims' allegations by collaborating with other professionals such as police, child and family services, and College investigators.

This advisory helps clarify members' responsibilities to the profession — to govern their own conduct and to understand clearly what conduct by other members does not conform to professional standards, provincial law and the Criminal Code.

Understanding the legal, ethical and professional parameters of behaviour is central to a member's successful career. This advisory helps members recognize when they are at risk of breaching those parameters.

Even though many of the behaviours described here may be unthinkable to most members, the College has the obligation to identify them so that the parameters of professional behaviour are clear.

Ignorance of the law or College regulations is not an acceptable excuse. Engaging in sexual abuse of students or sexual misconduct is a form of professional misconduct and will result in an investigation and disciplinary action by the College. Consequences may include the suspension or revocation of a member's certificate of qualification and membership in the teaching profession.

Sexual abuse

Sexual abuse is a form of professional misconduct. The *Student Protection Act* defines sexual abuse of a student and amends the *Ontario College of Teachers Act* to include this definition:

(i) sexual intercourse or other forms of physical sexual relations between the member and a student,

(ii) touching, of a sexual nature, of the student by the member, or

(iii) behaviour or remarks of a sexual nature by the member towards the student.

Accordingly, members should avoid:

- sexual relations or sexual intercourse with a student
- any form of sexual touching of a student
- any sexual contact including behaviour or remarks of a sexual nature, regardless of the age of the student or any apparent consent by the student.

Professional misconduct

Professional misconduct includes, but is not limited to, sexual abuse of a student by a member. Professional misconduct of a sexual nature could involve a member's own students, other students or children, or even adults, if the Discipline Committee of the College determines that the behaviour amounts to an act defined as professional misconduct.

There may be forms of professional misconduct that do not fall within the definition of sexual abuse but which may be considered sexual misconduct. These behaviours could nonetheless fall within the definition of sexual misconduct and constitute professional misconduct. These behaviours may include sexual harassment and sexual relationships with students or any conduct which may lead to an unprofessional and inappropriate relationship with a student. The latter is often called grooming behaviour.

The College deals with complaints made by members, employers and the public. Written complaints of alleged sexual abuse of a student or sexual misconduct have to be investigated by the College if they fall within the definition of professional misconduct.

Ultimately, the determination of whether particular behaviour constitutes professional misconduct will be made by the Discipline Committee based on the definition of sexual abuse, as well as the other definitions of professional misconduct contained in Regulation 437/97 - The Professional Misconduct Regulation — including:

1(5)   failing to maintain the standards of the profession

1(7)   abusing a student physically, sexually, verbally, psychologically, or emotionally

1(14)   failing to comply with the [Ontario College of Teachers] Act, the regulations or the bylaws

1(15)   failing to comply with the *Education Act* or the regulations made under that Act, if the member is subject to that Act

1(16)   contravening a law if the contravention is relevant to the member's suitability to hold a certificate of qualification and registration

1(17)   contravening a law if the contravention has caused or may cause a student who is under the member's professional supervision to be put at or to remain at risk

1(18)   an act or omission that, having regard to all the circumstances, would reasonably be regarded by members as disgraceful, dishonourable, or unprofessional

1(19)   conduct unbecoming a member.

Sexual harassment

Inappropriate behaviour or remarks of a sexual nature which may constitute professional misconduct include, but are not limited to, conduct that would amount to sexual harassment or sexual discrimination under the *Ontario Human Rights Code*. These need not be overtly sexual but may nonetheless demean or cause personal embarrassment to a student, based upon a student's gender, race or sexual orientation.

Members should avoid even a single event that may constitute sexual harassment, including but not limited to:

*   objectionable conduct or comments incompatible with the role of a member, regardless of whether the affected students appear to be offended by the conduct or comments

*   sexual harassment of non-students or of co-workers

*   reprisals or threatened reprisals for rejecting sexual advances.

Sexual relationships

Regardless of the age of a student and whether there are any criminal law considerations, a member engaging in or attempting to establish a sexual relationship with a student is unacceptable.

Professional misconduct includes but is not limited to any sexual relationship with

(i)   a student, regardless of the student's age

(ii)   a former student under the age of 18

(iii) a former student who suffers from a disability affecting his or her ability to consent to a relationship.

Responsibility for ensuring that a member-student relationship is professional and appropriate rests with the member and not with the student. This remains the case even when it is the student who attempts to initiate an inappropriate relationship. Any conduct directed to establishing such a relationship may constitute professional misconduct.

It is not necessary that the student be in the member's own class. A student may be a student who is in the school or school system where the member is employed, or in relation to whom a member is otherwise considered to hold a position of trust and responsibility.

Members should not engage in activity directed to establishing a sexual relationship. This includes, but is not limited to:

*   sending intimate letters to students

*   making telephone calls of a personal nature to students

*   engaging in sexualized dialogue through the Internet with students

*   making suggestive comments to students

*   dating students.

Such conduct is inappropriate even if the conduct does not result in the establishment of a relationship.

Engaging in a sexual relationship with a person who is under the age of 18, or in relation to whom the member holds a position of trust or authority, may also constitute professional misconduct, regardless of whether the person is a student or former student.

Knowing the limits - the responsibility of each member

There are situations, activities and actions where members should be cautious. Even though an action or event may seem to be in a student's best interest, members need to consider thoroughly the implications and appearance of the action or event beforehand.

Members have an additional responsibility to avoid activities that may reasonably raise concerns as to their propriety. Keeping this in mind can help members avoid complaints to either their employer or to the College, and can help protect students by detecting and preventing sexual abuse or sexual misconduct by others.

Using good judgement

Members understand that students depend on teachers to interpret what is right and wrong. This judgement can be difficult when certain acts seem innocent, but may be considered later as a prelude to sexual abuse or sexual misconduct.

In the interests of student safety, when members use their professional judgement about their own or others' activities they should be mindful of these and other considerations:

- whether the activities are known to, or approved by, supervisors and/or parents or legal guardians
- whether the student is physically isolated from other observers, for example, behind closed doors
- whether the circumstances are urgent or an emergency (providing transportation in a blizzard, for example)
- whether the educational environment might be detrimentally affected by the activities
- whether the activity would reasonably be regarded as conduct intended to promote or facilitate an inappropriate personal relationship with a student
- the extent to which the activities might reasonably be regarded as posing a risk to the personal integrity or security of a student, or as contributing to any student's level of discomfort
- whether the conduct would reasonably be regarded as being in the best interests of the student.

Members should avoid:

- inviting individual students to their homes
- seeing students in private and isolated situations
- exchanging personal notes, comments or e-mails
- becoming personally involved in students' affairs
- giving personal gifts to students
- sharing personal information about themselves
- making physical contact of a sexual nature.

When meeting with students, members should, whenever possible, ensure that:

- classroom and office doors are left open
- a third party is present or aware of the meeting
- the student is not physically isolated from other observers, for example, behind closed doors
- they are not alone with an individual student except in urgent or emergency circumstances.

Reporting suspected or alleged inappropriate sexual behaviour

If a member of the College has reasonable grounds to suspect sexual abuse of students or sexual misconduct, a member has a responsibility to report suspected or alleged cases to appropriate authorities. This includes one or more or all of the following: child and family services, police, the employer and the Ontario College of Teachers.

Adverse report and anti-reprisal provisions

The *Student Protection Act* also amended the *Teaching Profession Act*. A member who makes an adverse report about another member respecting suspected sexual abuse of a student by that other member need not provide him or her with a copy of the report or with any information about the report.

Members of the College may not engage in, or threaten to engage in, reprisals against anyone who discloses, reports or otherwise provides information with respect to alleged or suspected professional misconduct of a sexual nature.

Employer responsibilities

Similarly, employers were previously required to report to the College members who had been convicted of an offence under the Criminal Code involving sexual conduct and minors. The *Student Protection Act* stipulates that employers must now report to the College at the time a member is charged with a sexual offence.

Responsibility of the Ontario College of Teachers

The Investigation Committee of the College is responsible for investigating complaints relating to a member's alleged professional misconduct, incompetence or incapacity. Allegations of misconduct may result in charges under Regulation 437/97 made under the *Ontario College of Teachers Act*. If the Investigation Committee refers a case to the Discipline Committee, a panel of the Discipline Committee will conduct a hearing to determine whether the alleged conduct constitutes professional misconduct.

If members of the College or the public have questions about the content of this advisory, please contact the College at 416-961-8800 or toll free in Ontario at 1-888-534-2222, or e-mail info@oct.on.ca.

Legislative references

Ontario College of Teachers Act
Education Act
Regulation 437/97, Professional Misconduct made under the Ontario College of Teachers Act
Teaching Profession Act
Child and Family Services Act
Ontario Human Rights Code

Ontario College of Teachers
121 Bloor Street East, 6th Floor Toronto ON M4W 3M5
www.oct.on.ca

APPENDIX 2

CRIMINAL CODE, R.S.C. 1985, c. C-46

Amendments to reproduced sections: R.S. 1985, c. 19 (3rd Supp.), ss. 1, 7, 10; 1992, c. 38, s. 1; 1993, c. 46, s. 2; 1994, c. 44, s. 19; 1995, c. 39, s. 145; 1998, c. 9, s. 2; 2002, c. 13, s. 5.

150.1 (1) — **Consent no defence**. Where an accused is charged with an offence under section 151 or 152 or subsection 153(1), 160(3) or 173(2) or is charged with an offence under section 271, 272 or 273 in respect of a complainant under the age of fourteen years, it is not a defence that the complainant consented to the activity that forms the subject-matter of the charge.

(2) **Exception** — Notwithstanding subsection (1), where an accused is charged with an offence under section 151 or 152, subsection 173(2) or section 271 in respect of a complainant who is twelve years of age or more but under the age of fourteen years, it is not a defence that the complainant consented to the activity that forms the subject-matter of the charge unless the accused

(a) is twelve years of age or more but under the age of sixteen years;

(b) is less than two years older than the complainant; and

(c) is neither in a position of trust or authority towards the complainant nor is a person with whom the complainant is in a relationship of dependency.

(3) **Exemption for accused aged twelve or thirteen** — No person aged twelve or thirteen years shall be tried for an offence under section 151 or 152 or subsection 173(2) unless the person is in a position of trust or authority towards the complainant or is a person with whom the complainant is in a relationship of dependency.

(4) **Mistake of age** — It is not a defence to a charge under section 151 or 152, subsection 160(3) or 173(2), or section 271, 272 or 273 that the accused believed that the complainant was fourteen years of age or more

at the time the offence is alleged to have been committed unless the accused took all reasonable steps to ascertain the age of the complainant.

(5) **Idem** — It is not a defence to a charge under section 153, 159, 170, 171 or 172 or subsection 212(2) or (4) that the accused believed that the complainant was eighteen years of age or more at the time the offence is alleged to have been committed unless the accused took all reasonable steps to ascertain the age of the complainant.

[R.S., 1985, c. 19 (3rd Supp.), s. 1 (in force January 1, 1988).]

151. Sexual interference — Every person who, for a sexual purpose, touches, directly or indirectly, with a part of the body or with an object, any part of the body of a person under the age of fourteen years is guilty of an indictable offence and liable to imprisonment for a term not exceeding ten years or is guilty of an offence punishable on summary conviction.

[R.S., 1985, c. 19 (3rd Supp.), s. 1 (in force January 1, 1988).]

152. Invitation to sexual touching — Every person who, for a sexual purpose, invites, counsels or incites a person under the age of fourteen years to touch, directly or indirectly, with a part of the body or with an object, the body of any person, including the body of the person who so invites, counsels or incites and the body of the person under the age of fourteen years, is guilty of an indictable offence and liable to imprisonment for a term not exceeding ten years or is guilty of an offence punishable on summary conviction.

[R.S., 1985, c. 19 (3rd Supp.), s. 1 (in force January 1, 1988).]

153. (1) **Sexual exploitation** — Every person who is in a position of trust or authority towards a young person or is a person with whom the young person is in a relationship of dependency and who

(a) for a sexual purpose, touches, directly or indirectly, with a part of the body or with an object, any part of the body of the young person, or

(b) for a sexual purpose, invites, counsels or incites a young person to touch, directly or indirectly, with a part of the body or with an object, the body of any person, including the body of the person who so invites, counsels or incites and the body of the young person,

is guilty of an indictable offence and liable to imprisonment for a term not exceeding five years or is guilty of an offence punishable on summary conviction.

(2) **Definition of "young person"** — In this section, "young person" means a person fourteen years of age or more but under the age of eighteen years.

[R.S., 1985, c. 19 (3rd Supp.), s. 1 (in force January 1, 1988).]

153.1 (1) **Sexual exploitation of person with disability** — Every person who is in a position of trust or authority towards a person with a mental or physical disability or who is a person with whom a person with a mental or physical disability is in a relationship of dependency and who, for a sexual purpose, counsels or incites that person to touch, without that person's consent, his or her own body, the body of the person who so counsels or incites, or the body of any other person, directly or indirectly, with a part of the body or with an object, is guilty of

  (a) an indictable offence and liable to imprisonment for a term not exceeding five years; or
  (b) an offence punishable on summary conviction and liable to imprisonment for a term not exceeding eighteen months.

(2) **Definition of "consent"** — Subject to subsection (3), "consent" means, for the purposes of this section, the voluntary agreement of the complainant to engage in the sexual activity in question.

(3) **When no consent obtained** — No consent is obtained, for the purposes of this section, if

  (a) the agreement is expressed by the words or conduct of a person other than the complainant;
  (b) the complainant is incapable of consenting to the activity;
  (c) the accused counsels or incites the complainant to engage in the activity by abusing a position of trust, power or authority;
  (d) the complainant expresses, by words or conduct, a lack of agreement to engage in the activity; or
  (e) the complainant, having consented to engage in sexual activity, expresses, by words or conduct, a lack of agreement to continue to engage in the activity.

(4) **Subsection (3) not limiting** — Nothing in subsection (3) shall be construed as limiting the circumstances in which no consent is obtained.

(5) **When belief in consent not a defence** — It is not a defence to a charge under this section that the accused believed that the complainant consented to the activity that forms the subject-matter of the charge if

  (a) the accused's belief arose from the accused's
    (i) self-induced intoxication, or
    (ii) recklessness or wilful blindness; or

(b) the accused did not take reasonable steps, in the circumstances known to the accused at the time, to ascertain that the complainant was consenting.

(6) **Accused's belief as to consent** — If an accused alleges that he or she believed that the complainant consented to the conduct that is the subject-matter of the charge, a judge, if satisfied that there is sufficient evidence and that, if believed by the jury, the evidence would constitute a defence, shall instruct the jury, when reviewing all the evidence relating to the determination of the honesty of the accused's belief, to consider the presence or absence of reasonable grounds for that belief.

[1998, c. 9, s. 2 (in force June 30, 1998)]

163.1 (1) **Definition of "child pornography"** — In this section, "child pornography" means

(a) a photographic, film, video or other visual representation, whether or not it was made by electronic or mechanical means,
  (i) that shows a person who is or is depicted as being under the age of eighteen years and is engaged in or is depicted as engaged in explicit sexual activity, or
  (ii) the dominant characteristic of which is the depiction, for a sexual purpose, of a sexual organ or the anal region of a person under the age of eighteen years; or
(b) any written material or visual representation that advocates or counsels sexual activity with a person under the age of eighteen years that would be an offence under this Act.

(2) **Making child pornography** — Every person who makes, prints, publishes or possesses for the purpose of publication any child pornography is guilty of

(a) an indictable offence and liable to imprisonment for a term not exceeding ten years; or
(b) an offence punishable on summary conviction.

(3) **Distribution, etc. of child pornography** — Every person who transmits, makes available, distributes, sells, imports, exports or possesses for the purpose of transmission, making available, distribution, sale or exportation any child pornography is guilty of

(a) an indictable offence and liable to imprisonment for a term not exceeding ten years; or
(b) an offence punishable on summary conviction.

(4) **Possession of child pornography** — Every person who possesses any child pornography is guilty of

(a) an indictable offence and liable to imprisonment for a term not exceeding five years; or

(b) an offence punishable on summary conviction.

(4.1) **Accessing child pornography** — Every person who accesses any child pornography is guilty of

(a) an indictable offence and liable to imprisonment for a term not exceeding five years; or

(b) an offence punishable on summary conviction.

(4.2) **Interpretation** — For the purposes of subsection (4.1), a person accesses child pornography who knowingly causes child pornography to be viewed by, or transmitted to, himself or herself.

(5) **Defence** — It is not a defence to a charge under subsection (2) in respect of a visual representation that the accused believed that a person shown in the representation that is alleged to constitute child pornography was or was depicted as being eighteen years of age or more unless the accused took all reasonable steps to ascertain the age of that person and took all reasonable steps to ensure that, where the person was eighteen years of age or more, the representation did not depict that person as being under the age of eighteen years.

(6) **Defences** — Where the accused is charged with an offence under subsection (2), (3), (4) or (4.1), the court shall find the accused not guilty if the representation or written material that is alleged to constitute child pornography has artistic merit or an educational, scientific or medical purpose.

(7) **Other provisions to apply** — Subsections 163(3) to (5) apply, with such modifications as the circumstances require, with respect to an offence under subsection (2), (3), (4) or (4.1).

[1993, c. 46, s. 2 (in force August 1, 1993); 2002, c. 13, s. 5 (in force July 23, 2002).]

173. (1) **Indecent acts** — Every one who wilfully does an indecent act

(a) in a public place in the presence of one or more persons, or

(b) in any place, with intent thereby to insult or offend any person, is guilty of an offence punishable on summary conviction.

(2) **Exposure** — Every person who, in any place, for a sexual purpose, exposes his or her genital organs to a person who is under the age of fourteen years is guilty of an offence punishable on summary conviction.

[R.S., 1985, c. 19 (3rd Supp.), s. 7 (in force January 1, 1988).]

265. (1) **Assault** — A person commits an assault when

(a) without the consent of another person, he applies force intentionally to that other person, directly or indirectly;

(b) he attempts or threatens, by an act or a gesture, to apply force to another person, if he has, or causes that other person to believe on reasonable grounds that he has, present ability to effect his purpose; or

(c) while openly wearing or carrying a weapon or an imitation thereof, he accosts or impedes another person or begs.

(2) **Application** — This section applies to all forms of assault, including sexual assault, sexual assault with a weapon, threats to a third party or causing bodily harm and aggravated sexual assault.

(3) **Consent** — For the purposes of this section, no consent is obtained where the complainant submits or does not resist by reason of

(a) the application of force to the complainant or to a person other than the complainant;

(b) threats or fear of the application of force to the complainant or to a person other than the complainant;

(c) fraud; or

(d) the exercise of authority.

(4) **Accused's belief as to consent** — Where an accused alleges that he believed that the complainant consented to the conduct that is the subject-matter of the charge, a judge, if satisfied that there is sufficient evidence and that, if believed by the jury, the evidence would constitute a defence, shall instruct the jury, when reviewing all the evidence relating to the determination of the honesty of the accused's belief, to consider the presence or absence of reasonable grounds for that belief.

271. (1) **Sexual assault** — Every one who commits a sexual assault is guilty of

(a) an indictable offence and is liable to imprisonment for a term not exceeding ten years; or

(b) an offence punishable on summary conviction and liable to imprisonment for a term not exceeding eighteen months.

(2) [Repealed, R.S., 1985, c. 19 (3rd Supp.), s. 10 (in force January 1, 1988)]

[R.S., 1985, c. 19 (3rd Supp.), s. 10 (in force January 1, 1988); 1994, c. 44, s. 19 (in force February 15, 1995).]

272. (1) **Sexual assault with a weapon, threats to a third party or causing bodily harm** — Every person commits an offence who, in committing a sexual assault,

- (a) carries, uses or threatens to use a weapon or an imitation of a weapon;
- (b) threatens to cause bodily harm to a person other than the complainant;
- (c) causes bodily harm to the complainant; or
- (d) is a party to the offence with any other person.

(2) **Punishment** — Every person who commits an offence under subsection (1) is guilty of an indictable offence and liable

- (a) where a firearm is used in the commission of the offence, to imprisonment for a term not exceeding fourteen years and to a minimum punishment of imprisonment for a term of four years; and
- (b) in any other case, to imprisonment for a term not exceeding fourteen years.

[1995, c. 39, s. 145 (in force January 1, 1996).]

273.1 (1) **Meaning of "consent"** — Subject to subsection (2) and subsection 265(3), "consent" means, for the purposes of sections 271, 272 and 273, the voluntary agreement of the complainant to engage in the sexual activity in question.

(2) **Where no consent obtained** — No consent is obtained, for the purposes of sections 271, 272 and 273, where

- (a) the agreement is expressed by the words or conduct of a person other than the complainant;
- (b) the complainant is incapable of consenting to the activity;
- (c) the accused induces the complainant to engage in the activity by abusing a position of trust, power or authority;
- (d) the complainant expresses, by words or conduct, a lack of agreement to engage in the activity; or
- (e) the complainant, having consented to engage in sexual activity, expresses, by words or conduct, a lack of agreement to continue to engage in the activity.

(3) **Subsection (2) not limiting** — Nothing in subsection (2) shall be construed as limiting the circumstances in which no consent is obtained.

[1992, c. 38, s. 1 (in force August 15, 1992).]

273.2 Where belief in consent not a defence — It is not a defence to a charge under section 271, 272 or 273 that the accused believed that the complainant consented to the activity that forms the subject-matter of the charge, where

    (a) the accused's belief arose from the accused's
        (i)   self-induced intoxication, or
        (ii) recklessness or wilful blindness; or
    (b) the accused did not take reasonable steps, in the circumstances known to the accused at the time, to ascertain that the complainant was consenting.

[1992, c. 38, s. 1 (in force August 15, 1992).]

APPENDIX 3

CHILD AND FAMILY SERVICES ACT, R.S.O. 1990, C. C.11

Amendments to reproduced sections: S.O. 1993, c. 27, Sched.; S.O. 1994, c. 27, s. 43(2); S.O. 1999, c. 2, ss. 1, 9, 15, 22, 24, 29, 30.

1. (1) **Paramount purpose** — The paramount purpose of this Act is to promote the best interests, protection and well being of children.

(2) **Other purposes** — The additional purposes of this Act, so long as they are consistent with the best interests, protection and well being of children, are:

1. To recognize that while parents may need help in caring for their children, that help should give support to the autonomy and integrity of the family unit and, wherever possible, be provided on the basis of mutual consent.
2. To recognize that the least disruptive course of action that is available and is appropriate in a particular case to help a child should be considered.
3. To recognize that children's services should be provided in a manner that,
   i. respects children's needs for continuity of care and for stable family relationships, and
   ii. takes into account physical and mental developmental differences among children.
4. To recognize that, wherever possible, services to children and their families should be provided in a manner that respects cultural, religious and regional differences.
5. To recognize that Indian and native people should be entitled to provide, wherever possible, their own child and family services, and that all services to Indian and native children and families should be provided in a manner that recognizes their culture, heritage and traditions and the concept of the extended family.

[S.O. 1999, c. 2, s. 1.]

37. (1) **Definitions** — In this Part,

"child" does not include a child as defined in subsection 3 (1) who is actually or apparently sixteen years of age or older, unless the child is the subject of an order under this Part;

"child protection worker" means a Director, a local director or a person authorized by a Director or local director for the purposes of section 40 (commencing child protection proceedings);

"extended family", when used in reference to a child, means the persons to whom the child is related by blood, marriage or adoption;

"parent", when used in reference to a child, means each of,

    (a) the child's mother,

    (b) an individual described in one of paragraphs 1 to 6 of subsection 8 (1) of the *Children's Law Reform Act*, unless it is proved on a balance of probabilities that he is not the child's natural father,

    (c) the individual having lawful custody of the child,

    (d) an individual who, during the twelve months before intervention under this Part, has demonstrated a settled intention to treat the child as a child of his or her family, or has acknowledged parentage of the child and provided for the child's support,

    (e) an individual who, under a written agreement or a court order, is required to provide for the child, has custody of the child or has a right of access to the child, and

    (f) an individual who has acknowledged parentage of the child in writing under section 12 of the *Children's Law Reform Act*,

but does not include a foster parent;

"place of safety" means a foster home, a hospital, and a place or one of a class of places designated as such by a Director under subsection 17 (2) of Part I (Flexible Services), but does not include,

    (a) a place of secure custody as defined in Part IV (Young Offenders), or

    (b) a place of secure temporary detention as defined in Part IV.

(2) **Child in need of protection** — A child is in need of protection where,

    (a) the child has suffered physical harm, inflicted by the person having charge of the child or caused by or resulting from that person's,

        (i) failure to adequately care for, provide for, supervise or protect the child, or

        (ii) pattern of neglect in caring for, providing for, supervising or protecting the child;

(b) there is a risk that the child is likely to suffer physical harm inflicted by the person having charge of the child or caused by or resulting from that person's,

(i) failure to adequately care for, provide for, supervise or protect the child, or

(ii) pattern of neglect in caring for, providing for, supervising or protecting the child;

(c) the child has been sexually molested or sexually exploited, by the person having charge of the child or by another person where the person having charge of the child knows or should know of the possibility of sexual molestation or sexual exploitation and fails to protect the child;

(d) there is a risk that the child is likely to be sexually molested or sexually exploited as described in clause (c);

(e) the child requires medical treatment to cure, prevent or alleviate physical harm or suffering and the child's parent or the person having charge of the child does not provide, or refuses or is unavailable or unable to consent to, the treatment;

(f) the child has suffered emotional harm, demonstrated by serious,

(i) anxiety,

(ii) depression,

(iii) withdrawal,

(iv) self-destructive or aggressive behaviour, or

(v) delayed development,

and there are reasonable grounds to believe that the emotional harm suffered by the child results from the actions, failure to act or pattern of neglect on the part of the child's parent or the person having charge of the child;

(f.1) the child has suffered emotional harm of the kind described in subclause (f) (i), (ii), (iii), (iv) or (v) and the child's parent or the person having charge of the child does not provide, or refuses or is unavailable or unable to consent to, services or treatment to remedy or alleviate the harm;

(g) there is a risk that the child is likely to suffer emotional harm of the kind described in subclause (f) (i), (ii), (iii), (iv) or (v) resulting from the actions, failure to act or pattern of neglect on the part of the child's parent or the person having charge of the child;

(g.1) there is a risk that the child is likely to suffer emotional harm of the kind described in subclause (f) (i), (ii), (iii), (iv) or (v) and that the child's parent or the person having charge of the child does not provide, or refuses or is unavailable or unable to consent to, services or treatment to prevent the harm;

(h) the child suffers from a mental, emotional or developmental condition that, if not remedied, could seriously impair the child's development and the child's parent or the person having charge of the child does not provide, or refuses or is unavailable or unable to consent to, treatment to remedy or alleviate the condition;

(i) the child has been abandoned, the child's parent has died or is unavailable to exercise his or her custodial rights over the child and has not made adequate provision for the child's care and custody, or the child is in a residential placement and the parent refuses or is unable or unwilling to resume the child's care and custody;

(j) the child is less than twelve years old and has killed or seriously injured another person or caused serious damage to another person's property, services or treatment are necessary to prevent a recurrence and the child's parent or the person having charge of the child does not provide, or refuses or is unavailable or unable to consent to, those services or treatment;

(k) the child is less than twelve years old and has on more than one occasion injured another person or caused loss or damage to another person's property, with the encouragement of the person having charge of the child or because of that person's failure or inability to supervise the child adequately; or

(l) the child's parent is unable to care for the child and the child is brought before the court with the parent's consent and, where the child is twelve years of age or older, with the child's consent, to be dealt with under this Part.

[S.O. 1999, c. 2, s. 9.]

57. (1) **Order where child in need of protection** — Where the court finds that a child is in need of protection and is satisfied that intervention through a court order is necessary to protect the child in the future, the court shall make one of the following orders, in the child's best interests:

1. **Supervision order** — That the child be placed with or returned to a parent or another person, subject to the supervision of the society, for a specified period of at least three and not more than twelve months.

2. **Society wardship** — That the child be made a ward of the society and be placed in its care and custody for a specified period not exceeding twelve months.

3. **Crown wardship** — That the child be made a ward of the Crown, until the wardship is terminated under section 65 or expires under subsection 71 (1), and be placed in the care of the society.

4. **Consecutive orders of society wardship and supervision** — That the child be made a ward of the society under paragraph 2 for a specified period and then be returned to a parent or another person under paragraph 1, for a period or periods not exceeding an aggregate of twelve months.

(2) **Court to inquire** — In determining which order to make under subsection (1), the court shall ask the parties what efforts the society or another agency or person made to assist the child before intervention under this Part.

(3) **Less disruptive alternatives preferred** — The court shall not make an order removing the child from the care of the person who had charge of him or her immediately before intervention under this Part unless the court is satisfied that alternatives that are less disruptive to the child, including non-residential services and the assistance referred to in subsection (2), would be inadequate to protect the child.

(4) **Community placement to be considered** — Where the court decides that it is necessary to remove the child from the care of the person who had charge of him or her immediately before intervention under this Part, the court shall, before making an order for society or Crown wardship under paragraph 2 or 3 of subsection (1), consider whether it is possible to place the child with a relative, neighbour or other member of the child's community or extended family under paragraph 1 of subsection (1) with the consent of the relative or other person.

(5) **Idem: where child an Indian or a native person** — Where the child referred to in subsection (4) is an Indian or a native person, unless there is a substantial reason for placing the child elsewhere, the court shall place the child with,

(a) a member of the child's extended family;
(b) a member of the child's band or native community; or
(c) another Indian or native family.

(6) REPEALED: S.O. 1999, c. 2, s. 15(2), effective March 31, 2000 (O. Gaz. 2000 p. 451).

(7) **Idem** — When the court has dispensed with notice to a person under subsection 39 (7), the court shall not make an order for Crown wardship under paragraph 3 of subsection (1), or an order for society wardship under paragraph 2 of subsection (1) for a period exceeding thirty days, until a further hearing under subsection 47 (1) has been held upon notice to that person.

(8) **Terms and conditions of supervision order** — Where the court makes a supervision order under paragraph 1 of subsection (1), the court may impose reasonable terms and conditions relating to the child's care and supervision on,

- (a) the person with whom the child is placed or to whom the child is returned;
- (b) the supervising society;
- (c) the child; and
- (d) any other person who participated in the hearing.

(9) **Where no court order necessary** — Where the court finds that a child is in need of protection but is not satisfied that a court order is necessary to protect the child in the future, the court shall order that the child remain with or be returned to the person who had charge of the child immediately before intervention under this Part.

[S.O. 1999, c. 2, s. 15.]

72. (1) **Duty to report child in need of protection** — Despite the provisions of any other Act, if a person, including a person who performs professional or official duties with respect to children, has reasonable grounds to suspect one of the following, the person shall forthwith report the suspicion and the information on which it is based to a society:

1. The child has suffered physical harm, inflicted by the person having charge of the child or caused by or resulting from that person's,
   i.   failure to adequately care for, provide for, supervise or protect the child, or
   ii. pattern of neglect in caring for, providing for, supervising or protecting the child.
2. There is a risk that the child is likely to suffer physical harm inflicted by the person having charge of the child or caused by or resulting from that person's,
   i.   failure to adequately care for, provide for, supervise or protect the child, or
   ii. pattern of neglect in caring for, providing for, supervising or protecting the child.
3. The child has been sexually molested or sexually exploited, by the person having charge of the child or by another person where the person having charge of the child knows or should know of the possibility of sexual molestation or sexual exploitation and fails to protect the child.
4. There is a risk that the child is likely to be sexually molested or sexually exploited as described in paragraph 3.

5. The child requires medical treatment to cure, prevent or alleviate physical harm or suffering and the child's parent or the person having charge of the child does not provide, or refuses or is unavailable or unable to consent to, the treatment.

6. The child has suffered emotional harm, demonstrated by serious,
   i.   anxiety,
   ii.   depression,
   iii. withdrawal,
   iv.   self-destructive or aggressive behaviour, or
   v.   delayed development,
   and there are reasonable grounds to believe that the emotional harm suffered by the child results from the actions, failure to act or pattern of neglect on the part of the child's parent or the person having charge of the child.

7. The child has suffered emotional harm of the kind described in subparagraph i, ii, iii, iv or v of paragraph 6 and the child's parent or the person having charge of the child does not provide, or refuses or is unavailable or unable to consent to, services or treatment to remedy or alleviate the harm.

8. There is a risk that the child is likely to suffer emotional harm of the kind described in subparagraph i, ii, iii, iv or v of paragraph 6 resulting from the actions, failure to act or pattern of neglect on the part of the child's parent or the person having charge of the child.

9. There is a risk that the child is likely to suffer emotional harm of the kind described in subparagraph i, ii, iii, iv or v of paragraph 6 and that the child's parent or the person having charge of the child does not provide, or refuses or is unavailable or unable to consent to, services or treatment to prevent the harm.

10. The child suffers from a mental, emotional or developmental condition that, if not remedied, could seriously impair the child's development and the child's parent or the person having charge of the child does not provide, or refuses or is unavailable or unable to consent to, treatment to remedy or alleviate the condition.

11. The child has been abandoned, the child's parent has died or is unavailable to exercise his or her custodial rights over the child and has not made adequate provision for the child's care and custody, or the child is in a residential placement and the parent refuses or is unable or unwilling to resume the child's care and custody.

12. The child is less than 12 years old and has killed or seriously injured another person or caused serious damage to another

person's property, services or treatment are necessary to prevent a recurrence and the child's parent or the person having charge of the child does not provide, or refuses or is unavailable or unable to consent to, those services or treatment.

13. The child is less than 12 years old and has on more than one occasion injured another person or caused loss or damage to another person's property, with the encouragement of the person having charge of the child or because of that person's failure or inability to supervise the child adequately.

(2) **Ongoing duty to report** — A person who has additional reasonable grounds to suspect one of the matters set out in subsection (1) shall make a further report under subsection (1) even if he or she has made previous reports with respect to the same child.

(3) **Person must report directly** — A person who has a duty to report a matter under subsection (1) or (2) shall make the report directly to the society and shall not rely on any other person to report on his or her behalf.

(4) **Offence** — A person referred to in subsection (5) is guilty of an offence if,

    (a) he or she contravenes subsection (1) or (2) by not reporting a suspicion; and

    (b) the information on which it was based was obtained in the course of his or her professional or official duties.

(5) **Same** — Subsection (4) applies to every person who performs professional or official duties with respect to children including,

    (a) a health care professional, including a physician, nurse, dentist, pharmacist and psychologist;

    (b) a teacher, school principal, social worker, family counsellor, priest, rabbi, member of the clergy, operator or employee of a day nursery and youth and recreation worker;

    (c) a peace officer and a coroner;

    (d) a solicitor; and

    (e) a service provider and an employee of a service provider.

(6) **Same** — In clause (5) (b),

"youth and recreation worker" does not include a volunteer.

(6.1) **Same** — A director, officer or employee of a corporation who authorizes, permits or concurs in a contravention of an offence under subsection (4) by an employee of the corporation is guilty of an offence.

(6.2) **Same** — A person convicted of an offence under subsection (4) or (6.1) is liable to a fine of not more than $1,000.

(7) **Section overrides privilege** — This section applies although the information reported may be confidential or privileged, and no action for making the report shall be instituted against a person who acts in accordance with this section unless the person acts maliciously or without reasonable grounds for the suspicion.

(8) **Exception: solicitor client privilege** — Nothing in this section abrogates any privilege that may exist between a solicitor and his or her client.

[1993, c. 27, Sch.; 1999, c. 2, s. 22.]

74. (1) **Definition** — In this section and sections 74.1 and 74.2,

"record" means recorded information, regardless of physical form or characteristics.

(2) **Motion or application, production of record** — A Director or a society may at any time make a motion or an application for an order under subsection (3) or (3.1) for the production of a record or part of a record.

(3) **Order** — Where the court is satisfied that a record or part of a record that is the subject of a motion referred to in subsection (2) contains information that may be relevant to a proceeding under this Part and that the person in possession or control of the record has refused to permit a Director or the society to inspect it, the court may order that the person in possession or control of the record produce it or a specified part of it for inspection and copying by the Director, by the society or by the court.

(3.1) **Same** — Where the court is satisfied that a record or part of a record that is the subject of an application referred to in subsection (2) may be relevant to assessing compliance with one of the following and that the person in possession or control of the record has refused to permit a Director or the society to inspect it, the court may order that the person in possession or control of the record produce it or a specified part of it for inspection and copying by the Director, by the society or by the court:

1. An order under clause 51 (2) (b) or (c) that is subject to supervision.
2. An order under clause 51 (2) (c) or (d) with respect to access.
3. A supervision order under section 57.
4. An access order under section 58.

5. An order under section 65 with respect to access or supervision.

6. A restraining order under section 80.

(4) **Court may examine record** — In considering whether to make an order under subsection (3) or (3.1), the court may examine the record.

(5) **Information confidential** — No person who obtains information by means of an order made under subsection (3) or (3.1) shall disclose the information except,

(a) as specified in the order; and

(b) in testimony in a proceeding under this Part.

(6) **Application: solicitor client privilege excepted** — Subject to subsection (7), this section applies despite any other Act, but nothing in this section abrogates any privilege that may exist between a solicitor and his or her client.

(7) **Matters to be considered by court** — Where a motion or an application under subsection (2) concerns a record that is a clinical record within the meaning of section 35 of the *Mental Health Act*, subsection 35 (6) (attending physician's statement, hearing) of that Act applies and the court shall give equal consideration to,

(a) the matters to be considered under subsection 35 (7) of that Act; and

(b) the need to protect the child.

(8) **Same** — Where a motion or an application under subsection (2) concerns a record that is a record of a mental disorder within the meaning of section 183, that section applies and the court shall give equal consideration to,

(a) the matters to be considered under subsection 183 (6); and

(b) the need to protect the child.

[S.O. 1999, c. 2, s. 24.]

75. (1) **Definitions** — In this section and in section 76,

"Director" means the person appointed under subsection (2);

"register" means the register maintained under subsection (5);

"registered person" means a person identified in the register, but does not include,

(a) a person who reports to a society under subsection 72 (2) or (3) and is not the subject of the report, or

(b) the child who is the subject of a report.

(2) **Director** — The Minister may appoint an employee of the Ministry as Director for the purposes of this section.

(3) **Duty of society** — A society that receives a report under section 72 that a child, including a child in the society's care, is or may be suffering or may have suffered abuse shall forthwith verify the reported information, or ensure that the information is verified by another society, in the manner determined by the Director, and if the information is verified, the society that verified it shall forthwith report it to the Director in the prescribed form.

(4) **Protection from liability** — No action or other proceeding for damages shall be instituted against an officer or employee of a society, acting in good faith, for an act done in the execution or intended execution of the duty imposed on the society by subsection (3) or for an alleged neglect or default of that duty.

(5) **Child abuse register** — The Director shall maintain a register in the manner prescribed by the regulations for the purpose of recording information reported to the Director under subsection (3), but the register shall not contain information that has the effect of identifying a person who reports to a society under subsection 72 (2) or (3) and is not the subject of the report.

(6) **Register confidential** — Despite any other Act, no person shall inspect, remove, alter or permit the inspection, removal or alteration of information maintained in the register, or disclose or permit the disclosure of information that the person obtained from the register, except as this section authorizes.

(7) **Coroner's inquest, etc.** — A person who is,

(a) a coroner, or a legally qualified medical practitioner or peace officer authorized in writing by a coroner, acting in connection with an investigation or inquest under the *Coroners Act*; or

(b) the Children's Lawyer or the Children's Lawyer's authorized agent,

may inspect, remove and disclose information in the register in accordance with his or her authority.

[S.O. 1994, c. 27, s. 43 (2), in force April 3, 1995 (Act, s. 64 (2), O. Gaz. 1995 p. 101).]

(8) **Minister or Director may permit access to register** — The Minister or the Director may permit,

(a) a person who is employed by,

(i) the Ministry,

      (ii)   a society, or

      (iii) a recognized child protection agency outside Ontario; or

  (b) a person who is providing or proposes to provide counselling or treatment to a registered person,

to inspect and remove information in the register and to disclose the information to a person referred to in subsection (7) or to another person referred to in this subsection, subject to such terms and conditions as the Director may impose.

(9) **Director may disclose information** — The Minister or the Director may disclose information in the register to a person referred to in subsection (7) or (8).

(10) **Research** — A person who is engaged in research may, with the Director's written approval, inspect and use the information in the register, but shall not,

  (a) use or communicate the information for any purpose except research, academic pursuits or the compilation of statistical data; or

  (b) communicate any information that may have the effect of identifying a person named in the register.

(11) **Registered person** — A child, a registered person or the child's or registered person's solicitor or agent may inspect only the information in the register that refers to the child or registered person.

(12) **Physician** — A legally qualified medical practitioner may, with the Director's written approval, inspect the information in the register that is specified by the Director.

(13) **Amendment of register** — The Director or an employee of the Ministry acting under the Director's authority,

  (a) shall remove a name from or otherwise amend the register where the regulations require the removal or amendment; and

  (b) may amend the register to correct an error.

(14) **Register inadmissible: exceptions** — The register shall not be admitted into evidence in a proceeding except,

  (a) to prove compliance or non-compliance with this section;

  (b) in a hearing or appeal under section 76;

  (c) in a proceeding under the *Coroners Act*; or

  (d) in a proceeding referred to in section 81 (recovery on child's behalf).

76. (1) **Definition** — In this section, "hearing" means a hearing held under clause (4) (b).

(2) **Notice to registered person** — Where an entry is made in the register, the Director shall forthwith give written notice to each registered person referred to in the entry indicating that,

    (a) the person is identified in the register;

    (b) the person or the person's solicitor or agent is entitled to inspect the information in the register that refers to or identifies the person; and

    (c) the person is entitled to request that the Director remove the person's name from or otherwise amend the register.

(3) **Request to amend register** — A registered person who receives notice under subsection (2) may request that the Director remove the person's name from or otherwise amend the register.

(4) **Director's response** — On receiving a request under subsection (3), the Director may,

    (a) grant the request; or

    (b) hold a hearing, on ten days written notice to the parties, to determine whether to grant or refuse the request.

(5) **Delegation** — The Director may authorize another person to hold a hearing and exercise the Director's powers and duties under subsection (8).

(6) **Procedure** — The *Statutory Powers Procedure Act* applies to a hearing and a hearing shall be conducted in accordance with the prescribed practices and procedures.

(7) **Hearing** — The parties to a hearing are,

    (a) the registered person;

    (b) the society that verified the information referring to or identifying the registered person; and

    (c) any other person specified by the Director.

(8) **Director's decision** — Where the Director determines, after holding a hearing, that the information in the register with respect to a registered person is in error or should not be in the register, the Director shall remove the registered person's name from or otherwise amend the register, and may order that the society's records be amended to reflect the Director's decision.

(9) **Appeal to Divisional Court** — A party to a hearing may appeal the Director's decision to the Divisional Court.

(10) **Hearing private** — A hearing or appeal under this section shall be held in the absence of the public and no media representative shall be permitted to attend.

(11) **Publication** — No person shall publish or make public information that has the effect of identifying a witness at or a participant in a hearing, or a party to a hearing other than a society.

(12) **Record inadmissible: exception** — The record of a hearing or appeal under this section shall not be admitted into evidence in any other proceeding except a proceeding under clause 85 (1) (d) (confidentiality of register) or clause 85 (1) (e) (amendment of society's records).

79. (1) **Definition** — In this section, "abuse" means a state or condition of being physically harmed, sexually molested or sexually exploited.

(2) **Child abuse** — No person having charge of a child shall,

    (a) inflict abuse on the child; or
    (b) by failing to care and provide for or supervise and protect the child adequately,
        (i)   permit the child to suffer abuse, or
        (ii) permit the child to suffer from a mental, emotional or developmental condition that, if not remedied, could seriously impair the child's development.

(3) **Leaving child unattended** — No person having charge of a child less than sixteen years of age shall leave the child without making provision for his or her supervision and care that is reasonable in the circumstances.

(4) **Reverse onus** — Where a person is charged with contravening subsection (3) and the child is less than ten years of age, the onus of establishing that the person made provision for the child's supervision and care that was reasonable in the circumstances rests with the person.

(5) **Allowing child to loiter, etc.** — No parent of a child less than sixteen years of age shall permit the child to,

    (a) loiter in a public place between the hours of midnight and 6 a.m.; or
    (b) be in a place of public entertainment between the hours of midnight and 6 a.m., unless the parent accompanies the child or

authorizes a specified individual eighteen years of age or older to accompany the child.

(6) **Police may take child home or to place of safety** — Where a child who is actually or apparently less than sixteen years of age is in a place to which the public has access between the hours of midnight and 6 a.m. and is not accompanied by a person described in clause (5) (b), a peace officer may apprehend the child without a warrant and proceed as if the child had been apprehended under subsection 42 (1).

(7) **Child protection hearing** — The court may, in connection with a case arising under subsection (2), (3) or (5), proceed under this Part as if an application had been made under subsection 40 (1) (child protection proceeding) in respect of the child.

81. (1) **Definition** — In this section, "to suffer abuse", when used in reference to a child, means to be in need of protection within the meaning of clause 37 (2) (a), (c), (e), (f), (f.1) or (h).

(2) **Recovery on child's behalf** — When the Children's Lawyer is of the opinion that a child has a cause of action or other claim because the child has suffered abuse, the Children's Lawyer may, if he or she considers it to be in the child's best interests, institute and conduct proceedings on the child's behalf for the recovery of damages or other compensation.

[S.O. 1994, c. 27, s. 43 (2), in force April 3, 1995 (Act, s. 64 (2), O. Gaz. 1995 p. 101.]

(3) **Idem: society** — Where a child is in a society's care and custody, subsection (2) also applies to the society with necessary modifications.

[S.O. 1994, c. 27, s. 43; S.O. 1999, c. 2, s. 29.]

85. (1) **Offences** — A person who contravenes,

(a) an order for access made under subsection 58 (1);
(b) REPEALED: S.O. 1999, c. 2, s. 30(1), effective March 31, 2000 (O. Gaz. 2000 p. 451).
(c) subsection 74 (5) (disclosure of information obtained by court order);
(d) subsection 75 (6) or (10) (confidentiality of child abuse register);
(e) an order made under subsection 76 (8) (amendment of society's records);
(f) subsection 79 (3) or (5) (leaving child unattended, etc.);
(g) a restraining order made under subsection 80 (1);
(h) section 82 (unauthorized placement);
(i) any provision of section 83 (interference with child, etc.); or

(j) clause 84 (a) or (b),

and a director, officer or employee of a corporation who authorizes, permits or concurs in such a contravention by the corporation is guilty of an offence and on conviction is liable to a fine of not more than $1,000 or to imprisonment for a term of not more than one year, or to both.

(2) **Idem** — A person who contravenes subsection 79 (2) (child abuse), and a director, officer or employee of a corporation who authorizes, permits or concurs in such a contravention by the corporation is guilty of an offence and on conviction is liable to a fine of not more than $2,000 or to imprisonment for a term of not more than two years, or to both.

(3) **Idem** — A person who contravenes subsection 45 (8) or 76 (11) (publication of identifying information) or an order prohibiting publication made under clause 45 (7) (c) or subsection 45 (9), and a director, officer or employee of a corporation who authorizes, permits or concurs in such a contravention by the corporation, is guilty of an offence and on conviction is liable to a fine of not more than $10,000 or to imprisonment for a term of not more than three years, or to both.

[S.O. 1999, c. 2, s. 30.]

APPENDIX 4

R.R.O. 1990, REG. 71

REGISTER

Amended to O. Reg. 213/00

1. REVOKED: O. Reg. 213/00, s. 1 effective March 31, 2000 (O. Gaz. April 15, 2000).

2. (1) A society that receives information under section 72 of the Act concerning the abuse of a child shall enquire of the Director who maintains the register established under subsection 75 (5) of the Act, within three days after receiving the information, to determine whether any person referred to in the information has been previously identified in the register.

(2) A society that makes a report of verified information concerning the abuse of a child under subsection 75 (3) of the Act to the Director shall make the report within fourteen days after the information is verified by the society unless the Director extends the period of time.

(3) Upon receiving an inquiry from a society under subsection (1), the Director shall forthwith notify the society whether any person referred to in the information received by the society under section 72 of the Act has been previously identified in the register, the date of any such prior identification and the society or other agency that reported the prior identification.

(4) A report by a society to the Director of verified information concerning the abuse of a child made under subsection 75 (3) of the Act shall be in Form 1.

(5) Where a case concerning the abuse of a child has been reported by a society under subsection 75 (3) of the Act and the case is not closed by the society, the society shall make a further report in Form 2 to the Director within four months after making of the original report under subsection 75 (3) of the Act.

(6) Where a case is not closed, a society shall make a subsequent report to the Director in Form 2 on each anniversary of the original report until the case is closed by the society.

(7) REVOKED: O. Reg. 213/00, s. 2 effective March 31, 2000 (O. Gaz. April 15, 2000).

(8) REVOKED: O. Reg. 213/00, s. 2 effective March 31, 2000 (O. Gaz. April 15, 2000).

3. (1) The Director shall record information reported to the register under subsection 75 (3) of the Act in Form 3.

(2) The Director shall maintain information in the register established under subsection 75 (5) of the Act for at least twenty-five years from the date of the recording of the information unless the information has been previously expunged or amended pursuant to a decision by the Director.

4. (1) Every society shall ensure that each child in care of the society is given a medical and dental examination as soon as is practical after the admission of the child to care.

(2) Every society shall ensure that each child who is in care of the society is given a medical examination and dental examination at least once a year.

(3) Every society shall keep a record of each medical examination and dental examination of each child admitted into care by the society.

(4) Every society shall ensure that the treatment recommended as a result of a medical examination or dental examination of a child admitted into care by the society is carried out within the times recommended.

(5) Psychological and psychiatric assessments or treatment or both shall be provided for each child in the care of a society in accordance with the needs of the child where the society is of the opinion that the behaviour and condition of the child indicate that an assessment or treatment or both is necessary in the circumstances.

(6) The results of each assessment and treatment carried out under subsection (5) shall be recorded by the society.

5. (1) No society that admits a child into care shall place the child in a foster home or other home unless the child has previously visited the home at least ten days before the placement.

(2) Subsection (1) does not apply where it is not practical in the circumstances to have the child visit the home at least ten days before the placement.

(3) Every society shall ensure that each child placed in a foster home or other home by the society is visited by a social worker,

    (a) within seven days after the child's admission to the home;
    (b) at least once within thirty days of the placement; and
    (c) at least once every three months after the visit referred to in clause (b),

or at such other interval as the local director directs.

6. Every society that receives an application to adopt or board a child that is in the care of the society shall, within thirty days after receiving the application, begin an investigation of the applicant and the home of the applicant.

7. (1) Every society shall open and maintain a separate file with respect to,

    (a) each person who is a parent within the meaning of subsection 137 (1) of the Act who relinquishes a child to the society for adoption;
    (b) each prospective adoptive parent;
    (c) each child who is placed or who is intended to be placed for adoption by the society; and
    (d) each foster parent who provides services to the society in connection with an adoption.

(2) The society shall review each file referred to in subsection (1) and bring the file up to date at least every six months until the file is closed.

(3) The society shall permanently retain a record of the contents of each file referred to in subsection (1).

[**Ed. note:** Forms 1, 2 and 3 have been omitted.]

APPENDIX 5

PROFESSIONAL MISCONDUCT O. REG. 437/97

NO AMENDMENTS

1. The following acts are defined as professional misconduct for the purposes of subsection 30 (2) of the Act:

1. Providing false information or documents to the College or any other person with respect to the member's professional qualifications.
2. Inappropriately using a term, title or designation indicating a specialization in the profession which is not specified on the member's certificate of qualification and registration.
3. Permitting, counselling or assisting any person who is not a member to represent himself or herself as a member of the College.
4. Using a name other than the member's name, as set out in the register, in the course of his or her professional duties.
5. Failing to maintain the standards of the profession.
6. Releasing or disclosing information about a student to a person other than the student or, if the student is a minor, the student's parent or guardian. The release or disclosure of information is not an act of professional misconduct if,
    i. the student (or if the student is a minor, the student's parent or guardian) consents to the release or disclosure, or
    ii. if the release or disclosure is required or allowed by law.
7. Abusing a student physically, sexually, verbally, psychologically or emotionally.
8. Practising or purporting to practise the profession while under the influence of any substance or while adversely affected by any dysfunction,
    i. which the member knows or ought to know impairs the member's ability to practise, and
    ii. in respect of which treatment has previously been recommended, ordered or prescribed but the member has failed to follow the treatment.

9. Contravening a term, condition or limitation imposed on the member's certificate of qualification and registration.
10. Failing to keep records as required by his or her professional duties.
11. Failing to supervise adequately a person who is under the professional supervision of the member.
12. Signing or issuing, in the member's professional capacity, a document that the member knows or ought to know contains a false, improper or misleading statement.
13. Falsifying a record relating to the member's professional responsibilities.
14. Failing to comply with the Act or the regulations or the by-laws.
15. Failing to comply with the *Education Act* or the regulations made under that Act, if the member is subject to that Act.
16. Contravening a law if the contravention is relevant to the member's suitability to hold a certificate of qualification and registration.
17. Contravening a law if the contravention has caused or may cause a student who is under the member's professional supervision to be put at or to remain at risk.
18. An act or omission that, having regard to all the circumstances, would reasonably be regarded by members as disgraceful, dishonourable or unprofessional.
19. Conduct unbecoming a member.
20. Failing to appear before a panel of the Investigation Committee to be cautioned or admonished, if the Investigation Committee has required the member to appear under clause 26 (5) (c) of the Act.
21. Failing to comply with an order of a panel of the Discipline Committee or an order of a panel of the Fitness to Practise Committee.
22. Failing to co-operate in a College investigation.
23. Failing to take reasonable steps to ensure that the requested information is provided in a complete and accurate manner if the member is required to provide information to the College under the Act and the regulations.
24. Failing to abide by a written undertaking given by the member to the College or by an agreement entered into by the member with the College.
25. Failing to respond adequately or within a reasonable time to a written inquiry from the College.
26. Practising the profession while the member is in a conflict of interest.

27. Failing to comply with the member's duties under the *Child and Family Services Act.*

2. A finding of incompetence, professional misconduct or a similar finding against a member by a governing authority of the teaching profession in a jurisdiction other than Ontario that is based on facts that would, in the opinion of the Discipline Committee, constitute professional misconduct as defined in section 1, is defined as professional misconduct for the purposes of subsection 30 (2) of the Act.

APPENDIX 6

ONTARIO COLLEGE OF TEACHERS ACT, 1996, S.O. 1996, c. 12

Amendments to reproduced sections: S.O. 1997, c. 31, s. 161; S.O. 2001, c. 14, Sched. B, ss. 1, 6-8; S.O. 2002, c. 7, ss. 2-4.

1. In this Act,

. . . . .

"sexual abuse" of a student by a member means,

    (a) sexual intercourse or other forms of physical sexual relations between the member and the student,

    (b) touching, of a sexual nature, of the student by the member, or

    (c) behaviour or remarks of a sexual nature by the member towards the student.

[S.O. 1997, c. 31, s. 161; S.O. 2001, c. 14, Sched. B, s. 1; S.O. 2002, c. 7, s. 2.]

40. (1.1) **Sexual abuse** — The definition of "professional misconduct" under paragraph 31 of subsection (1) shall be deemed to include sexual abuse of a student by a member.

[S.O. 2001, c. 14, Sched. B, ss. 6- 8; S.O. 2002, c. 7, s. 3.]

43. (1) **Regulations and by-laws: general or specific** — A regulation or by-law made under any provision of this Act may be general or specific.

(2) **Same** — Without limiting the generality of subsection (1), a regulation or by-law may be limited in its application to any class of members, certificates or qualifications.

(3) **Classes** — A class under this Act may be defined with respect to any attribute and may be defined to consist of or to exclude any specified member of the class, whether or not with the same attributes.

PART IX.1
REPORTING REQUIREMENTS RELATED
TO PROFESSIONAL MISCONDUCT

43.1 (1) **Application of Part** — For the purposes of this Part, an employer shall be considered to employ or to have employed a member only if the employer employs or employed the member,

    (a) to teach a person who is 18 years old or less or, in the case of a person who has special needs, 21 years old or less; or

    (b) to provide services, including support services, related to the education of a person who is 18 years old or less or, in the case of a person who has special needs, 21 years old or less.

(2) **Special needs** — For the purposes of subsection (1), a person has special needs if,

    (a) in the opinion of the employer, the person, by reason of some mental or physical disability, is particularly vulnerable to sexual abuse; or

    (b) the employer, exercising reasonable diligence, should have formed the opinion that the person, by reason of some mental or physical disability, is particularly vulnerable to sexual abuse.

(3) **Crown bound** — This Part binds the Crown.

43.2 (1) **Employer reports re: termination, etc.** — An employer of a member who terminates the member's employment or imposes restrictions on the member's duties for reasons of professional misconduct shall file with the Registrar within 30 days after the termination or restriction a written report setting out the reasons.

(2) **Same** — If an employer of a member intended to terminate the member's employment or to impose restrictions on the member's duties for reasons of professional misconduct but the employer did not do so because the member resigned, the employer shall file with the Registrar within 30 days after the resignation a written report setting out the reasons on which the employer had intended to act.

(3) **Same** — If a member resigns while his or her employer is engaged in an investigation into allegations of an act or omission by the member that would, if proven, have caused the employer to terminate the member's employment or to impose restrictions on the member's duties for reasons of professional misconduct, the employer shall file with the Registrar within 30 days after the resignation a written report stating the nature of the allegations being investigated.

(4) **Registrar to report back** — Where an employer makes a report to the Registrar under subsection (1), (2) or (3), the Registrar shall, as soon as is reasonably possible, provide the employer with a written report respecting the action, if any, taken by the Registrar in response to the employer's report.

43.3 (1) **Employer reports re: certain offences, conduct** — An employer shall promptly report to the College in writing when the employer becomes aware that a member who is or has been employed by the employer,

(a) has been charged with or convicted of an offence under the *Criminal Code* (Canada) involving sexual conduct and minors;

(b) has been charged with or convicted of an offence under the *Criminal Code* (Canada) that in the opinion of the employer indicates that students may be at risk of harm or injury; or

(c) has engaged in conduct or taken action that, in the opinion of the employer, should be reviewed by a committee of the College.

(2) **Same** — An employer who makes a report under subsection (1) respecting a charge or conviction shall promptly report to the College in writing if the employer becomes aware that the charge was withdrawn, the member was discharged following a preliminary inquiry, the charge was stayed, or the member was acquitted.

43.4 (1) **College reports to employers** — The College shall provide employers of members with information respecting certain decisions and orders under this Act in accordance with the following rules and with subsection (2):

1. If a decision respecting a member is made under subsection 26 (5), the Registrar shall provide the documents referred to in subsection 26 (7) to the member's employer.

2. If an order respecting a member is made under subsection 29 (3), the Registrar shall provide a copy of the order to the member's employer.

3. If an order respecting a member is made under section 30 or 31, the Discipline Committee or the Fitness to Practise Committee, as the case may be, shall provide the employer with the same material as is served on the parties under subsection 32 (13).

4. If a decision respecting a member is made under section 33, the Discipline Committee or the Fitness to Practise Committee, as the case may be, shall provide the employer with the same material as is served on the parties under subsection 33 (13) or (14).

5. If an order respecting a member is made under section 34, the Registrar shall provide a copy of the order to the member's employer.

6. If a court order respecting a member is made under section 35, the Registrar shall provide a copy of the order, with reasons, if any, to the member's employer.

(2) **Same** — The following are the employers who shall receive the information referred to in subsection (1):

1. An employer who employed the member at the time the relevant decision or order referred to in subsection (1) was made.

2. An employer who made a report respecting the member under section 43.3, if the subject of the report is related to the decision or order referred to in subsection (1).

[S.O. 2002, c. 7, s. 4.]

APPENDIX 7

PROTOCOL FOR REPORTING TEACHER PROFESSIONAL MISCONDUCT

Ontario Public School Boards' Association
Labour Relations Services
September 2002

1.   Purpose

The purpose of this protocol is to effect a process which will attempt to ensure that the Board's reporting obligations under the *Student Protection Act* are met and in order to effect greater protection to students.

2.   Reporting Obligations

2.1   The Board must promptly report to the Ontario College of Teachers ("the College") where the Board becomes aware that a teacher or temporary teacher:
- has been charged with or convicted of a *Criminal Code* offence involving sexual conduct with any person under 18 years of age, or 21 years of age in the case of a person with special needs (i.e. a person who by reason of mental or physical disability is particularly vulnerable to sexual abuse);
- has been charged with or convicted of a *Criminal Code* offence which, in the Board's opinion, indicates that students may be at risk [of] injury; or
- having been charged with or convicted of an offence as noted above, has the charge withdrawn from against him/her, is discharged during a preliminary inquiry, has the charge against him/her stayed, or is acquitted;
- has engaged in conduct which in the Board's opinion, should be the subject of review by a Committee of the College (e.g. Investigation, Discipline, Fitness to Practice);

- having been reported by the Board to the College of being charged with or convicted of a criminal offence, is subsequently acquitted, or where the charge is withdrawn, stayed or the teacher discharged following a preliminary inquiry.

2.2 The Board <u>must</u> report to the College <u>within 30 days</u> where a teacher or temporary teacher:
- is dismissed by the Board for reasons of professional misconduct, including "sexual abuse";
- has restrictions imposed on his/her duties for reasons of professional misconduct, including "sexual abuse";
- resigns before the Board, which intended to impose restrictions upon or dismiss this teacher, could do so.

"Restrictions" include limiting the classes which a teacher may teach, limiting the teacher's presence from certain areas within the school or from certain activities in the school, or any other limitation which might be imposed on the teacher's normal duties and activities within the school or the school community.

2.3 All employees should be aware that failure to comply with any of these reporting obligations may lead to charges against the Board.

3. <u>Expanded Definition of "Sexual Abuse"</u>

3.1 "Sexual abuse" for purposes of defining professional misconduct by a teacher, includes:
- sexual intercourse or other forms of physical sexual relations between the teacher and the student;
- touching of a sexual nature of the student by the teacher;
- behaviour or remarks of a sexual nature by the member towards the student.

4. <u>Duty of Employees</u>

4.1 It is the duty of every employee of the Board to promptly report to the Principal of the school in which he/she works, the Superintendent responsible to the school or the Superintendent/or Manager responsible for Human Resources, any situation of sexual abuse by a teacher towards a student.

4.2 It is the duty of every employee of the Board to report to the Principal of the school in which he/she works, the Superintendent responsible to the school or the Superintendent/or Manager responsible for Human Resources where the employee becomes aware that any employee (including himself or herself) has been charged with or convicted of a *Criminal Code* offence involving sexual conduct with any person under 18 years of age, or with any offence which involves drugs, violence or theft.

4.3 It is the duty of any Principal, Superintendent/or Manager of Human Resources who receives information under 4.1 or 4.2 to immediately report such information to the Director of Education or designate.

4.4 It is the duty of every Principal who believes that a teacher has engaged in conduct which the principal believes should be the subject of a review by the College's investigation, discipline or fitness to practice committee, to promptly consult with his/her Superintendent and, where the Superintendent agrees that the matter should be referred to the College, to so advise the Director of Education or Designate.

4.5 It is the duty of every Principal who imposes restrictions on any teacher's duties for the reason that the teacher engaged in professional misconduct, including sexual abuse, to promptly report this to his/her Superintendent and the Director of Education and/or designate.

5. Report to the Ontario College of Teachers

5.1 It is the responsibility of the Director of Education or designate to send a letter to the College where the Director becomes aware of any situation, as defined in Part II of this protocol, in which the Board is required to make a report to the College.

5.2 The Director will advise the Board of any report which its Director or designate makes to the College concerning any employee of the Board.

SUGGESTED COMMUNIQUE TO PRINCIPALS

Sexual Abuse Legislation: New Reporting Requirements for Boards

I. Introduction

The *Student Protection Act, 2002* requires school boards to report to the Ontario College of Teachers ("the College") in certain cases where the Board becomes aware that a teacher (including a temporary teacher, principal, vice principal or supervisory officer who is a member of the

College) has been convicted of a criminal offence <u>and</u> in certain circumstances of professional misconduct by a teacher.

II.   Criminal Code Conviction or Charges

The Board must "<u>promptly</u>" report to the College where a teacher:
  i)   has been charged with or convicted of a criminal offence involving sexual conduct with persons under 18 years of age, or 21 years of age in the case of a person with special needs (i.e. a person who by reason of mental or physical disability is particularly vulnerable to sexual abuse);
  ii) has been charged with or convicted of a criminal offence which, in the Board's opinion indicates that students may be at risk [of] injury; or
  iii) has engaged in conduct which, in the Board's opinion, should be the subject of review by a Committee of the College. [Note: Committees include: investigator, discipline and fitness to practice]

Moreover, where a teacher has been charged with a *Criminal Code* offence, as noted above, the teacher <u>must</u> be removed from the classroom and contact with pupils until the charges have been withdrawn or stayed or the teacher has been acquitted.

If the Board has reported to the College that charges have been laid against a teacher and those charges are subsequently withdrawn, dismissed or the teacher is discharged following a preliminary inquiry, or the teacher is acquitted of the charges, the Board must report this promptly to the College as soon as the Board becomes aware of the fact.

III.   Professional Misconduct (Including Sexual Abuse)

The Board must report to the College <u>within 30 days</u> where a teacher or temporary teacher:
  i)   is dismissed by the Board for reasons of professional misconduct;
  ii) has restrictions imposed on his/her duties for reasons of professional misconduct;
  iii) resigns before the Board, which intended to impose restrictions or dismiss for professional misconduct, could do so.

"Professional misconduct" is defined as including sexual abuse. The definition of "sexual abuse" under the *Ontario College of Teachers Act* and the *Teaching Profession Act* is modified by the new legislation. It is broadly defined to include the following:
  a)   sexual intercourse or other forms of physical sexual relations between the member and the student;
  b)   touching of a sexual nature, of the student by the member; or

    c) behaviour or remarks of a sexual nature by the member towards the student.

It is important to note that while the Bill defines "professional misconduct" as <u>including</u> sexual abuse, "professional misconduct" covers <u>all</u> of the actions addressed by O. Reg. 437/97 under the *College of Teachers Act*. In other words, a School Board's obligation to file a report arises in respect to any professional misconduct in which any limitation on the teacher's duties is imposed, and not just sexual misconduct or sexual abuse. [See attached Regulation to *Ontario College of Teachers Act* defining "professional misconduct".] [**Ed. note:** Regulation omitted]

The College has a reciprocal duty to keep a Board informed of its orders and actions in respect of a member employed by that Board.

The legislation will not require that teachers who are aware of, or have suspicions of, sexual abuse or sexual misconduct by one of their colleagues to report this to the Board or the College, although there is nothing preventing a Board from requiring such disclosure by its employees. The new legislation will, however, amend the *Teaching Profession Act* to make clear that a teacher's obligation to inform another teacher that he/she has made an adverse report about the other, does <u>not</u> include a report of suspected sexual abuse of a student.

IV.   Conclusion

It will be important, where a principal or any other manager becomes aware of any matter which should be reported to the College, that the Superintendent of Human Resources or Director of Education be informed immediately in order that the Board can comply with its obligations under the legislation. The Board will be implementing a Protocol to facilitate this process.

APPENDIX 8

POLICY OF THE TORONTO DISTRICT SCHOOL BOARD

Number C.07   Dealing With Abuse and Neglect of Students

Statement

The Toronto District School Board is committed to providing each and every student with a safe, nurturing, positive and respectful learning environment.

Every year, thousands of cases of child abuse and neglect are reported to child welfare authorities in Toronto. Both the Ontario Child and Family Services Act and the Criminal Code of Canada demonstrate our society's commitment to protecting children from abuse and neglect. The employees of the Toronto District School Board have a special role and responsibility in the protection of children and students of all ages.

Whether a child suffers from physical, sexual or emotional abuse or is a victim of neglect, the long-term effects can be enormous. Increased rates of suicide, addiction, and mental health disorders of all kinds are directly related to child abuse or neglect. Experience has shown that it is not only younger children who are victims of abuse, but that older students can also be victimized in the home, at school, or in the community.

The Toronto District School Board has a duty to prevent, detect, intervene in and report abuse or neglect of any students.

Early identification of child abuse and neglect can occur through disclosure or as the result of reasonable suspicions on the part of Board employees and volunteers. Reporting disclosures or suspicions may not only prevent future victimization of children, it may also permit both the victim and perpetrator to receive the help they need. Early intervention may ameliorate the long-term effects of abuse and break the ongoing cycle of further victimization and harm.

By pursuing an integrated program of prevention education and intervention and by providing the necessary resources to support these initiatives for all students, we will demonstrate the Board's commitment to the goal of eradicating abuse and neglect.

The Toronto District School Board, therefore, shall have zero tolerance in all of its learning environments for physical, sexual and emotional abuse and/or neglect of students.

Policy of the Toronto District School Board

Number C.07: Dealing With Abuse and Neglect of Students

For the purpose of this policy, abuse is any form of physical harm, sexual mistreatment, emotional harm, or neglect, which can result in injury or psychological damage. The four categories of abuse of students are described in the procedures document.

Policy of the Toronto District School Board

Number C.07: Dealing With Abuse and Neglect of Students

1. Principles

    (a)   No student shall experience corporal punishment, physical mistreatment, sexual, emotional or verbal abuse by staff. In addition, students shall be protected from violence and harassment, including threats and/or bullying and inappropriate sexual behaviour by other students.

    (b)   The Toronto District School Board will educate all of its students about their right to live without fear of physical, sexual, and emotional abuse and neglect and will support disclosure of such abuse.

    (c)   The Toronto District School Board will establish a series of age-appropriate programs in the elementary and secondary panels to explicitly educate all of its students about the issues of abuse and neglect. In addition, the Board will educate all its employees, volunteers and parents about the issues of abuse and neglect and their duty to maintain safe and abuse-free learning environments. While the Board respects the diversity of its school communities, child abuse prevention and reporting practices must be consistent with Canadian law.

    (d)   The Toronto District School Board will hold all employees and volunteers accountable for the following:

        (i)   Board staff and volunteers working directly with a student of any age in their professional capacity (see (iii) below) will not enter into a sexual relationship with that student during the course of the professional relationship or for a period of one year thereafter.

        (ii)   In the case of students and former students under the age of 18, any such relationship, in addition to being a serious breach of Board policy, is also a criminal offence of sexual exploitation or sexual assault.

        (iii)   Professional capacity shall mean working or volunteering in the same school as the student is enrolled or otherwise supervising, counselling, coaching or assisting in extra curricular activities in which the student is participating regardless of which school the student is enrolled.

    (e)   The Toronto District School Board will ensure that all prospective employees are screened for records of criminal conviction for sexual offences and offences involving children.

2. Detecting and Reporting Abuse or Neglect

Policy of the Toronto District School Board

Number C.07: Dealing With Abuse and Neglect of Students

(a) All Toronto District School Board employees and volunteers must remain vigilant about neglect and abuse. In the event a Toronto District School Board employee or volunteer suspects that abuse or neglect has occurred, the employee or volunteer will forthwith report her/his suspicions to the police and/or a children's aid society in accordance with the procedures attached to this policy and in compliance with the Child and Family Services Act. The legal responsibilities under the Child and Family Services Act are described in the administrative procedures.

(b) All employees are expected to support victims of abuse and neglect in accordance with the procedures attached to this policy.

(c) All student disclosures shall be reported to the police and/or children's aid society as is appropriate.

(d) The dignity and all legal rights to privacy of those affected by an abuse disclosure will be respected.

(e) Where the alleged perpetrator of abuse is an adult, every effort will be made to protect the student in the learning environment from further contact or reprisals by the adult.

(f) If a Board employee is convicted of abusing a student or if an internal investigation determines, on a balance of probabilities, that the employee abused a student, the employee will be dismissed from employment. Any volunteer found to have abused a student will no longer be permitted to volunteer.

(g) Where the alleged perpetrator is a student, he/she will be separated from the alleged victim and, where appropriate, an alternative learning environment and support and counselling will be provided.

3. Sexually Intrusive Behaviour By Students

The Toronto District School Board also recognizes that not all perpetrators of abuse are of the age of criminal responsibility and that sexually intrusive behaviours can occur between students of all ages. For the purpose of this policy sexual intrusion includes behaviour of a sexual nature that may put a child or children at risk of physical or emotional harm. These include any behaviours for which a person over the age of 12 might be charged under the Criminal Code. Other sexually problematic behaviours include persistent sexually explicit talk or enactments, sex play between children of different ages or developmental levels and the inability of a child to stop engaging in sexual behaviour.

Policy of the Toronto District School Board

Number C.07: Dealing With Abuse and Neglect of Students

The Toronto District School Board will offer support for both victims and perpetrators of sexually intrusive behaviour.

4.   After Abuse Is Reported

Where abuse has been reported, the Toronto District School Board will co-operate fully with the investigating agency.   In the case of child sexual abuse, the Toronto Child Sexual Abuse Protocol (MCSA) will be followed.

The Toronto District School Board is committed to the goal of obtaining appropriate emotional and psychological support for all victims of neglect and abuse and for their families.   In addition, where appropriate, support and as much information as may be legally shared will be provided to the greater school community. In some sexual abuse situations, a response team will be convened to provide support to the school and the community. The response team will draw upon designated staff who are trained in sexual abuse issues.

APPENDIX 9

PROCEDURES DEALING WITH SEXUAL ABUSE AND/OR SEXUAL ASSAULT

Toronto District School Board

4. Procedures Dealing With Sexual Abuse and/or Sexual Assault: Victim is Student Who is Under the Age of 16, Alleged Perpetrator is Board Employee or Volunteer

4.1. Board Policy on Sexual Relationships Between Staff and Students/Former Students

    4.1.1. Board staff/volunteers working directly with a student of any age in their professional capacity (see 4.1.3. below) will not enter into a sexual relationship with that student during the course of the professional relationship or for a period of one year thereafter.

    4.1.2. In the case of students/former students under the age of 18, any such relationship, in addition to being a serious breach of Board policy, is also a criminal offence of sexual exploitation or sexual assault.

    4.1.3. Professional capacity shall mean working or volunteering in the same school as the student is enrolled or otherwise supervising, counselling, coaching or assisting in extra curricular activities in which the student is participating regardless of which school the student attends.

4.2. Notice to Board Resource Person/Convening a Response Team

The principal or designate will immediately contact one of the following child abuse resource persons so that a response team can be convened to assist the school. In most cases, this response team will be comprised of a representative of the Communications and Public Affairs Office, the appropriate school superintendent, a social worker, and the principal or designate of the school. The response team will use Board staff who are specialists in sexual abuse/sexual assault issues to implement any intervention in the school including informing students and staff, counselling students and staff and providing advice to parents.

When a response team has been established under this procedure, the team shall designate a member of the team whose responsibility shall be to liaise with, on an ongoing basis, and assist the police.

Toronto District School Board

Child Abuse Resource Persons (see page 52)

4.3. Reporting to Children's Aid Society and Police

The responsibility to report to C.A.S. lies with the employee or volunteer who received the disclosure or who suspected abuse/neglect.

4.3.1. Inform the Principal or Designate

- Report to the principal or designate what you suspect or what has been disclosed to you.
  - The principal or designate will immediately notify the appropriate superintendent.

  - Under no circumstances shall the implicated staff member be contacted regarding allegations or disclosures until specific instructions are received from the investigating police. This procedure is designed to secure the safety of the students, to ensure that the rights of the victim and alleged abuser are protected, and to prevent possible destruction of evidence or flight by the alleged abuser.

  - While the duty to report lies with the person who has formed the suspicion or heard the disclosure, she/he may request the principal's or designate's presence while making the report to the Children's Aid Society.

•   In situations where the person with the duty to report is unable to discharge this duty, the principal or designate will, where possible, make the report in the presence of the person who has formed the suspicion or heard the disclosure.

•   Once a person has formed the suspicion or heard a disclosure, the principal or designate shall not prevent a report to the Children's Aid Society being made nor will there be sanction or reprisal as a result of such action taken.

4.3.2.   Inform the Children's Aid Society

•   All suspicions and disclosures of abuse/neglect **MUST** be reported to the appropriate Children's Aid Society **IMMEDIATELY**.

•   If advised by the Children's Aid Society worker that the suspicion or disclosure(s) does not warrant an investigation, ensure that you record the worker's name, the date, and time of the consultation.

Children's Aid Societies:
   Children's Aid Society of Toronto 924-4646
   Catholic Children's Aid Society of Toronto 395-1500
   Jewish Family and Child Services of Toronto 638-7800

•   When reporting to the appropriate Children's Aid Society, provide the required information as outlined in the "Record of Report of Abuse/Neglect" form D:001A, attached. [**Ed. note:** form omitted]

•   Make sure that the C.A.S. knows what the timelines are (such as when the child is expected at home) so its response can be prioritized accordingly. The C.A.S. also requires time to make arrangements for an investigation. This is an especially important factor when dealing with kindergarten children attending half-day programs.

- As the safety and protection of the student is the Board's paramount concern, the reporter should inform the C.A.S. regarding the child or her/his family circumstances which may help in the investigation. In addition, the reporter should ask the following questions:

    - How and when should the parents be contacted?
    - Will the child be interviewed?
    - Do the investigators plan to come to the school or home? When? Will they be investigating or only consulting?
    - May the child go home at lunch or after school if the interview has not yet taken place?
    - What information can be shared with the child and her/his parent(s) if the interview has not yet taken place?

REMEMBER: No notice to parent(s)/guardians(s) of victim without approval. After a report has been made to the police, the parent/guardian should not be notified until there has been consultation with the police.

- After reporting, the reporter should take the following steps:

    - Have a trusted person (most likely the person to whom the child disclosed) stay with the child until the police/C.A.S. team arrives at the school (recognizing that the child requires support during this period).
    - The child may wish to have a support person with her/him during the interview. If the child indicates that she/he wants support, the police should be advised and permission sought. The support person should be a person of the child's choosing.

- If <u>unsure</u> whether the abuse/neglect should be reported, <u>consult</u>:

    - Student Services can be consulted (see Student and Community Services Co-ordinators, page 52).
    - A child abuse resource person can also be consulted (see Student and Community Services Co-ordinators, page 52).

-    An intake worker for a Children's Aid Society can also be consulted without naming the suspected victim.

> **REMEMBER: Do not investigate disclosure**. Once a disclosure has been made, the disclosing student/former student will not be questioned by any other school staff, nor shall any other inquiries be made until specific directions are received from the investigating police and/or CAS.

4.4. Procedures for Dealing With Alleged Perpetrator (Board Employee [or] Volunteer)

 4.4.1. Alternate Assignments For Implicated Staff During Investigation

Where a student/former student discloses sexual abuse/sexual assault by a staff member and the police have begun an investigation, that staff member will be assigned, as soon as possible, to suitable alternate duties outside the school, not involving contact with students until the police investigation has been completed. In the case of a teacher or unionized employee, she/he must be notified of the right to contact her/his federation/union representative.

 4.4.2. After Charges Laid

Where a staff member is charged with a criminal offence of a sexual nature involving students or young persons under the age of 16, whether or not they are students/former students of the Toronto District School Board, that staff member will be assigned immediately to suitable alternative duties outside the school, not involving contact with students until the charges have been disposed of.

The charged perpetrator should be informed that notification will be given to the school community regarding the charges.

 4.4.3. Upon Completion of Police Investigation/Acquittal/Conviction or Where No Investigation

Upon completion of a police investigation, acquittal or conviction, or where no criminal investigation has been undertaken, the assignment/status of the employee will be reviewed by the Office of the Director. Such review may include an internal investigation and subsequent action such as discipline or support including counselling.

The employee will be dismissed from employment if convicted of a sexual offence against a student, or if an internal investigation determines, on a balance of probabilities, that the employee sexually abused, sexually exploited or sexually assaulted the student. Where the employee is a member of a professional college/society/association, a report of professional misconduct will be made to that college/society/association by the Director of Education or designate.

4.5. Document the Incident(s)

- Documentation of suspected abuse/neglect cases should be carefully prepared and maintained in accordance with the "Record of Report of Abuse/Neglect" form D:001A, attached. [**Ed. note:** form omitted] The report must:

  - be factual (including dates and time) and contain no opinions;
  - be brief and to the point; and,
  - contain questions asked of the student, information seen or heard by the teacher, principal or designate, and other observers.

- The "Record of Report of Abuse/Neglect" form will be forwarded, in a sealed envelope marked "Private and Confidential," to the Executive Officer of Student and Community Services or designate for secure storage. The Ontario Student Record (O.S.R.) of the student will contain a notice that a report was made to the Children's Aid Society and that a copy of the form is on file in Student Services.

- The "Record of Report of Abuse/Neglect" form and any other written records may be subject to subpoena or disclosure in any subsequent court hearing.

4.6. Follow-up With Police/Children's Aid Society

- If it is not apparent that an investigation has commenced within 24 hours, it is the responsibility of the principal or designate to contact the police/Children's Aid Society to ascertain the status of the case.

- It is the responsibility of the principal or designate to notify the police/Children's Aid Society when a child is known to have been reported to be at risk or found to be in need of protection and has transferred schools or moved to another Board.

4.7. Notify Social Worker/Student Services Worker

- It is the responsibility of the principal or designate to notify the social worker or Student Services worker assigned to the school so that appropriate support and counselling can be offered to the child and family.

4.8. Support for Students, Parents and Staff

- In the case of criminal charges being laid, as outlined above, the Board will, under the co-ordination of the response team, provide appropriate support for the affected school community. The response team will meet with the staff of the school as soon as possible to advise of the charges, the status of the accused staff member and describe a plan of action for dealing with students and the school community. Individual counselling for staff will be offered.

- The response team (see 4.1) will, in most cases, inform students about the charges, the status of the accused staff member and offer individual counselling to students.

- A meeting with parents will be scheduled as soon as possible to explain the school response, answer questions and provide advice for dealing with the personal safety of their children.

4.9. Communications Subsequent to Disclosure

- Principals and staff shall not communicate with other students, other parents, or the community about the disclosure or criminal charges until the appropriate superintendent and resource person have been consulted and the superintendent has consulted with the Director of Education about the specific communication.

APPENDIX 10

TEACHING PROFESSION ACT, R.S.O. 1990, C. T.2

Amendments to reproduced sections: S.O. 1997, c. 31, s. 180; S.O. 2000, C. 12, s. 8; S.O. 2002, c. 7, s. 7.

12. (1) **Regulations** — Subject to the approval of the Lieutenant Governor in Council, the Board of Governors may make regulations,

    (a) prescribing a code of ethics for teachers;

    (b) REPEALED: S.O. 1997, c. 31, s. 180(4), effective March 31, 1998 (O. Gaz. 1997 p. 2841).

    (c) providing for voluntary membership in the Federation of persons who are not members thereof and prescribing the duties, responsibilities and privileges of voluntary members;

    (d) prescribing the duties, responsibilities and privileges of associate members;

    (e) providing for the suspension and expulsion of members from the Federation and other disciplinary measures;

    (f) REPEALED: S.O. 2000, c. 12, s. 8, effective June 23, 2000 (R.A.).

    (g) providing for the holding of meetings of the Board of Governors and of the executive and prescribing the manner of calling and the notice to be given in respect of such meetings;

    (h) prescribing the procedure to be followed at meetings of the Board of Governors and of the executive;

    (i) providing for the payment of necessary expenses to the members of the Board of Governors and the executive;

    (j) conferring powers upon or extending or restricting the powers of and prescribing the duties of the Board of Governors and of the executive;

    (k) providing for the appointment of standing and special committees;

    (l) providing for the establishment of branches of the Federation or of the recognition by the Federation of local bodies, groups or associations of teachers which shall be affiliated with the Federation.

(2) **Reporting sexual abuse** — Despite any regulation made under subsection (1), a member who makes an adverse report about another member respecting suspected sexual abuse of a student by that other member need not provide him or her with a copy of the report or with any information about the report.

(3) **Definition** — In subsection (2),

"sexual abuse" of a student by a member means,

> (a) sexual intercourse or other forms of physical sexual relations between the member and the student,
> (b) touching, of a sexual nature, of the student by the member, or
> (c) behaviour or remarks of a sexual nature by the member towards the student.

[S.O. 1997, c. 31, s. 180; S.O. 2000, c. 12, s. 8; S.O. 2002, c. 7, s. 7.]

APPENDIX 11

TEACHING PROFESSION ACT REGULATION

[**Note:** Section 1 of the *Regulations Act*, R.S.O. 1990, c. R.21 expressly excludes regulations made under the *Teaching Profession Act* from the application of the *Regulations Act*, and consequently, they are not required to be published in *The Ontario Gazette*. For this reason, this *Teaching Profession Act* Regulation does not have a conventional "R.R.O. 1990, Reg.***" or an "O. Reg.***/**" citation.]

Duties of a Member to Fellow Members

18. (1) A member shall,

. . . . .

    (b) on making an adverse report on another member, furnish him with a written statement of the report at the earliest possible time and not later than three days after making the report;…

APPENDIX 12

EDUCATION ACT, R.S.O. 1990, C. E.2

Amendments to reproduced sections: S.O. 1991, c. 10; S.O. 1993, c. 11, s. 30; S.O. 1996, c. 11, s. 29; S.O. 1996, c. 12, s. 64; S.O. 1996, c. 13, s. 5; S.O. 1997, c. 31, ss. 32, 80, 128; S.O. 2000, c. 11, s. 3; S.O. 2000, c. 12, s. 3; S.O. 2001, c. 14, Sched. A; S.O. 2002, c. 7, s. 1; S.O. 2003, c. 2, s. 20.

58.5 (1) **Corporate status** — Every district school board is a corporation and has all the powers and shall perform all the duties that are conferred or imposed on it under this or any other Act.

(2) **Amalgamation or merger** — Subsection (3) applies where,

- (a) one or more old boards are merged or amalgamated with a district school board to continue as a district school board;
- (b) one or more school authorities are merged or amalgamated with a district school board to continue as a district school board; or
- (c) two or more district school boards are merged or amalgamated to continue as a district school board.

(3) **Same** — The district school board that is continued is a corporation and, except as otherwise provided by the regulations made under this Part, subsection 180(7) of the *Business Corporations Act* applies with necessary modifications as if the board had been continued under that Act.

[S.O. 1997, c. 31, s. 32.]

170. (1) **Duties of boards:** — Every board shall,

. . . . .

12.1 *duties - charges, convictions* — on becoming aware that a teacher or temporary teacher who is employed by the board has been charged with or convicted of an offence under the *Criminal Code* (Canada) involving sexual conduct and minors, or of any other offence under the *Criminal Code* (Canada) that in the opinion of the board indicates that pupils may be at risk, take prompt steps to ensure that the teacher or temporary teacher performs no duties in the classroom and no duties involving contact with pupils, pending withdrawal of the charge, discharge following a preliminary inquiry, stay of the charge or acquittal, as the case may be;

[S.O. 1993, c. 11, s. 30; S.O. 1996, c. 13, s. 5; S.O. 1996, c. 11, s. 29; S.O. 1996, c. 12, s. 64; S.O. 1997, c. 31, s. 80; S.O. 2000, c. 11, s. 3; S.O. 2001, c. 14, Sched. A, s. 2; S.O. 2002, c. 7, s. 1.]

264. (1) **Duties of teacher,** — It is the duty of a teacher and a temporary teacher,

teach
    (a) to teach diligently and faithfully the classes or subjects assigned to the teacher by the principal;

learning
    (b) to encourage the pupils in the pursuit of learning;

religion and morals
    (c) to inculcate by precept and example respect for religion and the principles of Judaeo-Christian morality and the highest regard for truth, justice, loyalty, love of country, humanity, benevolence, sobriety, industry, frugality, purity, temperance and all other virtues;

co-operation
    (d) to assist in developing co-operation and co-ordination of effort among the members of the staff of the school;

discipline
    (e) to maintain, under the direction of the principal, proper order and discipline in the teacher's classroom and while on duty in the school and on the school ground;

language of instruction
    (f) in instruction and in all communications with the pupils in regard to discipline and the management of the school,
        (i) to use the English language, except where it is impractical to do so by reason of the pupil not understanding English, and except in respect of instruction in a language other than English when such other language is being taught as one of the subjects in the course of study, or
        (ii) to use the French language in schools or classes in which French is the language of instruction except where it is impractical to do so by reason of the pupil not understanding French, and except in respect of instruction in a language other than French when such other language is being taught as one of the subjects in the course of study;

timetable
> (g) to conduct the teacher's class in accordance with a timetable which shall be accessible to pupils and to the principal and supervisory officers;

professional activity days
> (h) to participate in professional activity days as designated by the board under the regulations;

absence from school
> (i) to notify such person as is designated by the board if the teacher is to be absent from school and the reason therefor;

school property
> (j) to deliver the register, the school key and other school property in the teacher's possession to the board on demand, or when the teacher's agreement with the board has expired, or when for any reason the teacher's employment has ceased; and

textbooks
> (k) to use and permit to be used as a textbook in a class that he or she teaches in an elementary or a secondary school,
>> (i) in a subject area for which textbooks are approved by the Minister, only textbooks that are approved by the Minister, and
>> (ii) in all subject areas, only textbooks that are approved by the board.

duties assigned
> (l) to perform all duties assigned in accordance with this Act and the regulations.

(1.1) **Sign language** — Despite clause (1) (f), a teacher or temporary teacher may use American Sign Language or Quebec Sign Language in accordance with the regulations.

(2) **Refusal to give up school property** — A teacher who refuses, on demand or order of the board that operates the school concerned, to deliver to the board any school property in the teacher's possession forfeits any claim that the teacher may have against the board.

(3) **Teachers, conferences** — Teachers may organize themselves for the purpose of conducting professional development conferences and seminars.

[S.O. 1993, c. 11, s. 36; S.O. 2003, c. 2, s. 20.]

265. (1) **Duties of principal,** — It is the duty of a principal of a school, in addition to the principal's duties as a teacher,

discipline
> (a) to maintain proper order and discipline in the school;

co-operation
>   (b) to develop co-operation and co-ordination of effort among the members of the staff of the school;

register pupils and record attendance
>   (c) to register the pupils and to ensure that the attendance of pupils for every school day is recorded either in the register supplied by the Minister in accordance with the instructions contained therein or in such other manner as is approved by the Minister;

pupil records
>   (d) in accordance with this Act, the regulations and the guidelines issued by the Minister, to collect information for inclusion in a record in respect of each pupil enrolled in the school and to establish, maintain, retain, transfer and dispose of the record;

timetable
>   (e) to prepare a timetable, to conduct the school according to such timetable and the school year calendar or calendars applicable thereto, to make the calendar or calendars and the timetable accessible to the pupils, teachers and supervisory officers and to assign classes and subjects to the teachers;

examinations and reports
>   (f) to hold, subject to the approval of the appropriate supervisory officer, such examinations as the principal considers necessary for the promotion of pupils or for any other purpose and report as required by the board the progress of the pupil to his or her parent or guardian where the pupil is a minor and otherwise to the pupil;

promote pupils
>   (g) subject to revision by the appropriate supervisory officer, to promote such pupils as the principal considers proper and to issue to each such pupil a statement thereof;

textbooks
>   (h) to ensure that all textbooks used by pupils are those approved by the board and, in the case of subject areas for which the Minister approves textbooks, those approved by the Minister;

reports
>   (i) to furnish to the Ministry and to the appropriate supervisory officer any information that it may be in the principal's power to give respecting the condition of the school premises, the discipline of the school, the progress of the pupils and any other matter affecting the interests of the school, and to prepare such reports for the board as are required by the board;

care of pupils and property
>   (j) to give assiduous attention to the health and comfort of the pupils, to the cleanliness, temperature and ventilation of the

school, to the care of all teaching materials and other school property, and to the condition and appearance of the school buildings and grounds;

report to M.O.H.

    (k) to report promptly to the board and to the medical officer of health when the principal has reason to suspect the existence of any communicable disease in the school, and of the unsanitary condition of any part of the school building or the school grounds;

persons with communicable diseases

    (l) to refuse admission to the school of any person who the principal believes is infected with or exposed to communicable diseases requiring an order under section 22 of the *Health Protection and Promotion Act* until furnished with a certificate of a medical officer of health or of a legally qualified medical practitioner approved by the medical officer of health that all danger from exposure to contact with such person has passed;

access to school or class

    (m) subject to an appeal to the board, to refuse to admit to the school or classroom a person whose presence in the school or classroom would in the principal's judgment be detrimental to the physical or mental well-being of the pupils; and

visitor's book

    (n) to maintain a visitor's book in the school when so determined by the board.

(2) **Co-instructional activities** — In addition, it is the duty of a principal, in accordance with the board plan to provide for co-instructional activities under subsection 170 (1), to develop and implement a school plan providing for co-instructional activities.

(3) **School council** — The principal shall consult the school council at least once in each school year respecting the school plan providing for co-instructional activities.

[S.O. 1991, c. 10, s. 6; S.O. 2001, c. 14, Sched. A, s. 8.]

301. (1) **Provincial code of conduct** — The Minister may establish a code of conduct governing the behaviour of all persons in schools.

(2) **Purposes** — The following are the purposes of the code of conduct:

    1. To ensure that all members of the school community, especially people in positions of authority, are treated with respect and dignity.

2. To promote responsible citizenship by encouraging appropriate participation in the civic life of the school community.
3. To maintain an environment where conflict and difference can be addressed in a manner characterized by respect and civility.
4. To encourage the use of non-violent means to resolve conflict.
5. To promote the safety of people in the schools.
6. To discourage the use of alcohol and illegal drugs.

(3) **Notice** — Every board shall take such steps as the Minister directs to bring the code of conduct to the attention of pupils, parents and guardians of pupils and others who may be present in schools under the jurisdiction of the board.

(4) **Code is policy** — The code of conduct is a policy of the Minister.

(5) **Policies and guidelines governing conduct** — The Minister may establish additional policies and guidelines with respect to the conduct of persons in schools.

(6) **Same, governing discipline** — The Minister may establish policies and guidelines with respect to disciplining pupils, specifying, for example, the circumstances in which a pupil is subject to discipline and the forms and the extent of discipline that may be imposed in particular circumstances.

(7) **Same, promoting safety** — The Minister may establish policies and guidelines to promote the safety of pupils.

(8) **Different policies, etc.** — The Minister may establish different policies and guidelines under this section for different circumstances, for different locations and for different classes of persons.

(9) **Duty of boards** — The Minister may require boards to comply with policies and guidelines established under this section.

(10) **Not regulations** — Policies and guidelines established under this section are not regulations within the meaning of the *Regulations Act.*

302. (1) **Boards' policies and guidelines governing conduct** — Every board shall establish policies and guidelines with respect to the conduct of persons in schools within the board's jurisdiction and the policies and guidelines must address such matters and include such requirements as the Minister may specify.

(2) **Same, governing discipline** — A board may establish policies and guidelines with respect to disciplining pupils, and the policies and guidelines must be consistent with this Part and with the policies and guidelines established by the Minister under section 301, and must address such matters and include such requirements as the Minister may specify.

(3) **Same, promoting safety** — If required to do so by the Minister, a board shall establish policies and guidelines to promote the safety of pupils, and the policies and guidelines must be consistent with those established by the Minister under section 301 and must address such matters and include such requirements as the Minister may specify.

(4) **Same, governing access to school premises** — A board may establish policies and guidelines governing access to school premises, and the policies and guidelines must be consistent with the regulations made under section 305 and must address such matters and include such requirements as the Minister may specify.

(5) **Same, governing appropriate dress** — If required to do so by the Minister, a board shall establish policies and guidelines respecting appropriate dress for pupils in schools within the board's jurisdiction, and the policies and guidelines must address such matters and include such requirements as the Minister may specify.

(6) **Same, procedural matters** — A board shall establish policies and guidelines governing a review or appeal of a decision to suspend a pupil and governing, with respect to expulsions, a principal's inquiry, an expulsion hearing and an appeal of a decision to expel a pupil, and the policies and guidelines must address such matters and include such requirements as the Minister may specify.

(7) **Different policies, etc.**— A board may establish different policies and guidelines under this section for different circumstances, for different locations and for different classes of persons.

(8) **Role of school councils** — When establishing policies and guidelines under this section, a board shall consider the views of school councils with respect to the contents of the policies and guidelines.

(9) **Periodic review** — The board shall periodically review its policies and guidelines established under this section and shall solicit the views of pupils, teachers, staff, volunteers working in the schools, parents and guardians, school councils and the public.

(10) **Not regulations** — Policies and guidelines established under this section are not regulations within the meaning of the *Regulations Act*.

[S.O. 1997, c. 31, s. 128; S.O. 2000, c. 12, s. 3.]

INDEX